PERSONAL FICTION WRITING
★
MEREDITH SUE WILLIS

PERSONAL FICTION

WRITING

★

A GUIDE TO WRITING FROM REAL LIFE
FOR TEACHERS, STUDENTS, & WRITERS

★

MEREDITH SUE WILLIS

Teachers & Writers Collaborative

5 Union Square West   New York, N.Y. 10003

Funding for this publication has been provided by The New York State Council on the Arts and the National Endowment for the Arts.

Teachers & Writers Collaborative programs and publications are also made possible by funding from American Broadcasting Companies, Inc., American Stock Exchange, Atari Institute for Educational Action Research, Avon Products Foundation, Inc., Chemical Bank, Consolidated Edison Company, The Equitable Life Assurance Society, General Electric Foundation, The Hugh M. Hefner Foundation, Mobil Foundation, Inc., Morgan Guaranty Trust Company, Morgan Stanley, New York Foundation for the Arts, The New York Times Company Foundation, Henry Nias Foundation, Overseas Shipholding Group, Inc., Helena Rubinstein Foundation, The Scherman Foundation, and Variety Club.

Sixth printing

Library of Congress Cataloging in Publication Data

Willis, Meredith Sue
    Personal fiction writing.

    Includes index.
    1. Fiction—Technique.   I. Title.
PN3355.W595   1984   808.3   84-2622
ISBN 0-915924-13-7

Acknowledgments

Many of the writing exercises in this book were not so much invented by me as pulled out of the general sharing and discussion that has been a part of Teachers & Writers Collaborative for more than fifteen years. Other exercises were suggested to me by children's writings or talks with classroom teachers. I make no claim to originality, but only to having a quick eye for what works with helping people write.

There are, however, a few people I want to thank for particular ideas: Bob Sievert, a T&W painter with whom I have done a number of joint projects, for some of the drawing-writing connections; Janet Bloom, a poet and former T&W artist, for Dream Rooms; a New Jersey classroom teacher, whose name I have lost, who gave me an idea for writing about your favorite tree; and my sister, Christine Willis, for the Thoreau-Basho connection, which she came up with for a paper while working on her Master's degree in English and Education.

And I want to thank all the classroom teachers, administrators, and — above all — the students I have worked with over the past twelve years. These people have welcomed me and inspired me and are certainly the ultimate source of this book. Among the schools where I have had the privilege of working are P.S. 321, J.H.S. 51, P.S. 160, I.S. 218, J.H.S. 258, P.S. 48 (Brooklyn); P.S. 87, Hunter College Elementary School, Stuyvesant High School, P.S. 75, P.S. 84, Joan of Arc Junior High School (Manhattan); P.S. 3 (the Bronx); P.S. 48, P.S. 124, P.S. 183 (Queens); and Columbus School (New Rochelle).

A Note on Editing the Children's Writing in This Book

In most cases, spelling and punctuation have been made to fit the conventions of standard English usage. As often as possible, the revisions were made in editing sessions with the children, but in some cases minor changes had to be made without the student's participation. When considering these silent editorial changes, I imagined the child's face in front of me, and said, "Listen, do you want this change made so your piece will be like a regular published book?" And if the student in my mind said, "Sure, make it like a published book," then I went ahead.

This book is dedicated to the memory of two teachers:

Okey Jo Willis Mullins, 1921-1983

Paul Meredith, 1909-1967

Contents

Introduction

People who write well like to write. They may not like everything about writing, but they find satisfaction in the process, whether their talent is for writing lyric poetry or letters-to-the-editor or advertising copy. Liking writing doesn't mean that a good writer prefers a pencil and paper to a cream-filled pastry, and it certainly doesn't mean that writing is easy for anybody. Writing is, in fact, profoundly difficult; it is the making of a thing where there was no-thing before — and making this thing not out of fabric or boards, but out of one's own experience, knowledge, imagination, and understanding. My first objective in this book is to offer ways teachers can help their students get at these raw materials. My second objective is to show how the process for getting at these materials itself suggests the form they will take.

Consider the technique you might use for writing a letter to a friend. Most likely you have some special rituals: a preferred pen, certain stationery, pillows plumped behind you on the couch, knees drawn up under a blanket. You probably visualize the friend's face, too, as you begin to write, or perhaps you imagine all of her in the chair across the room. In your mind you start talking to her, writing down the words as fast as you can. "Well, you'll never guess what happened today." And you're on your way. You are comfortable, you trust that the person you are writing will be happy to receive the letter, and fairly soon you have a rhythm going — a kind of one-sided chat on paper. You feel in actual communication with this person through the medium of writing. You may have had to work yourself up to doing it — but once you get going, you feel a satisfaction in the process.

Another type of writing most of us are familiar with is the report for an office superior or a term paper for school. This is at another level of difficulty because of the critical eye at the receiving end of the communication.

Think of the term paper: the dreadful moment when all the books are gathered, and the notes, and the calendar with the deadline, and the knowledge of the grade to follow. The bad writer, that is to say, the writer who hasn't yet developed a technique for getting satisfaction out of writing, will assemble the notes and paraphrase the books with somewhat more sophistication than a seventh grader copying the *Encyclopaedia Britannica,* check back for spelling and topic sentences and conclusions and then copy it over. That's it. That's the paper. The good writer, on the other hand, may start out with equal panic and lack of interest in the topic, but somewhere along the line will find a place to get in something personal: a joke, a memory, a distinctive figure of speech. The good writer will engage in a little self-entertaining, perhaps even come up with a theory. It doesn't have to be a theory original to the world of letters; it doesn't have to be very deep. I imagine a young woman writing a paper and suddenly saying to herself, "I don't care if it *is* Shakespeare, I think Ophelia is wishy-washy." She starts looking through her notes and books for some support for this feeling and comes up with a good quotation and some information on how in Shakespeare's theater all the women's roles were played by young boys. When the professor reads the paper, I imagine him not agreeing about Shakespeare's women, but at the same time reading this particular paper without glancing at his watch. He has an urge to sit down with the student and explain to her that Shakespeare was actually very enlightened for his time on the woman question. He has this urge because there is no mistaking the paper writer's enthusiasm; she has actually gotten involved, found a way of connecting her own concerns in some small way with sixteenth-century literature. She is thinking more because she is interested. The paper becomes not an exercise for a grade, but real writing, about its own subject, about itself. I am not suggesting that my hypothetical student goes on to become a great Shakespeare scholar or even necessarily to get an A on her paper. There are many levels of interest in a piece of work: we do a paper for a teacher, letters and reports for a boss. There are hack writers who get paid by the word. But even hack writers of pulp fiction or the most hyped-up advertising copy work best when they find a way to get involved in their work.

•**Idea 1:** One of the best ways I know to get the writing juices flowing, and simultaneously to discover what is on your mind about a particular topic, is a technique called *directed freewriting.* If you have never done this, try it the next time you have to draft a letter or a report. Or try it just for the experience. Set a timer for ten or fifteen minutes and sit in front of it with pen, paper, and topic. The rule is to write without stopping, going back, or making any corrections, for the *full* amount of time. Don't even pause; move along steadily but without hurrying, and if your mind wanders, follow it. Most likely it will bring you back to the topic eventually. Consider this an exploration. Remember, you are looking for where *you* are in relation to this topic. The result will be rough, but that can always be cleaned up in a second draft. The point is to see what is really on your mind, to see where you connect to the topic at hand.

•**Idea 2:** The technique can also be used without a topic, as a completely automatic writing, also called *freewriting,* in which case you are exploring your thoughts and mood directly. Freewriting is a great way to loosen up and free yourself of the constraints of trying to be too correct too soon. Children love it too, from about third grade up, and are often delighted with the sheer volume of work they produce.

How to Use This Book

My metaphor for teaching writing is not that I come into a room full of cold little internal combustion engines and provide a spark that ignites them. Rather, I see myself walking in wonder among thirty barely contained chain reactions already in progress — each one flashing with personality and life experience, just waiting for a chance to inundate the room (the world!) with their energy. My job in this situation is to set up some power lines and give direction to the flow of energy.

The direction to the flow is provided by the assignments, the ways of getting started writing. The exercises in this book have been used with both children and adults, in classes ranging from first grade through junior high, high school, college, and adult classes. I think it will be obvious that certain exercises are more appropriate to one age group than another, but most have been tried with *all* age groups. The wonderful thing about writing is that since it deals with the materials we all have inside us, everyone is equally a real writer by virtue of the act of writing. The kind of writing taught in this book assumes the principle that six-year-olds, sixteen-year-olds, sixty-nine-year-olds, and ninety-six-year-olds all have real experience and vision to share. The techniques in this book, then, are not practice that will lead someday to the real thing. They are the real thing already.

It is particularly through the techniques of fiction writing that beginners can see the connections between their own lives and the written word. There is passion in the writing of a great philosopher and much of real life in the work of a historian or social scientist, but their writing is more or less abstracted and based on years of study and accumulated information. This book concerns itself with the kind of writing that works directly with what you already have — things you have experienced, seen, imagined. The first step is to get comfortable with writing, to make it your tool. The next, and perhaps simultaneous step, is to realize how much material you have to write about.

One basic technique which has to be mentioned for the sake of children who don't appear to be so full of ideas, the ones with little or no previous experience in writing, is how to make the connection between spoken and written language. Imagine this situation: everyone is scribbling away except one boy who sits staring at his paper, head down, obviously

3

hoping no one will notice him. I ask, "What were you going to say when you had your hand up?" or, "What animals were you thinking of when we were talking about animals?" I just want him to speak at this point. When he finally says something — "I wasn't thinking about anything," or "I wasn't thinking about animals, I was thinking about baseball" — I say, "Then write that down. Put it on paper." In other words, I want the student to learn how to dictate to himself, to learn how to talk on paper, to let loose the flow of language as material to be written. Once this is learned, everything else becomes possible.

I also want my students to write things that are interesting to read. The average fifth grader or even high school senior has done relatively little original thinking about world affairs, but that same student has had vivid personal experiences and fantasies. I like pieces of writing that cause me to respond with "Oh Wow! I had completely forgotten that feeling! I had the same thing happen to me!" Or, "I never thought about that before." I try to judge student work by the same criteria I use for adult books I read. Is there authenticity in the voice? Is the language concrete and vivid? Is this a real communication — perhaps of humor or even silliness — not something done to manipulate me into giving a good grade? I like to read, and I want to enjoy reading all the hundreds of student pieces that come my way in a school year.

The assignments and methods in this book, therefore, are not seeds to be planted in the soil of fertile young minds but a series of entries that students can make into their own personal materials. I rarely know in my writing just what I am going to say until I am well into it but something does always get me started. Part of what I want to do in this book is to share points of departure, paths for discovering what to write about.

Most of the lessons in this book were designed to fit into a period of forty-five minutes to an hour. This has to do with the classroom circumstances under which I work with students, but I think the organization of the lesson has its own logic. A typical period goes like this:

I. I begin with an introduction and a sharing of any games or materials I have brought with me. This often means passing out rexographed sheets with brief samples of adult writing. I read aloud and sometimes have students take a turn, giving the material a second reading.

II. Next comes an open discussion that goes on for as long as the class seems interested and ends with my presenting the day's specific writing assignment.

III. There is a period of about twenty minutes of in-class writing during which I move around the classroom helping slow starters and answering questions, being available on a one-to-one basis as much as possible. Twenty minutes is never enough time for all the students to finish writing, so I ask the classroom teacher to give extra time for them to work later, if possible. (For someone using this book in her or his own classroom, the tightly organized hour session is less important; occasional formal lessons with lots of time to work on continuing writing projects would make the most sense to me.)

IV. For those who have finished, I like to end with some kind of sharing of work. This can be a presentation by reading aloud (by the students or by me) or it can be children exchanging papers with one another. It is important, though, to have some culmination, because writing is meant to be received. At the end of a residency, whenever possible, I try to publish some of the work or to have a public reading.

The progression of lessons within each chapter runs very roughly from simple to complex. Thus each chapter begins with something that any young child could do — simple word games, for example — and proceeds to difficult samples of adult writing and ideas that you would probably not want to use with kids under, say, fourth grade. Many of the ideas in the latter parts of each chapter come out of work I have done with high school and college students and adults, but the vast majority of assignments in this book could be used well with students of almost any age.

The progression within chapters follows roughly this plan: each chapter opens with an exercise in describing the experience of the senses in the most vivid language possible. Next comes lessons about learning to manipulate raw materials in some particular way — often by exaggeration. This is essentially work in establishing a consciousness of style and level of diction. The third part of each chapter offers ideas that focus on organizing a piece of writing. The aim is to make the piece of writing move, have form, reach its own natural shape and conclusion. From time to time I also include exercises in revision aimed at making students aware of how to look at their work as something that can be extended and changed, but the focus of this book is the importance of the initial direction, the exploration and search into materials, rather than the finishing.

The chapters, too, have an order, which is roughly from most outward to most inward: Chapter 2 is description of place; Chapter 3 description of people from the outside; Chapter 4 description of action; Chapter 5 dialogue writing; and Chapter 6 monologue writing. The final chapter, Chapter 7, looks directly at form and organization. This order, too, moves more or less from simple to complex. Children in first grade can do the observation exercises in concrete writing in the early chapters; the more complex samples of internal monologue will most likely work best with older students. (See Appendix B for a list of writing ideas by grade level.)

Prominent in these pages you will see selections of writing by students and adults. It is from these examples, particularly from those by adults, that I have developed most of the methods and assignments in this book. There is a well-used and usually successful creative writing assignment I have seen done often in classrooms in which the students imagine they wake up and are turned into something else. How would it feel? What would they do? What if you were something really loathesome, like a cockroach? The source of this assignment, of course, is the splendid, searingly cruel and beautiful novella *The Metamorphosis* by Franz Kafka. This has always pointed up to me that the sources of literature are common to all of us. That is why I can use a brief but dense passage from Virginia Woolf to show sixth graders what I mean by interior monologue. They may not like the passage; they may not even understand every word, but the sense of what is happening comes across. Therefore with my classes I use everything from Jane Austen to the *New York Daily News Magazine.* I am proud to have eclectic sources, but mostly I just *like* the pieces I offer up for imitation.

Some teachers of writing balk at the idea of imitation and models. I myself do not recommend servile imitation. Anytime I give an assignment and halfway into the writing period someone comes up and says, "Listen, that gave me an idea for something, can I do that instead?" my response, almost always, is "Yes, yes, yes." This is what I mean when I call these assignments *entries* or *starters,* ways of finding a direction. I want the students to use my assignments in their own way, as picks and shovels to mine their own ores.

Children and adolescents are, however, great and natural imitators, and it behooves us to offer them good models to imitate because they are going to be imitating, whether we like it or not. They will imitate the books they read, or the television shows they watch, or the books we read them. Therefore, I want to give them good models to try on for size. Part of what I want to do is simply expose my students to the sound of language used in a variety of ways. I certainly don't analyze my samples in any great detail or spend time in weighty discussions. Rather, I use them to create an atmosphere, to suggest new patterns. My interest is not in the art of imitation, but in suggesting forms and directions the students would probably not have come to on their own. I want them to write with the words from my models in their ears, as it were. Some will pick up a theme or rhetorical device; others won't. My point in using adult literature is only to open doors.

Student pieces should be presented as models too. In fact, one of my most successful pieces for use in the classroom is a dream written by a fifth grader from my first year of teaching (See page 167). The main thing is to bring in samples of writing that *you* admire and can present enthusiastically.

Another kind of imitation is not literary at all but behavioral, and I sometimes think that the best thing a teacher could do for his or her students would be to write when they write, to let them see an adult writing, and perhaps to talk with them about what is hard and easy for you as a writer. Some of the best teaching experiences I have ever had were ones when I came into a classroom as a guest, and the teacher was not only attentive and interested, but picked up a pencil and paper and wrote along with the students.

My ideal classroom, then, would be one in which the teacher wrote regularly and the children wrote regularly, and they talked together about writing, and they read together and separately from the whole panoply of literature. I envisage children's classics on the shelves alongside books of adult poetry and fiction. Bring in samples of writing that you admire — things written by students you had in past years, articles or poems that amuse and move you. Your students would be fascinated by samples of your own writing too. If you are a journal keeper, bring in your journal and work on it while the class writes. If you have a pen pal from early childhood, get a pen pal project started. In other words, share your own expertise and enthiasms, whatever they are.

I imagine a teacher reading through this book and proceeding in one of several ways. Perhaps you already feel you have a good writing program: for you, this book is a resource. You will dogear pages and mark exercises that might enrich what you already do. You might, on the other hand, like to try a selection from each of the chapters: make a minicourse over, say, six weeks, doing Place writings week the first week, then Person writings, etc. You could quickly amass a lot of writing in this way. Another teacher might actually sketch out a year-long plan from this book — there is certainly enough material — skipping only the parts inappropriate to her or his class. I would be happy to see this book used in any of those ways. I would also be delighted to hear from you what worked well, what didn't — and why — and any new ideas that I might add in future editions of this book. This author too is eager for responses to her writing.

Regardless of how you use this book, have your class write often. A daily period for writing is not too much. One fact that has come out of numerous studies of writing in the classroom is that the more writing done, the better the students become at writing. Even when there is too much volume for a sane teacher to correct, writing still improves proportionally to the amount of time spent doing it. Writing is not something that you learn wrong habits by doing. *You learn wrong writing habits only if you are trying to please someone else instead of developing your own way of saying what you want to say.* So write often, not necessarily giving a lesson every day, but simply making a space for the class to work on things already started, to discuss them with another student, or to have a conference with the teacher.

And, finally, do something with the writing at the end of the term. Publications are useful and lovely — there is no motivation quite like the glory of being published. A book can be a simple rexographed affair, but even if you or your school can't manage a book, try for some culminating activity. Turn some of the younger children's pieces into plays. Stage readings where older students visit the classes of younger students and read aloud. Make covers and rewrite neatly the best pieces for a lending library. Rexograph handwritten stories and sell them in the halls. To local bookstores! This book is not about how to print or bind them, but those things are nonetheless important. You don't have to correct all the papers, but *do* read them all, "receive" them all. Writing is a solitary activity, but at some point it demands a receiver, another human being saying, "I hear you. I understand what you said on this paper."

Chapter I: Describing Place

One of my favorite ways to begin a writing course with new students is to write about places. We all know what a place is — we are in one right now. In fact, we are always in a place, at a particular time. We are in a room, or outside, or in a car or bus or train. There is always air around us, warm and close or cool and drafty. An odor of something cooking wafts in from the kitchen. Sounds distract us from the matter at hand, or perhaps our favorite music is playing in the background. In a familiar place, such as the classroom or our own living room, the objects around us may hardly be noticed, but in a new place we are alert, our senses taking in information. Is the bowl of porridge on the table still steaming? Is the window wide open on this cold day, curtains sucked in and out by the breeze? What sort of possessions do the people who live here have? Are the beds unmade, or neat, even fastidious, as if the inhabitants never relaxed?

Observe a Place

The simplest, most basic of the describe-a-place exercises is to record what is around you now, at this moment. We all *have* the place we are now as material for writing. This can be a great help to students who declare they can't think of anything to write. The teacher has only to reply, "Don't try to think. Use this place right here. Look at this classroom. What do you see? How many windows? What can you see out of them? How does this room smell? What do you hear? What does your desk feel like it's made of? What's that boy over there wearing?" The student already has all this information, possibly without being aware that it's usable. "That's all I have to do?" he says. "Well *I* can do that." The beginning assignment with Place, then, can be as simple as listing what is right here around the writer at this moment.

The novelist and diarist Anaïs Nin wrote such a description of her schoolroom when she was a child. She made this diary entry secretly, when she was supposed to be doing her schoolwork:

FEBRUARY 25, 1915

I brought my diary to school so that I could write a few words. We are reciting geography but I can't follow it. I am going to describe the classroom, that place I detest. The classroom is a large square room with gray woodwork, a glass door, and on the right, a big cloak closet with red curtains. After hanging up my coat and hat, I go to the 4th yellow desk in the 3rd row. Before that, when I come in, I say, Good Morning Miss Bring. I get out a pencil, a pen, an eraser and a ruler. I take a book and study. The teacher goes bing on her bell, we stand up and say a prayer made up of an Our Father, Glory to God, Hail Mary, and the blessing of the day. After that we recite the catechism, then geography, then we do arithmetic until noon. At 1 school starts again. We do dictation, composition, reading, and grammar. At 3 it's finished. There are 24 boys, 12 girls in our class. The teacher is stern, but not mean, but there are many unfair things because she has a favorite who is the meanest girl in the class and accuses everyone else very unfairly. The teacher is watching me, so I have to close my notebook.
— from *Linotte: The Early Diary of Anaïs Nin*

Students are interested to know that this was written by a twelve-year-old who had just immigrated to this country, and that she grew up to be a writer, best known for her diaries, which began as letters to her father in Spain. If you, as a teacher, received this paragraph in fulfillment of an assignment on describing the classroom, how would you react to it? How would you react if you actually caught her writing the diary when she was supposed to be taking down her homework? I personally find the beginning a little colorless, when she sets out as her project the objective description of the room, but I like it when she begins analyzing the teacher and how she plays favorites. Here are some basic assignments for writing about Place:

•**Idea 3:** Describe the place you are in now as objectively as possible, using nothing but the facts: sizes, shapes, colors, smells, etc.

•**Idea 4:** Do it for some other place where you go often but are not now.

•**Idea 5:** Describe one of the places again, this time showing how you feel about it, but without saying in so many words that you like it or don't like it.

•**Idea 6:** Describe your classroom following the same pattern that Linotte does. Start with how it looks, then give the schedule, number of boys and girls, how the teacher is, etc.

•**Idea 7:** As a class, go to some nearby place — the playground, a park, the auditorium, the lunchroom. Without looking at one another's writing, describe the place as fully as possible. It will be interesting to compare the different details that different people notice. Some will include the pigeons, others will spend a long time describing the hot dog cart.

•**Idea 8:** Do this "Write here, write now" assignment on a class trip. Try it during a rest period, after the bag lunches, maybe.

•**Idea 9:** Or do it *after* the trip is over.

•**Idea 10:** Describe in detail a room in your house while you are at school.

•**Idea 11:** For homework, describe the same room while you are actually in it. How are the two descriptions different. Is one more detailed than the other? More interesting? Why? (These are not meant to be a tendentious questions — some people write much better with the thing itself in front of them, or immediately after leaving it. Others work better through the process of memory and reconstruction. These questions have to do with students discovering something about the kind of writers they are.)

•**Idea 12:** Describe a place that always gives you some particular feeling: a favorite store, your church, your grandmother's house.

•**Idea 13:** Describe a place where someone you know works: your mother's office, your uncle's shop.

•**Idea 14:** Describe the place in the world you hate most.

•**Idea 15:** Describe the place in the world you love most.

MY COUNTRY HOUSE

I am at my country house
lying in my hammock
listening to the birds
looking at the colors of the warm
summer forest
listening to the rain and enjoying
the rainbow with my grandfather
by my side listening to his radio
here comes mother she will
make stew for a delicious country
supper in an old fashion log cabin.
    — Erica Stoltz, 4th, P.S. 321, Brooklyn

(I don't distinguish much between poetry and prose with younger children. I often use poems to stimulate prose writing, and from time to time a student writes in poetic form entirely of her own volition. I myself, almost strictly a prose writer, often read poetry because I believe it has a tightening and intensifying effect on my prose.)

  That piece by Erica Stoltz has a natural dependence on details of the senses, predominately hearing, although there is seeing too, and the imagined good taste of the coming supper. These sense details create the atmosphere or mood. I like to point out early to student writers that everything we know comes to us through our senses. Whether you are writing a newspaper article, a poem, a how-to book or a novel, at some crucial moment you have to depend on sense details to convey your meaning.

The sense details are also what makes a piece of writing alive and vivid. I like to make that point by telling the following story. (It needs to have the immediacy of real life behind it, so if the idea appeals to you, I would suggest that you tell some similar incident from your own life.) I say to the class, "I'm going to tell you two versions of something that happened to me. After I've completely finished talking, I want you to tell me which is more interesting to hear.

"Number One. When I was eight years old, I had to go to the dentist a lot.

"Number Two. The summer I was eight, I had to go to the dentist every week. I'll never forget what it was like, walking into that old-fashioned office building. Coming out of the hot day into the cool hall always gave me a shiver, and I would hear the echo of my shoes as I started up the stairs. I would smell, just a little bit, the odor of the dentist's medicine, and it reminded me of the taste in my mouth and made me shiver too. The hall upstairs was dim, and as I walked down it, I began to hear the drill in the dentist's office, and it made me almost feel the pain in my mouth. When I got to his door, I always remember looking at the glass and how his name was painted there: It said, 'Dr. Wolf.' "

No one has gotten the wrong answer yet, although I get a lot of variety when I ask exactly why the second version is so much more interesting to listen to. Some kids say, "You told more," and that is certainly true. It simply has more in it. That's one thing that student writing often needs, more words, more time spent on it, more patience, more details. Other students will say, "You told how you felt in the second one," and there is no doubt that emotional involvement helps and makes us want to read more. (It doesn't hurt if the subject is something many people have experienced in their own lives.) Some kids have said that more happens in the second version, and that is a more subtle point than it seems. The incident consists of going into a building, up some stairs, as far as a door. So on the one hand very little happens, but on the other hand the student who says that more happens is absolutely right, because much is experienced, much is anticipated and imagined.

Sometimes, for balance, I follow the incident from my real life with this poem that also has all the senses in it.

KNOXVILLE, TENNESSEE

I always like summer
best
you can eat fresh corn
from daddy's garden
and okra
and greens

12

and cabbage
and lots of
barbeque
and buttermilk
and homemade ice-cream
at the church picnic
and listen to
gospel music
outside
at the church
homecoming
and go to the mountains with
your grandmother
and go barefooted
and be warm
all the time
not only when you go to bed
and sleep.
— Nikki Giovanni

The assignment that follows is another simple one that can be done in many different ways.

•**Idea 16:** Write about a place that you like or don't like, including all five senses or as many as you can.

THE ZOO IN INDIA

I remember going to a zoo in India when I was two or three. I was hot, for it was about eighty degrees. I rode on a wagon pulled by two goats. I call it a goat wagon. I also remember feeding some kind of bird. I felt the bird nibbling on my thumb, but it didn't hurt. I wanted to go to a beach or in a pool, it was so hot. I could have gone, but there wasn't a beach for at least ten or twenty miles and I would have to pay to get in a pool. I could hear people walking by. I could hear the horses trotting along.

I remember I wanted to get out of the zoo because it smelled a lot. It was the disgusting smell of manure. I saw that the manure of the donkey had steam coming out of it. My father said it is hot inside a donkey. The cows were mooing and loose. The beautiful peacock was squawking and also loose. The cow and the peacock are sacred animals.
— Janice Patel, 5th, P.S. 183, Queens

ON MY VERY OWN SHIP

The ship that I was on was a luxury liner. I saw men and the captain. They were very nice to me. My mother and father wanted to take a swim, so my father saw a pool. My father said the last one in the pool is a funny alien. I smelled a good tasty smell. It felt like a chocolate chip. It was getting dark quicker and darker. My mother and father making jokes and riddles.

13

Around 12:00 my mother went down to her cabin. I was touching the walls and my bed I was in. In the morning I saw the sun and people passing my cabin door. There were people holding their wives' hands too. And I went back to sleep. I was tired. I ate pancakes, sausages, and a little Pepsi Cola. A few days later one of the captain's men died jumping in the ocean. The ocean was very deep. The ship was black and white.
— Sean Jones, 4th grade, P.S. 321, Brooklyn

PUERTO RICO

When I went to Puerto Rico I would hear the roosters crowing. I would taste the sweet avocado my grandmother bought. I would feel the goat walking up and down the street. I would see the goat eating grass. It had a big, fat belly and a very long beard. I would smell the rice and beans that my grandma cooked. It was very warm, but it would rain and I would get wet. It was very nice because our next door neighbor would let us pick some fruit from his tree.
— Jazmin Hines, 3rd, P.S. 183, Queens

This is an easy one to find the natural form of — especially if the five senses are listed on the blackboard. Everyone can come up with some place they can describe in terms of how it looks, sounds, smells, tastes, and feels. The very insistence of the pattern will make for concrete writing through the use of details — which comes automatically with using sense impressions. In order to demonstrate concrete writing even more thoroughly, I will sometimes do a group writing with a class. "Now what I want is vivid language," I will say. "Do you know what 'vivid' means? It's a sort of first cousin to the Spanish word 'vivir' which means 'to live.' I want life in the language, I want it as solid and concrete as life." I usually do a group writing by having a scribe (or me) write on the board what the class says. We pick out a place that they know, but where I have never been (a local candy store is good, or the school gymnasium or lunchroom). The group effort allows for weighing one word against another. "Big?" I say. "I've never been there. How big is it? As big as a classroom? As big as a supermarket?" We can take a vote on whether we prefer "huge" or "enormous" or "the size of a basketball court." The final product is not necessarily great writing, but the process of discussing and weighing words in this way teaches students that words are malleable, that words can be played with, reformed, discarded, and replaced.

I was once doing this group exercise in a seventh grade class, and we had come to the part where I was asking for a word to capture the smell of the gymnasium. Someone called out, without raising his hand, "Funky!" and the whole class broke up in laughter. They didn't think you are allowed to *write* words like that, words that they use often, with expressive vigor. I don't particularly admire the word myself, although it has a nice round sound, but I did love the way the class reacted, so I wrote on the board, "The gymnasium has a sweaty smell, funky!" For that class, at that moment,

14

"funky" was vivid; "funky" had life. It further suggested to them that *their* language, and thus *their* own lives, can be written.

At that same Bedford-Stuyvesant junior high school a workshop of teachers came up with a group description of their teacher cafeteria:

> Bare, no pictures on the wall, no curtains. Windows on one wall open up to a recessed area made of concrete off the schoolyard. There is a din of voices, loud discussion of what happened before lunch, snatches of complaints about supervisors, how many days till retirement, number of days to end of year, and till holidays, and problems of students. It smells stuffy and warm, and there is an odor of bacon. The salad is lovely, though, colorful! A profusion of green, yellow, and gold. Mounds of white cottage cheese. Toward the end of lunch there is a smell of ammonia, the signal to leave, like smelling salts, it brings you back to reality, back to "lifting that bale."

I think this is pretty good writing considering that it was done by committee. If I were revising it, I might rework the beginning because it starts off slowly. At that point the teachers weren't sure of what was expected of them. But then it begins to get more lively. I really like the rhythm of what people were saying in the overheard conversations, although I might change the order so that "number of days till retirement" becomes the culmination of the list of things to look forward to. I especially like the way the smell of ammonia brings the writers back to reality, and I must say that I have a strong sense of what that lunchroom is like, and what it means to those teachers: an unlovely, noisy refuge where adults can sympathize with each other and have at least one of life's pleasures — enjoying the sight and flavor of good food.

Writing As a "Moment of Being"

Writing that centers on the senses can also be extremely sophisticated. How I apprehend the place where I am can be a deep indicator of mood or even world view. Virginia Woolf speaks of "moments of being" in which everything around you seems alive. You are entirely awake and aware of the sensation of your finger tips, of the sounds of leaves, of your own mind at work. Today as I write this, it is bright and sunny outside, but windy, just before spring bursts out. Brilliant light falls into my room and my spirits soar, and I long to get up from this typewriter and run outside. On another day, though, in a different mood, I might be torn by the contrast between the day and some unhappiness I am feeling. I might notice that there are no leaves yet, that sunlight falling on concrete seems to intensify the absence of nature from city life.

In the following exquisite piece of prose from her novel *The Years*, Virginia Woolf allows the evidence of the senses to draw us through a young college man's reverie and experience of a moment:

He stood by the window again. It was raining, but the whiteness had gone. Save for a wet leaf shining here and there, the garden was all dark now — the yellow mound of the flowering tree had vanished. The college buildings lay round the garden in a low couched mass, here red-stained, here yellow-stained, where lights burnt behind curtains; and there lay the chapel, huddling its bulk against the sky which, because of the rain, seemed to tremble slightly. But it was no longer silent. He listened; there was no sound in particular; but, as he stood looking out, the building hummed with life. There was a sudden roar of laughter; then the tinkle of a piano; then a nondescript clatter and chatter — of china partly; then again the sound of rain falling, and the gutters chuckling and burbling as they sucked up the water. He turned back into the room.

It had grown chilly; the fire was almost out; only a little red glowed under the grey ash. Opportunely he remembered his father's gift — the wine that had come that morning. He went to the side table and poured himself out a glass of port. As he raised it against the light, he smiled. He saw again his father's hand with two smooth knobs instead of fingers holding the glass, as he always held the glass to the light before he drank.

(The father's hand, by the way, lost two fingers in an accident. The trouble with using excerpts from long fiction works is that one of a fiction writer's primary tools is referring to things that take place pages and even chapters back. The advantage of using poetry or prose poems or fables in the classroom is that you can have before you the entire text of a work, every word of it at once.)

Notice the many colors of light in this piece: red and yellow from the windows, while the other colors have faded and only masses remain. Then there are the sounds — some wonderful, unobtrusive examples of onomatopoeia: "clatter and chatter — of china partly" and the "gutters chuckling and burbling." The reader is not only told about sounds, but given them. The main character also experiences changes in temperature (sense of touch), and he takes a glass of wine, implying taste. The sensations move from seeing and hearing to the more intimate ones of touch, smell, and taste.

This sort of writing will not immediately attract most students. If you ask them if they liked this piece they will say, "No, it was boring" or "It had too much description." You may not particularly like it yourself, but I find the precision and painstaking care a good balance for young writers' full-speed-ahead tendencies. In fact, I don't usually ask if students *like* my more difficult pieces. I ask them to find the five senses and to tell me how many colors the light has. I don't particularly *want* them to like this — I certainly would be astounded if any of them ran off and read *The Years,* but I think exposure to this sort of writing in a judiciously small dose can have a good effect. For example, one of my sixth grade students who had a distaste for writing wrote this after hearing and reading the selection from Virginia Woolf:

We got in the boat. It was a small sailboat packed with adventure. We started off onto the deep blue bay. The sound of the waves hitting the boat was there all the time. It was a very windy day, and waves were coming over the top of the boat. My feet felt wet and soggy inside my soaked sneakers. There was a smell of fish as we passed by a fishing boat, so we left and headed for the shore.

— Stephen Jenkins, 6th, P.S. 6, Manhattan

What I like about Stephen's piece is that he allowed himself a little time to recall. The piece has a leisured pace that I attribute directly to the Virginia Woolf. I am not interested in "description" for its own sake, although it is a skill we need in writing. Nineteenth-century readers delighted in long descriptions of places and objects as a means of learning about them; today television and magazine illustrations fulfill the function of giving us information about how things look. We've all, by now, seen photographs of a tiger, if not the actual creature in the zoo, so a description of a tiger has to have more reason for being than to provide information about how the animal looks. I am interested in description as an approach to exploring experience. The senses offer a way of organizing that exploration.

Students, in their headlong rush of writing, often assume far too much. They forget that the reader doesn't know that their kitten Snowball is not only white and cute but also blue-eyed and deaf. They need to be made aware of what has to be included. In general, the demand for details that teachers more and more insist on in writing assignments is a good thing. A poet I know, Janet Bloom, invented something called the Detail Monster while working with some third graders. The Monster is an insatiable gobbling creature who cries, "More colors! More sounds! Shapes!" It means little to tell me a room was ugly unless you and I have both been there or you are absolutely certain that I share your taste exactly. What is ugly about the room? Its color scheme? Its lack of cleanliness? Is it dingy and barren or crowded with plaster statues of nude ladies? Another vital function of description is that it allows me to give you something of what my particular experience was. I try to imagine the thing so clearly that I am able to find just the right building blocks of words that will recreate in your mind what I experienced. I, the writer, have this thing I want to give you, that I want you to see in your inner mind: my first effort is to imagine it, and then to put it into words. The rest is up to you, the reader/receiver.

A BLUEBERRY FIELD

I like my friend's blueberry field with plants that feel prickly and berries that taste GREAT, all you can smell for miles are the blue smell of berries. It looks as though the painters just painted every berry purple or blue and you always feel the squish of berries in your hand and hear other people squishing too.

— Sarah Prior, 3rd, P.S. 321, Brooklyn

EAST HAMPTON

Fresh air, burned hot dogs, the dog barking, the clock bonging away, the wet sand clinging to my toes, sand castles, cars rushing by, the taste of homemade apple pie, cool iced tea, petting the neighborhood cat and the sound of her purring, pebbles scratching my feet, the sound of someone yelling because they lost a game or a race against someone. That's East Hampton in my eyes and ears.

— Kendra Rider, 5th, P.S. 87, Manhattan

•**Idea 17:** Describe a place by making up clues to the identity of the inhabitants. Tell what kind of furniture they have and what objects are on their tables, what pictures on their walls. You might do this in pairs or groups. Switch off and write what you think the people are like from the other person's clues while they do yours.

•**Idea 18:** Describe a room in such a way as to give away the personality of the person who lives there. A tomboy who loves the Yankees? A bedfast person who used to be a painter?

•**Idea 19:** Write an objective police report on a place where a crime has been committed.

•**Idea 20:** Without revealing the date, describe a town in such a way that it is clear what country and/or historical period it is in. Could you actually make it clear what the very year is by some clue? (Tea leaves floating around the wooden hulls of the ships at anchor....)

•**Idea 21:** Do the same thing for a country landscape or a beach.

•**Idea 22:** Do it with a room, or onboard a ship or other means of transportation.

•**Idea 23:** Do one of the above including people and their clothing and implements.

•**Idea 24:** Describe an imaginary setting in the future. What kind of society does it seem to be, judging by the vehicles, implements, buildings, etc. One that is more advanced than ours? One that has degenerated?

•**Idea 25:** Do this for a planet that never existed. Describe the landscape or cityscape. Include everything but the animate beings. Can you reveal anything about them, without actually describing what they look like?

•**Idea 26:** Do this same exercise for a deserted room or street on earth today as if you were a visitor from a distant galaxy. (What is that strange little spring of water in a porcelain container? It appears to be just the size for some domesticated animal to drink from....)

•**Idea 27:** A few years back there was a television series about a blind detective. Make up a story in which you explore a place using only the senses of hearing, touch, and smell.

•**Idea 28:** Pretend you are a dog or other animal whose primary sense is smell. Describe a place from that point of view.

•**Idea 29:** Describe a place using only *one* quality of *one* sense, color, for example, as Thoreau does in the piece on page 28.

•**Idea 30:** Still using your senses primarily, pretend to be a shrinking person and describe common objects as if they were places — a sink full of dirty dishes becomes a vast Badlands landscape. What do you hear and smell?

•**Idea 31:** Imagine you go inside a common object. Make up an imaginary landscape inside this thing. What is it like inside a wad of chewing gum? A light bulb? A computer? (The idea for this comes from a poem by Charles Simic called "The Stone," which can be found in many anthologies, such as *The Poetry Connection,* edited by Nyhart and Gensler and published by Teachers & Writers Collaborative.)

•**Idea 32:** Read any of the literature samples or student pieces in the body of this chapter or in the anthology that follows it. Underline the words and phrases you like best, and assemble them in a short poem of your own.

Exaggeration in Describing Places

Students love to be told to exaggerate. Exaggeration will appear again and again in this book as a good example of a style that is natural to most kids (it is one element of their humor). It is a good example, too, of a style that they can grasp immediately and have a good time with. It can also be a freeing experience for many students, possibly their first chance to have fun, go a little too far — be wild — with words.

From "The Aristocrat of Hustle"

This was not the Y, not your genteel basement rec room where secretaries pushed demure volleys at each other during lunch hour. The Fat Kid knew this was the place the *players* came, a subterranean inferno where only the best could stand the heat. Reputations rose and fell with each scorching smash. Losers slunk up the stairs and disappeared from the neighborhood; winners left at dawn, their pockets crammed with cash. And the most hardened bettors suddenly were overcome in the middle of a gut-wrenching match. Some fell to their knees on the cracked linoleum floor, others had to be pulled, quaking, from bathroom stalls.

The Fat Kid peered into the smoky room. Dangling 60 watt bulbs fought the gloom as little white spheres flew through the air at speeds the Fat Kid had never dreamed of. Tables dipped at precarious angles, propped by the stumps of broken paddles. People leaped, lunged, raced about, groaning in six languages. Korean masters dueled romance language professors; pinstriped stockbrokers pulled off their shirts and wiped their faces on monogrammed towels. In the corner, two gang members in leather jackets contested a point fiercely, a pile of chains and blades nestled in a sweatshirt beneath the table.

— Dave Hirshey, *New York Daily News Magazine*

19

This is an excerpt from an article about a man who owned and operated a ping pong emporium. It is not a particularly elegant piece of writing compared to the selection from Virginia Woolf on page 16 but it has a wonderful energy. I like to read it aloud to classes — you almost have to read it rapidly or you won't have enough breath to finish those crowded sentences. A fast reading also helps to give the full effect of jumbled detail and kaleidoscope turmoil. This is not a piece of writing to savor word by word. Rather, you should be drawn into a sort of word-malestrom, just as the Fat Kid himself is drawn into the place. Many of the words are used for effect — for atmosphere — rather than for their strict denotations. What, after all, are "Korean masters and romance language professors" supposed to look like? I think Dave Hirshey wants us to associate rapidly, a little vaguely perhaps, seeing some oriental practitioner of an arcane martial art, and a man in a dark moustache and cape. Or some such juxtaposition. Everything is extreme: he probably remembered some hoody-looking teenagers who became in his exaggerated style the "gang members in black leather jackets [who] contested a point fiercely, a pile of chains and blades nestled in a sweatshirt beneath the table." This kind of writing has a lot of energy, and a respectable pedigree, as demonstrated by the work of Tobias Smollett, Lawrence Sterne, Dickens, and even Rabelais. Today a writer like Thomas Pynchon works in this mode. (For more examples, see the selections on page 56.)

The first piece below is an exaggeration — I *think*. The student who wrote it claimed it was objective. The second piece is definitely exaggerated. Isn't it? At any rate, both were written after a discussion of exaggeration as a style, and after a reading of the selection by Dave Hirshey above.

•

The downstairs cafeteria — a dingy, dirty, greasy, grimy room cluttered with empty garbage cans, and mustard packets squeezed out on the floor. Chocolate milk and soda cartons are rolled out on the floor. Sticky orange soda stuck to all the tables. The back room smells of unsterilized walls and white floors with dirt, dust, and hair on them. High schoolers playing handball in and on every wall. The loud thumping noise of handballs fills the room. The crunch of potato chips muffles out the sound of talking.

— Jonathan Hatfield Hoefler, 5th, Hunter College
    Elementary school

DREAMS OF AN EPILEPTIC SCHOOLBUS

Screaming children are everywhere; one fifth grader breaks into a round of "we all live on a broken down bus," and two masked kids get on the bus with rubber knives, threatening to kill the driver if he doesn't take them straight to Disneyland.

The acrid, foul-smelling fumes of a 2-year-old barf lying on a seat turns your stomach; a war of bottle caps has broken out, and kids are betting on how long before the 70-year-old bus driver has a cardiac arrest. You can clearly see the blood-soaked, hole-ridden sweater riddled by B-B pellets.

Still you can very clearly hear kids screaming and smell a kid's bad breath. Someone just shot a piece of candy at you, and it lands in your mouth. You can taste the cheap cinnamon candy floating in your mouth.

You fall on the floor and now have 50,000 lbs. of kids' feet standing and/or walking on you, crushing you, while you hope and pray your stop comes soon.

> — Richard Lansky, 5th, Hunter College
> Elementary School, Manhattan

•**Idea 33:** Write an exaggerated description of a place. If it is, say, a noisy school lunch room, make it not just noisy, not merely deafening, but have the noise hit your ears like a bazooka.

•**Idea 34:** Write a description of a place in which you list many brand names. Try to use the words for effect, that is, if it is a snotty preppie's bedroom being described, tell all the brand names of the jeans and tee shirts etc.

•**Idea 35:** Write a description of a place using as many exotic strange words as you can find — names of places or plants or animals.

•**Idea 36:** Write about a place describing it very objectively, then do it again, exaggerating.

•**Idea 37:** Do the same thing, but exchange objective descriptions with a friend and exaggerate the friend's piece.

•**Idea 38:** Describe a place in which people are part of the decor — a demonstration, a disco.

•**Idea 39:** Describe a place where everything seems to be in motion — maybe the person doing the describing is drunk or even crazy.

•**Idea 40:** Describe an ordinary room as seen by a mad person.

•**Idea 41:** Bring in a book you like. Go through it looking for a description of a place. Copy it down, if it isn't too long, and then write an imitation of the description, using your own place.

•**Idea 42:** Consider in what ways the Dave Hirshey piece is different from the Virginia Woolf piece. Try to rewrite the Woolf piece as if it had been written by Hirshey, and then the Hirshey piece as if it had been written by Virginia Woolf.

Using Place to Get a Story Started

One way to go a step further with some of these ideas for writing about place is to suggest that the students use their places for the openings of stories. The place in this case becomes a setting and a mood creator for a story. An example of a place as an opening to a novel is the one from *The*

Dispossessed, a science fiction story, on page 27. Another is the following exaggerated place that begins a famous nineteenth-century novel by Charles Dickens. I like the extremity of this one; the weather described is so muddy that it seems the Deluge is just over and dinosaurs are walking around!

From BLEAK HOUSE

London. Michaelmas Term lately over, and the Lord Chancellor sitting in Lincoln's Inn Hall. Implacable November weather. As much mud in the streets as if the waters had but newly retired from the face of the earth, and it would not be wonderful to meet a Megalosaurus, forty feet long or so, waddling like an elephantine lizard up Holborn Hill. Smoke lowering down from chimney-pots, making a soft black drizzle, with flakes of soot in it as big as full-grown snow-flakes — gone into mourning, one might imagine, for the death of the sun.

Here are two student pieces that begin with a place and continue with the introduction of people and events.

•

This is a large field. The sun is shining in full blaze. The grass is a luscious green and the trees lining the field are in full bloom. Around the east side of the field there is a tree along with many others bearing pink and white flowers, it is a very special tree. In the far distance, there is a huge house, almost a mansion. Under the special tree on the east side, two girls are sitting on a checkered picnic blanket. Spread before them is a huge lunch of chicken, flounder, egg roll, and a dessert of apple and spice pie with whipped cream and ice cream. They are dressed in the same grand fashion. The girl on the right is wearing a white summer dress with dropped waist, and her hair ends at her neck and is straight and black. The girl next to her is dressed in a summer dress that is very light pink, with a dropped waist, and with the same hair style. Like most females of their time, their skin is smooth and correct. It is 1923.
— Danya Dayson, 5th, P.S. 87, Manhattan

•

I felt the cool breeze of the ocean swish against my dark hair as I walked on the hot sand. As I walked closer to the shore, I smelt the salty sea water. I can almost taste the salty water. At last I reached the cool moist sand. As I tip-toed through the freezing water, I saw a small crab waddle around me. I kneeled to get a closer look and at my surprise it snapped at me. I back off a few feet. I got bored, so I decided to run. It sounds stupid, but it's the only thing I could think of. I started to run. As I ran, the hot sand felt good as I swished through it. Suddenly I tripped and fell head over heels into the sand. "Poof! Yelch!" The sand tastes terrible. I got up and brushed the sand off me. I decided to walk home. As I walked on the rocky

road, I saw a round beige rock. I picked up the rock. It felt so smooth I threw it over a red barnyard fence. I heard glass shatter. A big lump went down my throat. A farmer came out in red overalls, black boots, blue checkered shirt, a straw hat, holding the rock in his hand. I was so scared I couldn't say anything. . . .
— Andrew Fearon, 3rd, P.S. 321, Brooklyn

Another way writing about place can get a story started in a fruitful direction is by offering a pattern or movement. The next selection from adult literature uses both objective description and place names for evoking a mood. You aren't really expected to run to your atlas and look up the Fedchenko Glacier or the Pamirs; rather, you should get a sense of great distance and exotic places from these.

From THE NAMES

West of Jemez Pueblo there is a great red mesa, and in the folds of the earth at its base there is a canyon, the dark red walls of which are sheer and shadow-stained; they rise vertically to a remarkable height. You do not suspect that the canyon is there, but you turn a corner and the walls contain you; you look into a corridor of geologic time. When I went into that place, I left my horse outside, for there was a strange light and quiet upon the walls, and the shadows closed upon me. I looked up, straight up, to the serpentine strip of the sky. It was clear and deep, like a river running across the top of the world. The sand in which I stood was deep, and I could feel the cold of it through the soles of my shoes. And when I walked out, the light and heat of the day struck me so hard that I nearly fell. On the side of a hill in the plain of the Hissar I saw my horse grazing among the sheep. The land inclined into the distance, to the Pamirs, to the Fedchenko Glacier. The river which I had seen near the sun had run out into the endless ether above the Narakoram range and the Plateau of Tibet.
— N. Scott Momaday

The author of this piece is a Native American who is describing a visit to an ancient mesa in the American Southwest. He uses this visit as a springing off place for memories, and the pace is slow. It should be read aloud slowly, too, with time for the words to sink in and a dignified, meditative mood to be established. Do you notice the importance of the sense of touch in this piece? The cool sand, the way the heat hits the speaker as he comes back out of the canyon? The place names at the end connect the present to the vastness of time and space, and perhaps the roots of the speaker's own people in faraway Asia.

One of the reasons I particularly like this piece is that it is organized as a walk. First the speaker describes the place seen from a great distance, the long cinematic view, the size and color of the mesa; then we come in a little closer, to one part of the mesa only, the canyon entrance. Then we walk into the canyon, and experience it from the inside, with the shadows closed in around us and the view of the strip of sky. We feel the temperature, the sand. Then the narrator looks back where he came from, and the view becomes vast again, even more vast than before he had entered the place and touched it. There is an interesting stylistic peculiarity, too, in that the speaker is addressing us, the readers, directly. Writing in the second person, to a "you" is unusual, but it has a way of pulling the reader into the writer's world, if there is sufficient sympathy. This selection is not easy, and its distant reflective quality is not natural to younger students, who take to the fun of exaggeration more easily, but the structure suggests interesting ways of giving form to impressions.

•**Idea 43:** Experiment with writing about a place using only the second person ("you").

•**Idea 44:** Write about a place as if you were walking through it. Approach, describing things from a distance, and then go closer so that you can actually touch things, then look back the way you came, as Momaday does in the preceding excerpt.

•**Idea 45:** Describe an abandoned place that seems very ancient.

•**Idea 46:** Describe something extremely distant, a range of mountains, the top of a distant building.

•**Idea 47:** Approach and enter a great thunderhead or other distant object. Imagine what it would be like to go inside it.

•**Idea 48:** Write about a place that has special meaning for you or your family or for people in your ethnic group. Go there, in your imagination, and describe the place, and try to include something of what it means to you.

•**Idea 49:** Imagine a real place you have always wanted to go to and haven't yet.

•**Idea 50:** Create (in words!) a horror or torture chamber with all the nastiest devices you can think up. Be sure to include psychological ones and the one that would be hardest for *you* to endure. Then take someone on a tour of it, describing the devices, saving the worst for last.

•**Idea 51:** Choose a point of view and write what you see from there. Use perhaps your own window. Then go to the place you were describing, look back at your vantage point, and describe *it* that way.

•**Idea 52:** Describe a dream room. Describe it in this order: how do you get there, and how do you enter it? What is the floor made of? The walls and ceiling? What holds it together? How long do you stay and how do you get out? How long will the room last?

MY VIOLET DREAM ROOM

The floor is made out of grass, but it is covered with pink-violet flowers so grass is unable to be seen.

The walls are made of vines growing up magically without falling. They are cemented with flowers in between. The ceiling is made of nothing but violet sunsetting sky for there is no ceiling. And there are pinkish clouds from the sky, and they are going over the sun which is almost set.

There is a little flowery bed which is coming up and one day it will be a tree with millions of flowers on it. I feel I should walk slowly, not knowing what's ahead of me, but so far liking what I see. When I go in there, I want to stay there because it's sunny and warm with a small pond. I go in, it's quiet except for animal sounds. Nothing happens to me except I feel as if I'm in a magical world, all alone with flowers and anything anyone would want in their own place. At the end it just dies away. The tree dies, the grass, the flowers, the vines, the sun, the clouds, the sky. It is lonely there. Nothing for miles except for dirt on the ground and gray sky. It is hard to believe it was once the wonderful dream room.
— Debbie Steinberg, 5th, P.S. 321, Brooklyn

•**Idea 53:** Try a mood room in the same style as the dream room, making the perfect place for you when you are in an angry mood, a sad one, a silly mood, etc.

•**Idea 54:** Write about a place that changes as you describe it. Start it, for example, extremely quiet, and then have music and activity begin to happen.

•**Idea 55:** Describe a place that you are reminded of by your senses. Bring some actual smells to class in small bottles or jars: perfume, coffee, cough medicine, etc. Without their knowing ahead of time what is in the bottles, have students close their eyes and sniff and then wait for that smell to carry them to some place and write about it. It can be an actual memory of a place or something made up that is stimulated by the smell.

COFFEE SMELL

An old-fashioned house with a fire and a smoking chimney. Soup on the fire. A room full of old books and pictures and hungry children and parents sitting at a table. A thin cat curled on the crimson and corn-colored rug. Outside, an old maple tree shedding its leaves. A small apple tree with unripe apples. The smell of winter. Inside again, the smell of soup, dust, and the sound of the fire crackling. A little brown chair and four wooden stools. In a white closet, a fur coat filled with mothballs.
— Lolly Jacobs, 1st, P.S. 6 Manhattan

•**Idea 56:** Choose a means of transportation and describe what you see as you travel on it.

•**Idea 57:** Take a trip through your own body, pretending to be tiny. What do you see and hear?

•**Idea 58:** Stand by, or pretend to stand by, your absolutely most favorite tree in the world and describe what you see, and what it makes you think of.

•**Idea 59:** Imagine you have arrived in the United States for the first time, immigrating from another country. What do you see, and how does it seem? (See Anais Nin's August 11, 1914 diary entry on page 132.)

•**Idea 60:** Take the reader on a tour of your house.

•**Idea 61:** Write about two places that are very different, or perhaps make it the same place seen at two greatly separated times.

A BEFORE AND AFTER STORY

Before

It is about noon and the animals are sheltered from the sun under scattered trees. The waves of long, brown grass stretch on forever, interrupted only by an occasional tree. A herd of small antelope play, running slowly in the sweltering heat.

The sky above is so blue it is unthinkable. It is like a giant bubble over the plain.

A waterhole nearby is brown mud and dirty water. Several trees grow nearby, and a few of the larger animals rest in their shade. Huge, fleshy, thick-skinned animals lie submerged in the water, only eyes and nostrils sticking out.

The rotted corpse of one of the great beasts lies festering, flies buzzing around its hindquarters. It has been devoured by one of the giant long-toothed cats which are the scourge of the plains.

The scene is quiet and peaceful, though later in the day, towards evening, it will be the scene of fierce battles and bloody killings.

After

A man in old greasy rags stands on the corner, a crumpled brown bag in his hand. Bright, garish neon lights flash in the half light of December at five o'clock. A group of sexy, well-formed women in tight pants, see-through blouses and lots of bright makeup are standing on the corner. The buildings are grey and dilapidated. A sign announces, "Topless waitresses." Bright, lurid neon signs grow pale in the gray washed-out light from the worn, dishrag sky.

Shouting erupts from a sordid alley. A door slams, a drunken man lurches out, cursing. He wobbles and weaves, and falls flat on his face in the gutter. Paper and garbage blow on the damp restless wind.

A baby wails, and a woman's voice curses. The sound of heavy blows is heard, and a child screams. The sky darkens to deep blue. Bright lights flash, loud raucous music blares. It is night.

— Megan Williams, 6th, Hunter College Elementary
School, Manhattan

•**Idea 62:** Describe a familiar place that suddenly becomes unfamiliar.

•**Idea 63:** Describe a garden of delights, with the most wonderful things you can imagine. Who goes there with you? What grows on the trees? (Make it something besides candy.)

•**Idea 64:** Describe the most interesting street corner you know. Or store. Or riverbank. etc.

•**Idea 65:** Describe a place that is all: horrible, new, old, still, lively, etc.

MORE PLACE PIECES BY ADULTS

From "The Fall of the House of Usher"

During the whole of a dull, dark, and soundless day in the autumn of the year, when the clouds hung oppressively low in the heavens, I had been passing alone, on horseback, through a singularly dreary tract of country, and at length found myself, as the shades of the evening drew on, within view of the melancholy House of Usher. I know how it was — but, with the first glimpse of the building, a sense of insufferable gloom pervaded my spirit. I say insufferable; for the feeling was unrelieved by any of that half-pleasurable, because poetic, sentiment with which the mind usually receives even the sternest natural images of the desolate or terrible. I looked upon the scene before me — upon the mere house, and the simple landscape features of the domain — upon the bleak walls — upon the vacant eye-like windows — upon a few rank sedges — and upon a few white trunks of decayed trees — with an utter depression of soul which I can compare to no earthly sensation more properly than to the icy afterdream of the reveller upon opium — the bitter lapse into everyday life — the hideous dropping off of the veil. There was an iciness, a sinking, a sickening of the heart — an unredeemed dreariness of thought which no goading of the imagination could torture into aught of the sublime. What was it — I paused to think — what was it that so unnerved me in the House of Usher?
    — Edgar Allan Poe

From THE DISPOSSESSED

There was a wall. It did not look important. It was built of uncut rocks roughly mortared. An adult could look right over it, and even a child could climb it. Where it crossed the roadway, instead of having a gate it degenerated into mere geometry, a line, an idea of boundary. But the idea was real. It was important. For seven generations there had been nothing in the world more important than that wall.

Like all walls it was ambiguous, two-faced. What was inside it and what was outside it depended upon which side of it you were on.

Looked at from one side, the wall enclosed a barren sixty-acre field called the Port of Anarres. On the field there were a couple of large gantry cranes, a rocket pad, three warehouses, a truck garage, and a dormitory. The dormitory looked durable, grimy, and mournful: it had no gardens, no children; plainly nobody lived there or was even meant to stay there long.
    — Ursula Le Guin

LYING ON A HAMMOCK
AT WILLIAM DUFFY'S FARM IN PINE ISLAND, MINNESOTA

Over my head I see the bronze butterfly,
Asleep on the black trunk,
Blowing like a leaf in green shadow.
Down the ravine behind the empty house,

The cowbells follow one another
Into the distances of the afternoon.
To my right,
In a field of sunlight between two pines,
The droppings of last year's horses
Blaze up into the golden stones.
I lean back, as the evening darkens and comes on.
A chicken hawk floats over, looking for home.
I have wasted my life.
                    — James Wright

NANTUCKET

Flowers through the window
lavender and yellow

changed by white curtains —
Smell of cleanliness —

a glass pitcher, the tumbler
turned down, by which

a key is lying — And the
immaculate white bed
                    — William Carlos Williams

From WALDEN

    All our Concord waters have two colors at least, one when viewed at
a distance, and another, more proper, close at hand. The first depends
more on the light, and follows the sky. In clear weather, in summer, they
appear blue at a little distance, especially if agitated, and at a great distance
all appear alike. In stormy weather, they are sometimes of a dark slate color
. . . . I have seen our river, when, the landscape being covered with snow,
both water and ice were almost as green as grass. Some consider blue "to be
the color of pure water, whether liquid or solid." But, looking directly down
into our waters from a boat, they are seen to be of very different colors.
Walden is blue at one time and green at another, even from the same point
of view. Lying between the earth and the heavens, it partakes of the color of
both. Viewed from a hill top, it reflects the color of the sky, but near at
hand, it is of a yellowish tint next to the shore where you can see the sand,
then a light green, which gradually deepens to a uniform dark green in the
body of the pond.
                    — Henry David Thoreau

From HIGHER GROUND

    At the top of the stairs was a great swell of grass and sky. I moved
forward cautiously, almost dizzy after being enclosed by hillside and weeds.

There was a path through this unfolding of sky, and then I really was on top, with everything spread around me: fields, woods, roads, barns, and I didn't recognize a single place among all this doubling and corrugating of hills.

Ahead of me was a weather-gray house with a porch. On one side, like crosses with their tops knocked off, were two clothes-line poles. Only the roof of the barn was visible as the hill started down again.

Dogs barked, and a person came out on the porch and stood in the shadows. . . .

— Meredith Sue Willis

MORE PLACE PIECES BY STUDENTS

•

One hollow tree all alone sitting in the field. You go inside, you smell pine and feel comfortable. It is cushioned all around and velvet wipes your skin. You hear all the birds and nature chirping away. Everything goes smoothly with warm fires and good food that just appears. You have a rocking chair and a small table you eat at. Then you go into the bedroom. It is all silk with a big round bed and a big furry rug. Everything is silent, you fall asleep. You go out and you are in the field standing in front of the hollow tree. Waiting for another night in the tree.

— Alice Finer, 5th, P.S. 321, Brooklyn

•

It's a cold and clammy dark place. Rough walls, icy rock. Smells like bacteria. Large poles, plain old wood, about to fall. You could hear the dropped water coming down. Chips of rock fall when you talk. You need a boat to travel. As you go deeper, it gets darker. There comes a person. Tall, dark teeth, long nose. It's a dog. He looks at me with a gloomy dark eyes. Tall eyes. He attacks me. I run, but as I run, the icy rock falls on me. When I look back, the dog is dead. A rock fell on his icy cold eyes. I went and saw nothing. I left there, not looking at it. I was afraid to tell anybody. When I look back, a big rock fell. I must go home, I said. And I did.

— Alvin Garcia, 7th, I.S. 184, The Bronx

•

My mansion is a very big house. It is white on the outside and has three floors. I have roses growing around the house, and two orange trees in the backyard. The inside smells as fresh as my roses. I had a beautiful big white chandelier and red light bulbs in it. The couches were beige, made out

29

of rabbit fur. The carpet was brown made out of bear fur. Then the kitchen was a beautiful pink with burgundy curtains. The bathroom downstairs was made out of blue satin and the bathroom upstairs was made out of a yellow satin. The dining area was big with a see-through glass table with chairs to match. My bedroom was a peach satin and I had an extra room with two water beds. Play area had all the toys a child could wish for. The third floor had its own kitchen, bathroom, and bedroom. All the upstairs colors were beige and brown....

  — Michele Lawrence, 7th, I.S. 184, The Bronx

●

  The hall room had been abandoned for a long time. Spider webs dangled from the ceiling, drawn like streamers. There were crates with wine bottles. A bar with six broken chairs. A bathroom near the bar. This dirty hole was it? This was the place I rented for three hundred dollars? This was where I was going to have my party? This place was too small for a rat, maybe even a mouse! There was no heat at all, no heat at all! Freezing! The windows were broken and the cold was seeping in! I walked into the dark bathroom. I turned on the faucet. A few flakes of rust came out, then some trickles of rusty water. The mirror was covered with a thin layer of dust. The paint on the walls was cracking. This place was awful! Not nearly fit for a king, not nearly fit for a bum. Three hundred dollars down the drain.

  — Geeta Tate, 6th, Hunter College Elementary School,
   Manhattan

●

  As I skated in the morning, the sun shone brightly on the frozen pond. It was cold and I felt my nose turning into an icicle, along with the rest of my face. The only sounds were the birds chatting about the new day and the blades of my skates striding on the ice. The fresh snow sparkled with an occasional patch of green. Suddenly the aroma of coffee came to my nose. I knew it was time for breakfast.

  — Rene Barseghian, 4th, P.S. 6,
   Manhattan

Chapter 2: Describing People

Many of the techniques for describing place can be used in describing people as well. Again it is the evidence of the writer's senses that creates the vivid impression in the reader's mind. Again it is concrete language and intense re-experiencing that sets the stage for good writing. A description of a person has many possible details: colors, sizes, shapes, tones of voice, textures of clothing, hair and skin, even odors. To demonstrate the variety of details, I like to tell a story.

"Which one of these is more interesting?" I say to the kids.

"Number One: I drove my car to your school last week, and when I went out after school I saw a man standing by my car. When I got close, he went away.

"Number two: I went out after school and saw a man standing beside my car. He was tall and had red hair and a red beard, and he was wearing a green jacket. As I got closer I noticed that he had the bluest eyes I had ever seen; they were so blue it was almost as if you could see through them, but in fact he seemed to be staring through me. He shouted in a harsh voice that sounded like he was half choking, 'Why did you park your car in front of my house? Nobody is supposed to park their car in front of my house!' and he brought down one rough-skinned hand on the hood of the car — wham! making a terrible loud noise. As I got closer, I smelled a whiff of liquor on him, and I started to shake. I had my key out and I jumped in my car and drove away as fast as I could."

I am very careful in this little story to include all the senses except taste — I smell liquor on the man's breath, I hear a particular kind of voice, I even notice that the skin on his hand is rough. It amuses kids to say in public what we all know, of course, and that is that the sense of touch and smell *are* involved in our apprehension of another being. If anyone is in doubt, have

31

someone talk (honestly) about a baby in their house: how the baby's hair and skin are so soft, and the sweet smell of fresh flesh and powder and then the unpleasantness of dirty diapers. I even remember my parents kissing and playing with my baby sister's feet and saying they tasted sweet, were good enough to eat.

One general lesson in this chapter, then, is an extension of the writing-with-your-senses message of the previous chapter. It can be demonstrated, as I have done with my two versions of the same story, that an incident is more interesting to hear or read when the senses are used extensively. Another good point to make is that there are two kinds of writing, and that they have different purposes. If someone had damaged my car and I had been in a big hurry to call the police and report it, the most efficient way of getting across my information would be something like the first version of my story of the man and my car. I would say something to the effect that my car is damaged and I saw a man near it. Later the details of his appearance and my opinion that he might be drunk would be important. If, on the other hand, I wanted to tell a good friend about it, I would use a style much more like the highly descriptive, sense-rich second version. I would share, demonstrate, *show* what the experience was like rather than simply telling a few salient details. Plain, concise *telling*, then, is one kind of writing (or talking), and it has its purposes. *Showing*, on the other hand, is the kind of writing used more often in fiction because the writer wants to convey not only the facts of the experience or event, but also the texture — the feeling, sound, and smell of it.

You can also use description of a person to explore character or create atmosphere. An old derelict on the street can be used as decor, part of a general impression of poverty. On the other hand, if you describe your particular derelict as an individual — perhaps revealing that under the layers of dirt and caked blood is a custom-made, tailored shirt — you are doing something else altogether. You may be setting up some facts that will be of use in furthering a plot, or you may be engaged in the more uniquely fictional activity of exploring and revealing the inner life and past history of a human being through his appearance and behavior.

Observation Games with Description of People

I have a series of describing games that I first used with younger children, but I've found them useful with older students too, especially on a stuffy winter day when the steam heat is too high and everyone has been sitting too long. The first exercise is an old-fashioned parlor game. Two students volunteer to come to the front of the class. One is "It" and he or she has ten or fifteen seconds to examine the other student closely, to observe. Then "It" goes out of the room, and the teacher or some other volunteer makes a tiny change in the clothing of the observed student: a button is unfastened, a sleeve rolled up, a watch moved from one wrist to the other. Then "It" returns and has to guess what was changed. After a few rounds of this, variety can be added by changing not the clothing, but the position of the arms and legs, or, even better, the expression on the observed student's face. Try crossed fingers or eyes or a neutral expression turned louring. The aim of the game is twofold: first to improve observation skills, and second to make a point about how many different details there are that make up a person's total appearance. At some point during the game I like to establish a list on the board of all the kinds of things we are changing: later I will enlarge this list in a class discussion about the things that we notice when we first meet a person. This list can be amazingly full: clothes (stylish, colorful, or dull), hair style, hair texture, expression on the face, color of skin, tone of voice, etc. Because students will tend to say that when you meet a person the first thing you notice is whether or not they are "nice," the teacher's job here is to make sure the list is primarily concrete.

•**Idea 66:** There are lots of variations on the observing game. Try having five people stand in front of the class with some textbook they all use, while "It" covers her or his eyes. The five read aloud, and "It" has to recognize them by voice.

•**Idea 67:** Try this with "It" touching five people's hair. Can you recognize a person by hair shape and teture?

At some point the class should brainstorm a list of sample words that are good for describing these details we are observing. Some details are easy to describe — we have lots of words for color and shape (although students usually need to be reminded of how many there are), but touch and smell and even sound take more thought. How would you describe Donny's voice? Deep? Like a person with a cold? More like a man's than a boy's? Was Lisa's hair puffy? Thick and soft? Like touching the babysbreath plant? Did it feel the way a cumulus cloud looks? This is an excellent opportunity to talk about how comparing one thing to another can extend the way we describe.

•**Idea 68:** Play the observation game by having all the students *write* their impressions of "It."

•**Idea 69:** Divide into groups and choose one person in each group for all the others to describe as completely as possible.

•**Idea 70:** Divide the task: one person is responsible for sound, one for sight, one for touch. Smell and taste are probably too intimate for this project, although it would be an interesting experiment, among friends, to know if Matthew's nose tastes the same as his fingertips.

•**Idea 71:** Describe in writing another person in the class right now. Don't give the name and don't say anything that would hurt anyone's feelings. Read the descriptions aloud and guess who was the subject.

DESCRIBING HER

She is a girl with long brown hair. She's wearing gray wooly socks and a

cornflower blue sweater and red silky jeans. She's got small brown leather shoes with rubber soles with leather strings hanging down them. She has light skin color. She has light rosy red cheeks. She has pretty brown eyes. She has a hair clip in her hair.
— Hilary Anger, 3rd, P.S. 321, Brooklyn

AS I OBSERVE MY FRIEND

When I look at her, I see brown eyes, brown hair that's curly at the bottom, and brown eyebrows. Personally I think she's very punky. In fact, last year for Halloween she was a punk clown. She has one hand of finger-nails painted pink and the other painted nothing. When the class is having a lesson, she slumps down in her chair and never raises her hand. Her ears are pierced, and the earrings that she wears are hooped. She really doesn't like them, but she has to wear them or her ears will close up. She also never wears dresses. Always the same old jeans or corduroys. She also never wears fancy shoes. Always the same old Adidas sneakers. And she hardly ever wears sweaters, just tee shirts or sweat shirts. She also wears purple socks usually, and her lips are always chapped. She likes to play board games and skate board, you know, stuff like that. You might say she's a tom boy. At the beginning of this story, I told you she has brown hair, but actually it's turning redder every day. She talks like a baby, kind of squeaky. Well, even though I've told you a lot of kind of bad stuff about this person, she's still my best friend. The reason why I like her is because we both have the same three qualities in common: freaky, funky, and punky. We both like the same things to eat, to wear, and to play.
— Tracy Charters, 5th, P.S. 87, Manhattan

One of the things I like about Tracy's piece is the way she starts out to be objective, but, after including lots of good details, moves into why she likes her friend — which was not part of the assignment — and reveals that she likes her because they two are a lot alike, and in fact that she, Tracy, would pretty much fit this same description. Often what a writer reveals in a description of one person is really something about herself or himself.

•**Idea 72:** Describe *only* a person's clothes; only the expressions; or any other single quality.

•**Idea 73:** Describe a person (real or imaginary) primarily by touch and/or smell. (See the Smollett excerpt on page 56.)

•**Idea 74:** Describe a person from the crown of the head down, or vice versa, starting from the shoes.

•**Idea 75:** Write a description of a person in the room but make it hard to guess who it is. You have to be perfectly accurate, but you can concentrate on something very small, like the green and red strawberry pattern on the person's tee shirt, or the brand name of the jeans and sneakers.

•**Idea 76:** Write a police blotter report, describing the alleged perpetrator as concisely and precisely as possible: "A male Caucasian, slim build, about 5'9", balding with glasses, wearing a blue nylon jacket, jeans and white Converse sneakers."

Using Description for Word Portraits

In the piece by Tracy above, the strict observation naturally expanded into a word portrait. Portraits in words have a long, respectable history. People have always tried to capture their friends and acquaintances in words. The experimental American writer Gertrude Stein wrote a series of portraits of painter friends of hers (Picasso, for example) using what she intended to be a style of language analogous to Cubism in painting. Much earlier, in seventeenth-century France, upper-class men and women wrote and published lengthy descriptions of one another that led to exciting controversies about who was being described, and who had dared to describe that person in that way.

Sometimes when I am feeling brave, I let a class do a group writing word portrait of me. I usually do this after a discussion and brainstorming in which we make a list (as discussed above) of the various things that can be included in such a portrait. I don't do it if I sense any kind of hostile atmosphere, but when the mood is right, the idea of writing in public a description of an adult causes wild delight. I think I understand something of the thrill; I certainly remember how closely I observed my teachers all through grade and high school. I was fascinated by their smoker's coughs and the runs in their stockings. I knew when they had a rash and when they wore the same sports jacket two days in a row. Students know if the hem is out of your skirt or if you got a haircut. There is a whole underground sport of teacher-watching, and sometimes certain students will even come up and say something quite direct: "Why don't you wear your hair down, Miss Sue?" "I like those shoes." "What kind of skirt is *that?*" One reason I like this particular exercise is that it brings out into the open something secret (such as teacher-watching) that has a lot of energy and can make for energetic writing. I remember at one teacher workshop in the Bronx I was working with a group of bilingual elementary school teachers who listened to me politely as I talked about how wonderful writing is, but they didn't seem very excited until I gave them this exercise of describing me. They burst into life, and members of the workshop who hadn't said anything suddenly had elements of the portrait to contribute. "No make-up," they said (this after I had actually put on lipstick and mascara that morning!). "Clothes that you can't tell if she's fat or thin" (that from the lone male member of the workshop, and his comment brought a lively discussion from the women who didn't agree at all, thought the clothes were fine.) "Earth colors," they said. An antique look. That intrigued me, so I asked for more specifics. "An antique hairstyle," someone volunteered. "Like one of those old brown pictures of your grandmother and great grandmother." I was a little disconcerted by their view of me, but when it was over, our scribe had taken down a solid piece of writing; I had the experience of getting a hint of how I look to other people; and the workshop was altogether more alive and friendly.

On a different occasion, a fourth grade class described me this way: "Blue jeans jumper with zipper. Green plastic bracelet. Colorful patchwork shirt. Blue clogs with blue nylon socks. Long brown hair in a pony tail bun." "Not bad," I said, "but try it now." I changed my face dramatically, and had them describe that.

•

Mad face, angry, wrinkled.
Looks like she wants to kill!
Mean, wicked, a hundred years old!
Thinks she's strong.
Wants to fight.
Going to rob.
Going to knock a head off.
Looks the way you do when you have to do something
    you don't want to do.

•**Idea 77:** Make as precise a word portrait as you can of any adult you know.

MR. MASON

    Mr. Mason is a kind, understanding teacher. He is not very tall, and has a dark complexion. On his face he wears a small smile and a little beard trickling down from his chin. He also has a thin moustache. When you look at him, his dark deep brown eyes stare at you in a joking way. His hair is a neat short brown afro. When teaching, he sweats under his arms and you can see great big patches of sweat. He has a powerful voice which is calm sometimes, but scares you and is hard if you don't hand in your homework. He takes medium size steps (for his size) which are quite quiet.
    — Jennifer David, 6th, Hunter College Elementary
    School, Manhattan

A PERSON CALLED SCARLET COHEN

    Scarlet Cohen is an adult who is very comforting. She is a person who is very skinny, wears classical clothes, and lots of necklaces. Her hair looks messy when it is already brushed. She is very pale; she has hazel eyes. She tells all your secrets. She is spaced out sometimes. And she also says words that aren't very nice and she has a boyfriend. She has a very low voice. She makes dolls that are bizarre. For instance, I was watching her once, and she made a doll with buttons and pins all over the body. She has a daughter Ali who's living with her father. Also she got married two times.
    — Georgia Emery, 4th, P.S. 87, Manhattan

•**Idea 78:** Make a class or family "album" of word portraits.
•**Idea 79:** Go for a walk and make a portrait in words of someone

you see. You can imagine things about them as well as writing down the details you observe.

•**Idea 80:** Make a collection of neighborhood characters: storekeepers, crossing guards, etc.

•**Idea 81:** Make a portrait of someone at work. (For more on this see the writings associated with the poem "Old Florist" in chapter 3, p. 69.)

Self-Portraits

Another portrait assignment is the one that asks the student to make a portrait of himself or herself.

•

I know a girl named Monsita.
She is a little fat.
She is too big.
She has a big butt.
She has big feet.
She has long hair.
She has brown eyes.
She is always putting on paint —
She has red nails.
She has bruises on her hands
and a little face.
She is not ugly,
and she is always clean.
— Monsita Torres, 4th, P.S. 321, Brooklyn

I love the honesty of that portrait, and particularly the way Monsita appears to be critical, but then comes around to some modest self-praise. It is, in fact, neither a critical nor a self-congratulatory portrait, but a case of a girl taking me very literally when I asked for a description of how she really looks.

Often junior high and high school students write particularly good self-portraits; they examine themselves with the care that younger children give to observing adults.

•

I am very nice to everyone. I like to sing songs and record them. I never like to hurt people's feelings and the most important thing is I care a lot for old people. I always get my way around my mother. And I like Melissa as if she were my own sister. I could never find another friend like her. I call her my bodyguard. I love her a lot. And I like a lot of boys, or rather, they like me.
— Stacey Cherry, 7th, J.H.S. 258, Brooklyn

A WORD PORTRAIT

My name is Willie Young.
I am a boy of fourteen.
My hair is short and black.
My feet are very large.
I stand 5 feet 9½ inches.
My clothes are a little middle class.
I don't wear glasses.
I don't smoke, drink, steal.
I am heavy set.
I don't wear make-up.
I love girls.
I don't like to fight.
I take every opportunity for a job and easily get mad
I love to stay out late.
And I love people but I am very shy.
— Willie Lee Young, 7th, J.H.S. 258, Brooklyn

With young children I sometimes set this up on drawing paper and have them draw a huge circle and tell them that this is their face, but they aren't supposed to draw it with pictures of eyes and noses. Rather, they are supposed to draw it with words. It is a "word-portrait." On one side we write what we look like (and second graders tend to drift off into other information about themselves too) and on the other side, in another large circle, we write our Secret Portraits: What I Am Really Like, the Me Nobody Knows, etc:

A WORD PORTRAIT OF ME

I look skinny. My hair
is dark brown. My eyes
are brown. My mother
always makes me wear
striped shirts. I am
getting tired, TIRED
of it. I wear always
blue jeans too. Cheeks,
never rosy.

A SECRET PORTRAIT

I don't think
anyone noticed my
nails are dirty.
Or if I always wore
sneakers.

— Andrew Torres, 2nd, P.S. 321, Brooklyn

•**Idea 82:** Another version of this (good with young children especially) includes drawing. On a sheet of paper make a large circle and draw a face that is funny, ugly, scary, beautiful, sad, angry, or whatever, but it should have an expression.

Before the picture is entirely finished, flip it over and trace the circle again. Write the inside thoughts of the face. When both sides are finished it is fun to have a reading with the children holding the faces in front of them as they read what is on the back.

•**Idea 83:** Do it with your own face.

•**Idea 84:** Do it with an animal face.

A more complex and structured kind of self-portrait, one appropriate to older students because of the fairly difficult form of it, is the "Self-Portrait As. . ." In the following example the speaker describes himself first as a lumbering hybrid of an animal, then turns out to have a lovely landscape inside him.

SELF-PORTRAIT, AS A BEAR

Here is a fat animal, a bear
that is partly a dodo.
Ridiculous wings hang at his shoulders
while he plods in the brickyards
at the edge of the city, smiling
and eating flowers. He eats them
because he loves them
because they are beautiful
because they love him.
It is eating flowers which makes him fat.
He carries his huge stomach
over the gutters of damp leaves
in the parking lots in October,
but inside that paunch
he knows there are fields of lupine
and meadows of mustard and poppy.
He encloses sunshine.

39

Winds bend the flowers
in combers across the valley,
birds hang on the stiff wind,
at night there are showers, and the sun
lifts through a haze every morning
of the summer in the stomach.
— Donald Hall

•**Idea 85:** The assignment is to do your own version of this in poetry or prose. What animal would you be if you were one, and what landscape would you have inside you? This could be done in two separate assignments. Here are two high school responses.

DRAGON

A strong, clever and cunning animal, ready to strike back at any time. At first it is shy, but later it opens up. It is a dragon. I, the unique animal that was said to have never existed. My scales protected me and I was invulnerable except for one spot. A scale was missing over my heart, making it vulnerable to anything and anyone. This is the spot that was hurt most through the years. And when this heart would groan with pain, a crowded city grew within me. People bustling and shoving, going in all directions. A pandemonium was going on inside me; total confusion was what was caused from this. All because of my vulnerable spot. But when this sore area healed, all was calm. There was no crowded city, although there was always that one place that could change all, and pain plus confusion would be brought back again.
— Kevin Chin, 10th, Stuyvesant High School, Manhattan

MONKEY

As I swing around from building to building this night in the big city of New York, I think about the other big city that's inside of me. The city I look down at is quiet and dark — deserted with only an occasional bum or kid. The city inside of me is different. My city is sparkling with people all dressed up, coming out of cabs to go to the theater. Or maybe they're going to a big party. The event of the year. Their laughter can be heard all over town. They're all very superficial, but they're all having a lot of fun, a much nicer sight that the very real people walking the dark streets of New York City.
— Melissa Krantz, 10th, Stuyvesant High School, Manhattan

•**Idea 86:** Write a portrait of the animal that is most like you. Talk about how it moves, the sounds it makes.
•**Idea 87:** Write the portrait of some famous person as if he or she were an animal.
•**Idea 88:** Describe the landscape inside you when things are going well and then when things are not going so well.

Portraits of Real Animals

For many children, and particularly young ones, descriptions of animals are even more popular than descriptions of people. All the points about using the senses and writing with vivid language hold true for animal writing. Be sure that the students are not just parroting some facts they have learned about general characteristics of a given animal: try to have them think of some specific animal, or at least to imagine that they are at this moment looking at the animal.

•

My cat named Zucchie has big glowing eyes and his nose is sensitive and the end has a pink triangle right over his little mouth. His teeth are as sharp as razor blades and his big, fat belly has white fur. His back is pitch black and his sides are striped black and white. Tail is long and fuzzy. He wants food after he takes his long naps. He likes to keep his claws razor sharp on his new scratching post. He likes to clean his silky fur by licking himself.
— Max Bruno, 4th, P.S. 321, Brooklyn

Inside/Outside Portraits

One of my nearly sure-fire one-shot assignments with younger children is to begin with the idea of describing a person or animal, and then, on the other side of the paper, or below a heavily drawn line, to give the *inside* portrait of the person or animal — its thoughts. I will have a lot more to say about writing thoughts in chapter 6, Monologue. For the moment, though, I would just like to mention this assignment as a way of rounding out portrait writing: this is the way this person or animal looks on the outside, and meanwhile, on the inside, this is what is going on.

•

Rough scales   hmmm I'm hungry
Large pointed teeth   short thrashing ripples
Small black eyes   Something is coming.
Long tail, flukes   Will attack it.
Swims smoothly   Hard, must bite
Wild attacker   harder. Broke
Fast swimmer   it. It's sinking
Large mammoth body   Something fell in the
Huge jaws   water. Hey what's
Carnivorous   this red stuff
Powerful body   tear it apart
Gills fins   now eat it.
— Erik Banks, 3rd, P.S. 6, Manhattan

THE ELEPHANT – THE OUTSIDE

The elephant is only a little smaller than a truck. He is all grey, with two holes in his nose which always sniff the floor. They have a little bit of rough skin. It's not bumpy. He smells very bad, I can't even tell. I can just taste all the food when they give it to the animals. I can see when all the people are buying the good food and it's just sitting there in its cage. I can hear them when they are hungry making sounds. I can see them when the people give them their food and they grab it when they are hungry. I can see their eyes when they are hungry and mad.

THE ELEPHANT – THE INSIDE

I'm hungry and the people don't give me food. I walk round and round my cage. Even if I'm not hungry, they stuff it in my mouth and I can imagine I can't breathe. Then they be calling me weird because I'm an elephant. They always be calling me dumb because I'm so fat and all gray. They say look at that dumb big trunk and say I'm so stupid because I'm all gray.

— Melissa Zapata, 3rd, P.S. 183, Queens

THE MAN ON THE TRAIN

Me and my mother were sitting in the train when a fat man and a lady walked in. I was hoping they would move on because there were only two seats next to me, and I knew they wouldn't be able to fit. Oops. Here they come. Plop, they sat down next to me. I was squished against my mother and could hardly breathe. I didn't want to anyway because soon a sickening smell was in the air. It would go away — then the man would move again and it would come back.

I tried to hide my nose without looking too obvious. I turned towards my mother and wrapped my scarf around my neck, nose and mouth. I prepared to go to sleep. It was going to be a long ride. I turned my head around just to get a quick look at him. He had on olive baggy pants and a funny colored jacket. I couldn't see the lady because the man was in the way. Luckily they got off after the next two stops. I surely was relieved.

The worst thing about riding the train is who you have to sit next to.

THE MAN ON THE TRAIN SPEAKS

Why did I sit next to that poor girl? She must be squished to death. I really ought to move but there's no more seats. Look at her holding her scarf over her nose and mouth. Do I smell that bad? My wife doesn't mind, but I guess she's use to it. Maybe it's because I didn't take a bath last night or the night before or even the night before that. I'll definitely take a bath tonight. Come to think of it, I don't think I have on any deodorant. I don't have any deodorant. No worry. I'll buy some when I get home I think. Oh good, it's my stop. I can relieve the poor girl from her misery. One little girl can make a man feel so low.

— Michelle Marshall, 5th, P.S. 183, Queens

Exaggerated Description and Caricature

In describing people, as in writing about place, exaggeration offers room for humor and study of style. Often exaggeration is the main ingredient in satire (see "Mr. Slope," page 56). Sometimes a character is exaggerated because of deep feeling or because of something extraordinary in the moment in which the observation was made. A selection from literature that shows this is the following piece from the original 1817 novel *Frankenstein* by Mary Shelley. The monster is made to be in all its aspects an exaggeration of a human being—in its appearance, and in its passions. Later in the book, the monster gets to speak for itself (see page 142 in this book), but here we have Dr. Victor Frankenstein's expression of horror at his creation:

> His limbs were in proportion, and I had selected his features as beautiful. Beautiful! Great God! His yellow skin scarcely covered the work of muscles and arteries beneath; his hair was of a lustrous black, and flowing; his teeth of a pearly whiteness; but these luxuriances only formed a more horrid contrast with his watery eyes, that seemed almost of the same color as the dun-white sockets in which they were set, his shrivelled complexion and straight black lips.

Like most other monsters, the Frankenstein monster is usually popular with kids. There are now dozens of versions of this story—movies, comics, dolls, Sons of, Brides of, Great Granddaughters of. For those who are interested, the original was written as a result of a game of ghost story-telling one stormy night among three young people: the poets Byron and Shelley, and the latter's new wife, Mary, who was the daughter of the great 18th-century feminist, Mary Wollstonecraft. (Wollstonecraft died giving birth to her daughter, and some like to psychologize that this fact had some influence on Mary Shelley's story of a monster child that destroys its parent.) At any rate, the three had a contest, and Mary's story was so far superior to the others and so terrifying, that the two young men encouraged her to write it out, and it became *Frankenstein*. The book itself is not easy to read with its old-fashioned diction and its several stories-within-stories, but some more advanced students might like to try it.

Whether they ever read the book or not, however, many students have an excellent natural sense of the sort of exaggerated writing that is so appropriate to the description of monsters.

•**Idea 89:** The assignment is simple. After reading or hearing the sample from *Frankenstein*, create your own monster in words.

The first example of one child's response to the assignment is by far the best piece of writing that particular student ever did for me. He became downright enthusiastic about his "Weirdest Man" and wrote at length, with lots of laughing and showing his friends as he went along.

THE WEIRDEST MAN ON EARTH

He's got monkey hands. He's got a giraffe's neck. He's got high eyes like if he was smoking pot. He's got a nose one hundred times bigger than Pinocchio. He's got a stomach bigger than Joaquin and mine put together. He's got a behind bigger than a hundred heads. He's got teeth one hundred times bigger than a beaver. He sometimes does right things. He is always tripping. He is very stupid. He is always eating his nails. His nails are eaten to one centimeter. He is always eating erasers. He eats TVs, radios, pencils, watches, stoves, refrigerators, pens, nails from his feet, sneakers, that's why he has holes in the front of his sneakers, eats books, belts, chairs, tables, eyeballs, teeth, and a couple of others. He is the weirdest man on earth because — he is the weirdest man on earth.
— Luis Rivera, 5th, P.S. 87, Manhattan

•

The skin was pale green. The hair dark black and stiff. Its teeth were dark yellow. The nose was large and oversized. Its eyes bulged. They were green and hideous. The lips were dark gray. Its body was disgusting. Its arms scarred and bloody. Its hands were covered with warts. Its bare chest was a slimy green. The legs were hairy and bloody. Together it made a disgusting, hideous, heartless, murderous monster. The monster moved as if it was holding two hundred pounds on its back. As it moves by, you get hit by a disgusting smell of rotten eggs and bananas. The expression on his face was like he was about to kill you. It could not make any noise except for a growl.
— Eric Quan, 6th, Hunter College Elementary School, Manhattan

The second piece is typical of this special genre of student writing. It is admirable for the way the senses get involved, although Eric could use a little work on synonyms for "hideous." I had just made a speech to the class about being sure to include sounds, so Eric dutifully tacked on the growl which rather spoils his ending, but overall, I think Eric succeeds in his project of getting a reader to want to retch and run. It always amazes me the way students, even ones who don't usually like to write, like Luis above, will pour on the warts and green skin.

It is interesting to note that in Eric Quan's monster description above, every word is one of ugliness and horror. In Mary Shelley's description of *her* monster, however, Dr. Frankenstein actually chose handsome parts for his creature: lustrous hair, good teeth, etc. The extremity of horror he feels at the result of his labors is largely because of the contrast to what he had hoped for and the distortion of what was once beautiful. Often the distance between what is expected and what occurs is the most chilling aspect of horror. Awful events that take place in broad daylight are potentially more shocking than the ones that take place in a deserted mansion on a stormy night. So I sometimes suggest that blood and guts and warts are not necessarily the most horrible things possible, but with this assignment I rarely have the heart to squelch real enthusiasm.

I have long imagined and never carried out a class project of A Child's Garden of Monsters in which a whole bulletin board is covered with vivid written monsters with gory illustrations and perhaps some nineteenth-century prints of the original Frankenstein's monster along with samples of how it has appeared in twentieth-century media. It is one of those projects, though, that is hard to prove has redeeming social value, although my instinct says that anything kids enjoy that much has to have some profound meaning.

Horror fiction, by the way, is an interesting genre for study from, say, fourth grade up. It has a style and typical structure that is relatively easy to analyze and imitate, although mastery is as difficult as in any other form. There are many good horror stories around — W.W. Jacob's "The Monkey's Paw" is my favorite, and of course Poe's stories are classics. (See the opening passage of "The Fall of the House of Usher" on page 27 of this book.) With advanced or high school students, a book like *Frankenstein* would also be an excellent introduction to the pleasures and difficulties of nineteenth-century fiction in general.

•**Idea 90:** Create a monster in writing. Include evidence of all your senses. How does it smell? What is its sound, the texture of its skin?

•**Idea 91:** Create a monstrous person. Begin with someone who seems at first glance to be perfectly ordinary. Bit by bit make changes, add details until the person is clearly a monster.

•**Idea 92:** Take partners. Write the first half of a monster description, then switch papers and finish the other person's.

•**Idea 93:** Write about a person who changes from normal to monstrous *à la* werewolves and Dr. Jekyll/Mr. Hyde. Concentrate on the face and what happens to it.

•**Idea 94:** Be a mad scientist trying to give life to a beautiful creature. Choose the most beautiful body parts (selected of course from the graveyard or morgue) and then tell how your creation comes out. You don't have to have the same thing happen to yours that happens to Dr. Frankenstein's.

•

Exaggeration is also used as a short cut to character description and for caricature and humor. It can be a sort of verbal cartoon, as in this description of Sam Spade in Dashiell Hammett's detective novel *The Maltese Falcon:*

Samuel Spade's jaw was long and bony, his chin a jutting v under the more flexible v of his mouth. His nostrils curved back to make another, smaller v. His yellow-gray eyes were horizontal. The *v motif* was picked up again by the thickish brows rising outward from twin creases above a hooked nose, and his pale brown hair grew down — from high flat temples — in a point on his forehead. He looked rather pleasantly like a blonde satan.

This caricature is not meant to make fun of Spade, who is the hero, but to capture him quickly on paper, in the reader's mind. This type of writing is very near to cartoon or comic-book drawing. This can be demonstrated by having someone with a reputation as class artist go to the board while the paragraph is read slowly. The artist draws exactly what is described: the horizontal eyes, the v-motif of the brows and mouth. A little sketch like this results:

This, then, is a caricature in the sense that Hammett is taking one feature and exaggerating it all out of proportion. Political cartoonists always do this. They draw Jimmy Carter all teeth and John Kennedy as all youthful cowlick. Ronald Reagan appears with a huge off-center tuft of hair and a myriad of neck wrinkles. I call this comic-book writing because it gives your character an immediately identifiable appearance that (in the comics) makes it easy to draw him or her repeatedly. It lends itself to writing in which events are more important than character development. Thus you can expect vivid, exaggerated description from Dashiell Hammett and Raymond Chandler, but not from Virginia Woolf or Henry James, who are capable of going through whole novels without telling what their characters look like. Another way of saying it is that caricature or exaggerated descriptions present people in a single, vivid state. Many things then happen to them, many things are revealed, but the people themselves change very little. Even when secrets are revealed about their characters, these secrets were present from the beginning rather than developed or changed. Character is a given quantity. This is typical of the best genre writing, but also of most imaginative writing of all kinds before the middle of the eighteenth century. Change in the spirit or psyche of a character is relatively rare before, say, Jane Austen's early nineteenth-century novels. The issue in the kind of writing we are talking about here is event, or perhaps idea. Mysteries, gothic romances, crime fiction, and most science fiction generally minimize interior development. I think this is part of their pleasure — there are unexpected turns and much excitement, but you have some dependably unchanging personalities at the center. An apparently good character may turn out to be evil, but you can usually flip back and see that there were lots of clues to the true state of the character's soul. Once all things are uncovered and explained, there is a great relief and satisfaction.

In writing caricature, the fun is to choose just the one or two salient qualities to emphasize. In exaggeration, the fun is in the elaboration. A paragraph begins with something simple and then adds details and colors and ridiculous comparisons. In the same book from which I took the caricature of Sam Spade, Dashiell Hammett also describes the Fat Man, the character played by Sidney Greenstreet in the famous movie version. In this description, detail is piled upon detail in reckless, wonderful abandon:

> The fat man was flabbily fat with bulbous pink cheeks and lips and chins and neck, with a great soft egg of a belly that was all his torso, and pendant cones for arms and legs. As he advanced to meet Spade, all his bulbs rose and shook and fell separately with each step, in the manner of clustered soap-bubbles not yet released from the pipe through which they had been blown. His eyes, made small by fat puffs around them, were dark and sleek. Dark ringlets thinly covered his broad scalp. He wore a black cutaway coat, black vest, black satin ascot tie holding a pinkish pearl, striped gray worsted trousers, and patent-leather shoes.
>
> His voice was a throaty purr. "Ah, Mr. Spade," he said with enthusiasm and held out a hand like a fat pink star.

Later, we'll use the rest of that scene in the chapter on dialogue, but what I am interested in now is the way the fatness is described. There is still a quality of comic-book sharpness — you could draw the egg-shaped body with the pendant cones, but other techniques are important in this piece too. Word sounds, for example. There is the alliteration in "flabbily fat" and the full-mouthed sensation of "bulbous" and "clustered soap-bubbles." There is an amplitude of words and sounds that corresponds to the excess flesh of the character. Hammett never stops with one thing: the man's pink cheeks are bulbous, but so are his "lips and chins and neck." He piles it on in a way that speaks of overflowing, spilling out, swelling. Wonderful, overblown choice of words!

If you read this selection aloud to your class, you need to have your tongue loosened up for all the curls of words. This piece and two other exaggerated writings on page 56 have a lot of complex clauses and hard words, but I like to ask students to close their eyes and see what impression this leaves on their minds. What picture do they see? What word from the reading sticks with them, is easiest to remember? I am not interested in a literary analysis or restatement to prove that they understand it: I want them to find a way of entering into something, even something with words they don't fully understand, of making it work for them. This works very well as long as the pieces are short. By the time a number of students have responded with the phrase or mental picture that impressed itself into their minds most, you begin to have a composite of the understanding the class *did* have, and at the same time students' memories will be jogged by what the others remembered.

The ultimate response to a piece of literature is, in my opinion, to write something of your own, a sort of answer to it. You might write an imitation, of course, or something of your own under the influence of what you have read. In college literature courses there is always a lot of discussion about how and where one writer influenced another, much of which is accurate but irrelevant. People who are deeply moved by books are often moved to write. There is a natural human tendency to respond in kind. Babies learn the language and habits of their parents; language students pick up the accents of their teachers. The relationship between the writing and the text that influences the writer is not one of analysis, though, and for that reason I would leave analysis of literature to other classes and other times. I prefer that the connection between samples from literature and the students' writing be impressionistic, reactive, and loose.

•**Idea 95:** Describe a person who is like a particular animal (perhaps with a walk like a pigeon, bobbing as if searching for grain).

•**Idea 96:** Choose any of the examples in this section or in the anthology on pages 56-60. Write a continuation of it. Try to add more of the same kind of description in the same style.

•**Idea 97:** Try to write something in the old-fashioned style of the Smollett and Trollope selections on page 56.

•**Idea 98:** Bring in some comic books with superheroes or funny-paper characters. Choose one and try to make a word portrait. Try to do with words what the pen has done in ink. It might be fun to have a contest and vote on which description of, say, the Hulk, is most like the drawing.

•**Idea 99:** Make up a caricature or comic-book character in writing. Have a partner draw on the board what you have written.

•**Idea 100:** Write a description of a facial expression and see if a living person can duplicate it.

•**Idea 101:** Can you write about a person in words that sound the way the person looks? Short quick sentences for a nervous type, or long skinny sentences for an extremely tall person? Words like punches for an aggressive fighter?

•**Idea 102:** Describe a person whose clothes contrast with the rest of the appearance.

•**Idea 103:** Describing only the clothes, give proof that a person is a bum, a movie star, a pimp, or a rich person trying to look poor. This might work best in small groups.

•**Idea 104:** Do the above in thirty words or fewer.

•**Idea 105:** Try writing over one of the exaggerated pieces in this section or the anthology at the end of the chapter and see if you can do it *without* exaggerating.

•**Idea 106:** Write a description of someone ugly whom you feel sympathetic to.

•**Idea 107:** The following exaggerated description by a sixth grader seems to be part of a longer story. Can you finish it? You might also want to write what comes before it.

•

A gaunt and tall figure, its shadow against the full moon seemed hideous and sinister. A long and feathery white beard seemed to keep growing from the prune-like face, which arose from the dark and rushing water behind it. The hunched candlestick body threatened to eclipse me any moment, its huge and thin moustache bristling, its eyes flashing fire, and a hideous grin upon its sallow cheeks and small mouth. I looked upward and saw some smooth and shiny hair gleaming from a peak on the figure's low brow, to the top of his neck, forming a ghost looking like a ghoulish demon of a devil. Then the apparition vanished.

— Orin J. Percus, 6th, P.S. 6, Manhattan

Using Description to Explore Character

One of the primary uses of description in fiction and in other kinds of writing is to explore and reveal. But there is another type of description that also discovers as it goes. In this type of writing you, the author, have an idea — something based on memory or on the merest glimpse of a real person or strictly made up from the imagination. Perhaps you know a certain person from your childhood who was very important to you, but you never really sat down to figure out why. Perhaps you saw a woman on the street who fascinated you and made you wonder what her life was like. You might not know yourself why either the memory or the observation caught your attention, but you want to write about it anyhow. There is a discipline of writing which consists of thinking about that person (although it could also be an incident, an event, a scrap of overheard conversation, or anything else) in a way that is almost a meditation. You see the person, try to hear and touch them, try by describing them in detail to discover what it was that fascinated you, what it was that this person meant. When you do this with an invented character, you add details to your invention just as you gathered details from your memory and in this way *discover* what the person was really like, or what he or she meant to you.

The following excerpt from a short-short story is a beautiful illustration of description of a person used in this way.

49

From "Alice"

Alice, tall like a man, with soft wooly hair spread out in tangles like a feathered hat and her face oily and her legs ashy, whose beauty I never quite believed because she valued it so little but was real. Real like wild flowers and uncut grass, real like the knotty sky-reach of a dead tree. Beauty of warm brown eyes in a round dark face and of teeth somehow always white and clean and of lips moist and open, out of which rolled the voice and the laughter, deep and breathless, rolling out the strong and secret beauty of her soul.

Alice of the streets. Gentle walking on long legs. Close-kneed. Careful. Stopping sometimes at our house on her way to unknown places and other people. She came wearing loose flowered dresses and she sat in our chairs rubbing her too-big knees that sometimes hurt, and we gathered, Momma, my sisters and I, to hear the beautiful bad-woman talk and feel the rolling laughter, always sure that she left more than she came for. I accepted the tender touch of her hands on my hair or my face or my arms like favors I never returned. I clung to the sounds of her words and the light of her smiles like stolen fruit.

— Paulette Childress White, in *Sturdy Black Bridges*

Do you see the way White starts with the sense details, and is amazed by how she never really knew there was beauty in Alice? But now, looking back, that is the first thing she remembers, a certain kind of beauty, which she then goes on to try to define, tries to find what is special about the beauty, and hits on the sound of the voice. Then she returns to the picture of Alice again, and this time sees Alice in action, sees that Alice was a sort of street person, saw how she came to their house and how they reacted to her. She ends this section of her portrait of Alice with the way Alice literally and figuratively *touched* her.

This is an excellent example of a piece of writing that does not demand a lot of analysis and discussion to have an effect on student writing. The following pieces were written after reading "Alice" and the assignment was not to imitate the selection, but to write about a person, real or made up. These two students quite naturally and on their own picked up their rhythm from the "Alice" piece.

TONY

Tony, tall like a man, afro short
and straight. His voice is like people
jogging down the street.
He's smart and wears designer
clothes. When he walks, his
back is straight. He likes
to make friends. When he
draws, he makes it look real.
His eyes are brown as a bear.

His skin is tan and his
manners are excellent.
His personality is like two
soft, furry rabbits gnawing on
a carrot.
— Peter Rodriguez, 5th, P.S. 124, Queens

SHELLY

Shelly, small and amiable. Her hair was very rough and continually growing. Her very dark eyes matched her dark complexion.

Shelly was a saint, only screaming when mad at her brother. Cheerful she was, always being able to make a joke out of something terrible.

I thought there was going to be war when I first saw her. Me, always thinking of terrible things. But then when she started speaking, the quickness of her voice, sometimes I hardly knew what she said. I knew it would be all right. Cheerful, caring, homely, amiable, sensible, always thinking of good ideas. That was Shelley.
— Nichola Davis, 6th, P.S. 124, Queens

•

Description of people can, of course, reveal much about their social station, economic condition, and personality. Often, however, a description actually reveals more about the author, or the narrator of a story, than about the ostensible subject. What we see may be an expression of what we are feeling or who we are. One day I will sit on the subway and see around me damaged, limping, ugly people. Another day I will see people with character and experience written in their fascinatingly individual faces. Fiction writers and poets use this technique all the time. The speaker or narrator sees and describes a woman in a foxfur coat. There is a sensation of anger. The lady made the speaker furious. It is revealed that the speaker was once fired peremptorily from a job by a snobbish lady in just such a foxfur coat.

Examine the following brief selection from Maxine Hong Kingston's wonderful memoir-fiction called *The Woman Warrior:*

She wore black bangs, and her cheeks were pink and white. She was baby soft. I thought that I could put my thumb on her nose and push it bonelessly in, indent her face. I could poke dimples into her cheeks. I could work her face around like dough.

Exactly what would you say are the speaker's feelings toward the girl with the black bangs? If you were reading the whole scene you would know that the speaker is remembering when she was in elementary school, so she is recalling events and feelings from twenty-five years ago. There is something repelling about the physical idea of working a face like dough — and the narrator wants us to be disturbed. She can't stand the passivity of the girl with the black bangs; she doesn't want to be like that herself.

•**Idea 108:** Write a description of a person (real or imaginary) to whom you would really like to do violence.

•**Idea 109:** Write a description of someone who looks good enough to eat.

In the next selection there is a feeling of envy in the speaker's description of a person, but there is also a lot more going on:

From THE BLUEST EYE

> This disrupter of seasons was a new girl in school named Maureen Peal. A high-yellow dream child with long brown hair braided into two lynch ropes that hung down her back. She was rich, at least by our standards, as rich as the richest of the white girls, swaddled in comfort and care. The quality of her clothes threatened to derange [my sister] Frieda and me. Patent-leather shoes with buckles, a cheaper version of which we got only at Easter and which had disintegrated by the end of May. Fluffy sweaters the color of lemon drops tucked into skirts with pleats so orderly they astounded us. Brightly colored knee socks with white borders, a brown velvet coat trimmed in white rabbit fur, and a matching muff. There was a hint of spring in her sloe green eyes, something summery in her complexion, and a rich autumn ripeness to her walk.
> – Toni Morrison

I love the flow of this paragraph, and its many levels. Notice that it begins and ends with a reference to the seasons: Maureen Peal is so rich, it suggests, that she has the colors of all the seasons in her body at once, as if she were a living hothouse. *She* can ignore the actual seasons: she wears Easter shoes in the winter. The main description centers on Maureen's clothes, all the tiny details of fluffy sweaters and velvet. Does the speaker want to destroy Maureen the way the speaker in the previous passage wanted to rework the face of the girl with the black bangs? I don't think so. I think that somehow the anger here is less personal. There is a fair amount of admiration, and a lifting of the level of Maureen's appeal to the height of a natural phenomenon. There appears also to be an awareness of the greater context of a society. Notice the race consciousness of phrases like "high-yellow dream child" and "hair braided like two lynch ropes." I am also interested in the way the sisters form a unit and seem to have a strength of unity from being two rather than one. This kind of fiction is not so much "made up" as grown, cultivated, out of the rich soil of truth.

•**Idea 110:** Describe the speaker and her sister from Maureen's point of view. Maybe Maureen envies their sisterhood, or perhaps she feels stifled by her new clothes.

•**Idea 111:** Write the next paragraph of this story, and the paragraph that came before it.

•**Idea 112:** Describe a person who is like a season: a wintery person or one who is like spring.

•**Idea 113:** Describe someone by his or her clothing. What do the clothes reveal? Are the clothes delicious or disgusting? Like jewels or like trash?

•**Idea 114:** Think of a real person you admire or even envy a little and describe him or her, showing how you feel without saying it directly.

•**Idea 115:** Describe a made-up person showing the way you (or your character who is the narrator) feel about him or her. It may be a mixture of many feelings.

•

Her sparkling, blue eyes twinkled in the bright sunlight. She had a merry face, her cheeks a rosy red. Her hair was golden with two spring curls on either side tied with yellow satin ribbons. She wore a yellow lacy dress with white ankle socks and black patent-leather shoes. She came happily skipping down the road, humming a splendid tune. She smelled like she had been in a rose garden. I felt so plain compared to her. I was wearing blue jeans and a yellow shirt and sneakers. I felt like a beggar looking at her.
— Lakmini Bresboda, 5th, Hunter College Elementary
  School, Manhattan

•**Idea 116:** Describe someone who makes you very angry.

•**Idea 117:** Make up a character who shows feelings toward a person he or she is observing. For example, "Frank stared at her, thinking she was the most beautiful girl he had ever seen. He loved the way her pale blonde hair fell in her eyes. . . ." If you are a girl, make your character be a boy. If you are a boy, make your character be a girl.

•**Idea 118:** Write a description in which you (or the character speaking) go through a change of attitude. Start with disgust and move to sympathy, or with admiration and move toward recognizing that the person is, say, a bully.

•**Idea 119:** Write a description of a person who seems to be one thing, but gives hints of something underneath that is different.

•**Idea 120:** Describe someone in a situation different from yours who seems to be like you would be if you were in that situation.

•

She is very rich
She has a bedroom
filled with money.
She has a silk
bed that she sleeps in.
When she goes to
school she wears
Sassons and a
shirt that is red.

53

She dreams in
school and thinks
of the ocean. When
she goes home
she takes off her
shoes and goes
to sleep in her
silk bed and
dreams about the ocean.
                    — Alexandra Hoyt, 6th, P.S. 6, Manhattan

Making an Abstract Specific

I use a lot of energy in the classroom trying to encourage
students to be less general and more specific in their language. I try,
as I'm sure most teachers of writing do, to get rid of the word "nice"
and replace it with something precise. Sometimes, of course, it is
not so much laziness holding students back from the exact word as
it is a kind of timidity about knowing their real feelings. Sometimes
we fall back on a much-used word or phrase because we have never
bothered to examine closely what we actually feel or think in such a
way that would give us the exact words. For example, if I write "I
saw an old woman," I could improve my writing by slowing down,
and saying to myself, "Now wait a minute. What did I really see?
Did I simply see a female human being over age sixty-five? Or did I
see someone who looked feeble and pathetic?" I might have to examine my attitudes toward old people a little, and I might end up
making no reference to the woman's age at all, but rather describing
a woman wearing elastic stockings and orthopedic shoes, walking
with a heavy limp and pain that showed in the lines around her
mouth. The point is not that general and abstract words are always
bad, but that often they don't do justice to what was actually experienced or thought or imagined. The quickest way to improve student writing in this area is to insist that they fully imagine their
"old" lady or "nice" friend — to see, hear, and smell the person. To
make it as specific and present as words can.
   An interesting writing exercise that carries this to its logical
conclusion is one that takes an actual abstract word and tries to give
it personality and flesh. This is an exercise in personification or
anthropormorphizing, in which an abstract quality is given a face
and body. My exercise comes from a lovely paragraph in Zora
Neale Hurston's *Their Eyes Were Watching God.*

So Janie began to think of Death. Death, that strange being with the
huge square toes who lived way in the West. The great one who lived in a
straight house like a platform without sides to it, and without a roof. What

54

need has Death for a cover, and what winds can blow against him? He stands in his high house that overlooks the world. Stands watchful and motionless all day with his sword drawn back, waiting for the messenger to bid him come. Been standing there before there was a where or a when or a then. She was liable to find a feather from his wings lying in her yard any day now. She was sad and afraid too.

•**Idea 121:** After hearing this piece, choose some abstract idea (a brainstorming on the board might help: hate, love, sadness, anger, etc.) and write its description. Kids seem to find this easy to latch onto. I was surprised by this at first, but when I started thinking about it I recalled how vividly and concretely I pictured God and the devil and a host of other ideas when I was a child.

DEPRESSION

Depression is a big dark being that has huge feet and giant dirty fingernails, and is weak and sick with yellow teeth and wicked uncombed hair and its head has a hairy green moustache. He looks a lot like Einstein.
— Hampton Finer, 4th, P.S. 321, Brooklyn

DEATH

I imagine Death as a mouse with a ski hat over his head. In his tail he holds a butcher knife and in one paw he pulls out a switchblade and in the other paw he holds a revolver. He's dressed in black pants and shirt.
— Carlo Cerruti, 4th, P.S. 321, Brooklyn

LOVE

Love is the Big Heart with red hair and red skin. He always takes target practice in his Big red palace, to shoot broken hearts. His face glows and he has a black robe and fire and lightning comes out.
— James Carroll, 4th, P.S. 321, Brooklyn

ANGER, ANGER, ANGER

A short beaming monkey always grinning at a town from a branch, the highest branch in the forest. "He is all rashed who hates me shall suffer anger!" he shouts. He goes running off to somebody who hates him and cuts a chunk of his rash off, makes it invisible and drops it on those who hate him.
— David Azcue, 4th, P.S. 321, Brooklyn

MORE PIECES DESCRIBING PEOPLE
BY ADULTS

From THE EXPEDITION OF HUMPHREY CLINKER

He would have measured above six feet in height had he stood upright; but he stooped very much; was very narrow in the shoulders, in black spatterdashes — As for his thighs, they were long and slender, like those of a grasshopper; his face was, at least, half a yard in length, brown and shrivelled, with projecting cheekbones, little grey eyes on the greenish hue, a large hook-nose, a pointed chin, a mouth from ear to ear, very ill furnished with teeth, and a high, narrow fore-head, well furrowed with wrinkles. His horse was exactly in the stile of its rider; a resurrection of dry bones which (as we afterwards learned) he valued exceedingly, as the only present he had ever received in his life.
— Tobias Smollett

From BARCHESTER TOWERS

Mr. Slope is tall and not ill-made. His feet and hands are large, as has ever been the case with all his family, but he has a broad chest and wide shoulders to carry off these excrescences, and on the whole his figure is good. His countenance, however, is not specially prepossessing. His hair is lank and of a dull pale reddish hue. It is always formed into three straight, lumpy masses, each brushed with admirable precision and cemented with much grease; two of them adhere closely to the sides of his face, and the other lies at right angles above them. He wears no whiskers and is always punctilliously shaven. His face is nearly of the same colour as his hair, though perhaps a little redder: it is not unlike beef — beef, however, one would say, of a bad quality. His forehead is capacious and high, but square and heavy and bloodless, and his big, prominent, pale-brown eyes inspire anything but confidence. His nose, however, is his redeeming feature: it is pronounced, straight and well formed; though I myself should have liked it better did it not possess a somewhat spongy, porous appearance, as though it had been cleverly formed out of a red-coloured cork.

I could never endure to shake hands with Mr. Slope. A cold, clammy perspiration always exudes from him, the small drops are ever to be seen standing on his brow, and his friendly grasp is unpleasant.
— Anthony Trollope

•

She reminded me of all the pictures I'd ever seen of Santa Claus. Chubby, happy, smiling face; round, red nose; soft gentle lips and eyes as merry and peaceful as a playful baby's. Of course there was no beard because this was my grandmother's face.

To be tightly folded into her lap was one of my greatest luxuries. All hurts mended, all tears dried and feelings soothed and smoothed over. Cuddling into her arms was pure joy.

She had a very special smell about her. It was good lunches and dinners — we never had breakfast except for coffee — sewing machine oil maybe, cotton or wool materials, freshly ironed clothes and Ivory soap. Her hair always smelled like Ivory soap.

Her voice was firm and sure, never shouting, but not a whiney, whispery sort of voice either. Her angry voice was full blown and tinged with sarcasm and bad words in a dialect foreign to most people. I enjoyed her anger; it was immediate, it was real and powerful, and it was soon over.

Her skin was hard and white like pure marble but not cold to the touch. It yielded to me always, especially as I slid my brown hand and arm around her neck as I pulled myself safely into her comforting, warm, lap.
   — Katherine Murray (Teacher, P.S. 124, Queens)

From HIGHER GROUND

On the table was a red and yellow Mickey Mouse record player with Mickey's gloved thumb pressing the needle into the record. But the center of attention, directly under the hanging bare bulb, was a red-headed boy and girl dancing together like teenagers. The boy wore glasses and a long-sleeved, white dress shirt, and his hair was greased back in a long, curved plume like Elvis Presley's. The girl was in black and white too, except she had a pink felt poodle appliqued to her circle skirt. When she whirled you could see a solid disk of crinoline slips, charms jangling on two separate bracelets. Her hair was even redder than her cousin's, and she wore it in many tiny red curls in a puff on her forehead and then another puff in the back. I didn't like the song; it was about parts of the body, a piece of bone, a hank of hair.
   — Meredith Sue Willis

MORE PIECES DESCRIBING PEOPLE BY STUDENTS

•

Her name is India. Red hair, green eyes, her voice warm and tender. When I touch her, joy goes through me. Her voice like tingling bells. I touch her very lightly. When she walks, she has a jump, a very light one. Light shines on her face. It seems to come all day, the light on her face. If not sunshine, moonlight, always on her face. She climbs a tree and jumps softly down. Roses bloom at her touch. When I see her, I sometimes pick her up. Only is she five, not any older. Her skin pure white, as white as sunlight.
   —Simone Dinnerstein, 4th, P.S. 321, Brooklyn

LIVING BRONZE

He was like a Greek statue. His body was hard and smooth like living bronze. His face was a work of art. His bathing suit was a shade darker than the beautiful blue sea, and his skin a few shades darker than the sand and his hair a few shades darker than that. His handsome grin was only a facade, for he longed for his deceased lover....
                    David Slocum, 6th, P.S. 6, Manhattan

BLUBBER BALL

She was tall. She wore a long beige heavy coat. Her face was broad and rounded. Her nose was shaped like a large red cherry. Her cheeks were red and rounded like a plum. Her lips looked like thick rubber erasers. Her body was shaped like a huge water barrel. Her stomach could reach from here to the library. When she walked, her stomach would stick out in front of her as if she was expecting a baby.
                    —Michelle Benicourt, 7th, I.S. 184, The Bronx

•

His glasses look monstrous, dwarfing his very small body. He wears purple (yes, purple) sneakers which clash with his plaid shirt and corduroy pants. His brownish-black hair looks like a stained mop. He never sits still unless you tie him up with very strong rope. When he moves, his hair flies like anything, getting in everyone's way. His nose is all shmushed up, and looks like someone threw flesh-colored mud at him.
                    —Robert Schonberg, 5th grade, Hunter College
                    Elementary School, Manhattan

•

Mitzi is my small sister. I think of how she calls me names. She calls me dummy stupid idiot punk blind deaf loud-mouth and when I come home from school she jumps on me like a maniac and punches my nose and when she comes off me she comes and trips me so that sometimes I fall on my mother.
                    —Carlos Perez, 2nd, P.S. 321, Brooklyn

•

I have a girl around my block. She's a bum who doesn't know how to dress. Everybody used to like her, but now she thinks she's better than everybody. She's dark skinned, tall, and has lots of bumps. She smells awful and always wears these ugly brown tap shoes. Known as roach killers around my block. She's the kind of girl who does anything to get attention. From anyone. She's very immature and very rude! Also disrespectful!
                    —Sharon Fowler, 7th, I.S. 184, The Bronx

MR. FRANCIS

Mr. Francis is a nice old man. He is very generous and kind. He always has on clean clothes.

Mr. Francis is a kind of man that likes to plant; he has his own garden. His wife is a kind person too. But she doesn't really like to help out with things.

Mr. Francis has a sweet warm loving soft voice. Whenever I see him, his clothes smell so fresh. Except when he's in the garden, because he smells like onions. I really like that man. I call him grandpa because he really seems like one.
— Betty Chandler, 6th, P.S. 124, Queens

HAPPINESS

Happiness is sitting on a back of a giant dog when it runs to its master. And when he licks him, you accidentally slide off. Then you hurry to get back on by climbing on his tail as if it was a rope. Then suddenly the dog starts to run to the kitchen because it's time for his lunch. And he drags you along. Then after he finishes eating, he has to get a drink and he flicks his tail and you fall into the hole of water and start laughing.
— Angel Estrada, 4th, P.S. 321, Brooklyn

DEATH

Death in the tall lingering shadow. Death on the roof's edge. Death in a heart and held within. He has a hood pulled over his head. Comes to pick up his victims at midnight. He lives in a cave that goes on and on. His victims wander there and about once a year he may meet one. But then he leaves to earth to get more. No man has met him and no one will, to the time doomsday has already fell.
— Andrew Delamarter, 4th, P.S. 321, Brooklyn

JOE KILLPATRICK

Joe has black, cold eyes with a patch over one. When he walks by, you see his cold knife and gun. You get the shivers when he looks at you. He rides through town on a black motorcycle that gives you the chills as it zooms by. No one likes him, no one can. You see him at night sneaking around. Some say he is a criminal, and some say he is just a nut. He lives in a small one room apartment. He is scary. He has green, uncared for buck teeth. He wears dirty, black clothes, including a leather jacket. He's tall, tough, and muscular. He lives in a dismal section of town. Everyone is afraid of him.
— Gus Christenson, 4th, P.S. 321, Brooklyn

•

My friend Victoria whom I met upstate at camp I thought was totally ugly. She's albino, and her hair was a long, rich white. She's thin, but with a hint of chubbiness on her. Her eyes were a light grey-ish blue and practically crosseyed. Her skin is a very pale white with small pink hands. In the beginning of the story I didn't mean totally ugly, but not pretty, just weirdly attractive. Her skin was as soft as a rose petal, and she smelled like plants. She walks with a long glide. The expression of her was rather angry but yet bland. Her voice sounded very stern, but yet not quite. Well, that's my friend.
— Candace O'Conner, 6th, Hunter College
Elementary School, Manhattan

•

Everyday while walking to school I see her. Everyday she wears the same loose fitting, tunic type sky blue dress. Everyday she wears the same cheap red belt around her dress. She has blond Farrah Fawcett type hairdo. Always she uses coral red lipstick, sexy blue eye shadow, and apple red rouge on her bony cheeks. She has a duck-like walk, head bobbing, and butt sticking out contrasting with her long strides. Everyday she has that snotty smug expression on her face, while stumbling on her high heel shoes. All in all I hate her guts.
— Chris Derek, 5th, P.S. 321, Brooklyn

JESSE

His eyes sparkling blue like the ocean at its deepest depths,
His short blond hair turned up at the sides.
His pants all worn at the knees.
With a rose in his hands.
A red rose with its light green stem with little thorns sticking out of it.
The rose dark red as dark red as you could dream of.
The rose has a drop of water on it
The sun reflecting on the dew drop turns the rose into a palace of many
    colors.
— Sarabinh Levy, 4th, P.S. 321, Brooklyn

Chapter 3: Describing Action

At some point, a writer always gets to the action. In writing about action, as in writing about place and people, we need that choice of words that helps the reader see what the writer sees. A good journalist is trained to get at it immediately with a minimum of background material. The idea is to tell what happened, when, where, who did it, and why — all within a couple of lines. Action is stripped to its bare essentials to convey information efficiently. We also find actions described on boxes and packages in the form of instructions on how to use or assemble the product. Home repair and hobby books abound in bookstores, and this book you are reading falls into the how-to category. I am giving instructions on how to do certain exercises and assignments and how to carry out a certain process. I also narrate from time to time examples of these exercises as they worked out for me. Even a poet or a writer who works almost entirely in the interior of a character's mind will eventually need to describe something in motion, to give some hint of what is happening. There is a sense in which all narratives (history as well as fiction) are actions writ large, general movements of change: progressions and degenerations, rises and falls.

Action, then, is an essential component of fiction. As with Place and People, I start students working on Action with Observation, the solid ground of our senses we all share, this time primarily the sense of sight. One of my favorite ways of encouraging students to observe action closely and experiment with putting it into words is by standing in front of the class and doing something with my hands. I don't mime a recognizable activity like cleaning teeth or hitting a tennis ball, but I make a brief, abstract combination of swoops, flutters, waves, and claps. I ask the students what I did, and someone will call out a simple answer like "Waved your hands in the air." I ask for more precision. Waved which hand first? Where did I hold them, at waist level or above my head? Was it the whole hand that waved or did I only wiggle my fingers? We either write a group description of my action, on the blackboard, or everyone writes individually. One ninth grader wrote:

A hand, closed tight like a jar. Suddenly it bloomed, each finger like a petal slowly unravelling gently moving as if it were a baby taking a first step. It brings itself up. Ta-dum, the hand is exposed.

Another student was even more elaborate with the same gesture:

Each finger, not quickly, but at medium speed, eases out of the clenched fist one at a time like a bird working its way out of an egg. Then the outstretched hand and fingers point towards the door, roll in a circle, again, you see the bird looking around quickly. They draw back into a fist, displeased with what they see. The fist is moved backwards to the shoulder, then they explode open as if they feel it's not so bad after all out there and they want to get on with the rest of the day.
— Nick Bazarini, 9th, Stuyvesant High School, Manhattan

I did not ask for figurative language in that assignment: I said simply to describe the action. Some students will fall naturally into metaphor or will use metaphor along with language that tries to describe directly the positions and speeds of things in motion. Since you will find students using both types of language naturally with this exercise, it is a handy time to discuss the two different kinds of writing, to talk about which kind is more appropriate in what situation.

A game using these abstract movements is to send an "It" out of sight while someone else makes one of the abstract movements and the class writes about it. "It" returns, and various people read their descriptions while "It" does what the description says. The object is to see whose words can tell "It" how to move in such a way that she or he duplicates the original movement. This again will point out the difference in the two types of description: for this exercise the more metaphoric writing will generally not work as well as an analytic breaking down of the action. "Birds working their way out of eggs" would probably get some interesting movements, but not necessarily the one that prompted the metaphor. This sort of writing is often used in a review of dance performance where the general tone of the action is wanted rather than the duplication of it. One reason we use figurative language so often in describing action is that it is very difficult to capture movement in words. Choreographic notation, for example, is notoriously cumbersome.

•**Idea 122:** An alternate form of the game above is to write metaphoric descriptions of an action and see how many different interpretations can be obtained.

•**Idea 123:** Another exercise at this point is for everyone to try writing up his or her description of the abstract action in each of two ways, one clinical and the other figurative.

•**Idea 124:** Younger students have trouble with the idea of an action being abstract, so an alternative game is to mime a common action and have people write or say in words how to do the action (without giving it away by saying something like "now pretend to pick up your toothbrush.") "It" goes through each movement described until he or she can guess what is being mimed. This game, like the previous one, makes clear to everyone why it is so hard to describe a spiral staircase without using your hands. "No, no," says the student describing. "I want your fist in *front* of your mouth, not up in the air." "Well," says It, "You didn't *say* that."

•**Idea 125:** Do the same exercise, working in pairs. Have the students decide on the clearest possible instructions, and then have them try their description on several other students, making revisions in the instructions as they go.

•**Idea 126:** Have everyone visualize an action mentally and write it out, then exchange slips of paper so that everyone gets to see how his or her description is performed. How close is it to what you visualized?

•**Idea 127:** If your class likes contests, you might try writing on the board two or three "boring" sentences. I have used these, among others:

> He struck out.
> The sun rose.
> The dentist drilled my tooth.
> The cat fell off the refrigerator.

The game is to make that boring sentence interesting by adding words that make the action vivid. Here are two fifth grade winners for the cat and refrigerator sentence:

> A furball was on the top of the fridge. Suddenly a screaming, hissing, mrowing, furry figure came flying down. Splat!

> •

> The cat fell off the refrigerator. The door was open, and he fell into the butter. Splat! He tumbled out of the butter dish into the tomato sauce and was cooked. Um, um!

The pleasures of fifth grade humor, and oh, those favorite words like Splat! and Zap! and Smoosh!

Writing How-to Instructions

A simple and highly effective follow-up exercise for these games is simply to write instructions on how to do something. How-to and step-by-step narrations of an action take us into the realm of structure and organization of a piece of writing. Analyzing an action into its parts and writing it up in this order is a natural form, as is a narrative of events in chronological order. Every time I offer one of these ideas for writing with a class, I am attempting to put into words and give order to an action. Of course, instructions for assembling a bicycle have to be exact in a way that I don't want to be in this book — there is only one right way to make the bicycle function properly, but there are thousands of right ways to teach writing. The bicycle assembly, in fact, requires such precision that the instructions often require *pictures* as well as words. The writing assignments using this structure, then, have at least two modes. One is the imitation of the bicycle assembly instructions where the object is maximum precision, and the other is a more open and serendipitous type of writing — an assignment on, say, How to Make a Friend or Enemy. This latter often turns into a narrative following the general pattern of the how-to.

To illustrate the bicycle-assembly type, I like to offer a sample of actual, professionally written instructions such as the ones below, although if you are working with younger children you might want some shorter ones — perhaps from a box of spaghetti.

A BETTER WAY TO CLEAN YOUR TEETH

To remove plaque, follow this
five-step procedure before going
to bed each night:

1. Make the plaque visible by
chewing a disclosing tablet or
painting the teeth with plaque
dye.

2. Brush your teeth, using a dry,
soft-bristle brush without toothpaste. Place the bristles at a
45-degree angle, pointing toward
the gum. Gently slide some of
bristles under the edge of the
gum, and move the brush back
and forth with short strokes.
Clean chewing surfaces with short
scrubbing strokes.

3. Use unwaxed dental floss to
clean between all the teeth and
under the edges of the gum (the
floss should actually disappear) to
remove plaque there. Slide the
floss up and down.

4. Rinse and examine the teeth
for any remaining stained areas.

5. Brush again, using toothpaste
and concentrating on areas that
still contain plaque.

For maximum effectiveness, don't
eat again before going to bed.
The gums may bleed a bit and
feel tender for the first few days
of regular flossing. If this per-
sists, see a dentist. In any case,
have a dental check-up twice a
year, and request that your dentist use a periodontal probe when
checking the teeth and gums.
— *The New York Times*

That selection always makes me feel guilty about how I clean my teeth.
Some supplementary assignments are:

•**Idea 128:** Describe how you clean your teeth in reality.

•**Idea 129:** Collect accounts of how various people clean their teeth
(or do some other pedestrian daily activity).

•**Idea 130:** Following the pattern of "A Better Way to Clean Your
Teeth," write a parody in which everything is opposite: "First smear your
teeth all over with blackberry jam making sure that the little seeds get caught
between your teeth...."

For many students who are just beginning to write, and especially for
those older students who have not had much success with writing, the form
of How-to (including even the numbers) can be a first success. The assignment should be to write instructions for how to do something you are good
at. A few years ago, I asked an eighth grade class to begin by simply writing
at the top of a paper one thing they knew how to do. When they had done
this much, I asked them to write instructions for how to do this thing. For
the first time since I'd been visiting their class, two boys in the back of the
room wrote instead of cradling their heads in their arms on their desks. John
wrote, "First you dribble around, then put up the ball real easy." He stopped. The rest of the class was still writing away, and he had already given it
his best shot, so to speak. I read over his shoulder and said, "That's good so
far, but how do you know *when* to put it up? Which hand do you use?" John
answered my questions, pointing out that there is a different approach for a
right-handed person and a left. I asked him to add the new information. The
other boy, Marcos, didn't need prompting from me because, as he explained
when I read his piece, he pretended he was teaching a younger player, and
that helped him break it down.

HOW TO DO A LAYUP

First you dribble to the backboard. Then if you are lefty you put it up with your right foot and your left hand. If you are righty you put it up with your left foot and your right hand. Right when you reach the small box, jump, and put it in gently.
> — John Santana, 8th, I.S. 184, Bronx

HOW TO SHOOT A BASKETBALL

First, hold your right hand behind the ball. Then put your left hand on the side of the ball, then you stay looking at the rim, the back of it, and you aim for it. You put the ball in any comfortable way you want to shoot, then flick your hand to push a little so the ball can go in.
> — Marcos Magnus, 8th, I.S. 184, Bronx

In that same class Sara gave a recipe for cooking white rice. It caused considerable debate because of the number of people who thought they knew a better way to cook it. Almost any recipe offers a clear model for this kind of writing.

HOW TO COOK WHITE RICE

1) Take some rice and put it in a bowl. You could put as much as you want.

2) Then wash the rice good with warm water.

3) After that, take a big pot and put cold water in it. The water that you are going to put on the pot depends on how much rice you are going to do.

4) Then heat up the water. Remember to put some salt in the water.

5) After that, put the rice in the water and add oil to the rice.

6) Then leave it heat up until it is done and dry. Remember to stir the rice every five minutes or so.
> — Sara Soto, 8th, I.S. 184, Bronx

•**Idea 131:** Write a recipe. Don't copy one out of a book, but ask your mother or father or someone who can cook how they do a favorite dish of theirs.

•**Idea 132:** Make a class collection of recipes.

•**Idea 133:** Make a class handbook on a favorite sport. Each person can give the instructions for one area of the sport — rules of the game, principles of defense, plus the various moves and skills. Someone who is good at drawing can make illustrations and appropriate stories and poems could be included. This would be a good book to do with rexograph masters that the students can draw on directly. Before making the final draft of the book, you might consult with coaches and gym teachers for accuracy.

•**Idea 134:** Make a handbook on this same pattern for some other skill: roller skating, dancing, a handicraft, etc.

•**Idea 135:** Make a set of instructions or a class booklet on how to teach some common process to young children.

HOW TO DRINK WATER OUT OF A GLASS

1. First you take the person to the kitchen.
2. Then you make them look in the cabinet and get a glass.
3. Then let them put the glass down.
4. Then make them turn on the water.
5. Then put the glass under the water.
6. Then move the glass when it is full.
7. Then turn the water off.
8. Drink the water.
9. Then put the glass in the sink.

This is what I did to teach my nephew. He learned very fast. I started teaching him when he was one, and now in March he will be two, and he knows how to drink out of the glass perfectly well.
— Cheryl Lindsey, 8th, I.S. 184, Bronx

•**Idea 136:** As you might imagine, some students begin to parody this kind of writing almost as soon as the assignment is given. Here are two, one by a student and one by a teacher. Both prefer to remain anonymous!

HOW TO TONGUE KISS

1. First give a small kiss.
2. Then another, but a better one.
3. Then you really go into action.
4. Don't go wild.
5. Kiss very gently.
6. Make sure that you give the tongue because the person won't feel secure.
7. Then try to make the kiss very comfortable and long.
8. And make sure that the person likes your kiss.
9. Make sure you know how to do all the famous kisses like Hot Kiss, French, Black power.

HOW TO LOOK BUSY DURING A PREP

1. First, always have plenty of papers on your desk. Do not keep them in an orderly fashion because it will be too easy to expose you. It is a good idea to keep a variety of papers, rexograph sheets, compositions, books, and folders.
2. Sit behind your desk.
3. Keep one of the side drawers open. Should someone walk in, you could simply reach into the drawer as if you were looking for something.

4. Hold a piece of paper (preferably students' work) in one hand. You could always make believe you are filing this paper in one of your many folders.
5. Sit back and relax.
6. Ignore the above and leave your room. Walk around the building. You can always say you are looking for a student, class, or teacher.

•**Idea 137:** Write instructions for doing something illegal.

•**Idea 138:** Tell how to do a piece of magic. This can either be researched so that you are telling how to do real magic, or it can be something you make up on your own, a love potion, or a curse.

•**Idea 139:** Read the lovely imaginary instructions in "To Paint the Portrait of a Bird" by Jacques Prévert below and then write your own imaginary instructions.

TO DO THE PORTRAIT OF A BIRD

Paint first of all a cage
with an open door
paint then
something pretty
something simple
something beautiful
something useful
for the bird
then place the canvas against a tree
in a garden
in a wood
or in a forest
hide behind the tree
without speaking
without moving
When the bird comes
if it comes
keep the deepest silence
wait for the bird to go into the cage
and when it has gone in
quietly close the door with the brush
Then do the portrait of the tree
choosing its most beautiful branches
for the bird
likewise paint the green foliage and the freshness of the wind
the dust of the sun
and the sound of the creatures of the grass in the summer heat
and then wait for the bird to decide to sing
If the bird doesn't sing
it's a bad sign
a sign that the painting is bad

but if it sings it's a good sign
a sign that you may sign the work
Then very softly you pull
a feather from the bird
and you write your name in a corner of the painting.
— Translated by Sheryl Treshan

•**Idea 140:** Write the narration of what actually happens when a real person tries to follow your instructions.

•**Idea 141:** Write a How-to for something more abstract like How to Get to Heaven or Hell.

Describing a Person at Work

One interesting series of action writings is based on the idea of observing (in fact or in your imagination or your memory) someone at work. This is again a good opportunity for using students' own experiences. Everyone has watched a person at work. Work ranges from a woman putting clothes in a washing machine to the man at the newsstand or the woman who is a crossing guard or your mother in her office dictating to a secretary, not to mention a teacher! I like to begin this lesson with a group piece describing someone we all have seen in motion — or at least with a brainstorming session listing words that describe people moving. How many different types of walks are there? How do you describe arm motions and muscle strains? You need to decide (if you are doing a group writing) whether you are going to cover the worker's whole day or only one movement, broken down and described in detail. Encourage your students to do the latter, because you are trying to make the language vivid and concrete rather to describe action over a lot of time, which necessitates generalization. Be sure and save one strong phrase or sentence to finish off the piece so it doesn't just trail off.

A very good model for this kind of writing is a poem by Theodore Roethke, whose family ran greenhouses. In language that I really admire he describes one worker:

OLD FLORIST

That hump of a man bunching chrysanthemums
Or pinching-back asters, or planting azaleas.
Tamping and stamping dirt into pots —
How he could flick and pick
Rotten leaves or yellowy petals,
Or scoop out a weed close to flourishing roots,
Or make the dust buzz with a light spray,
Or drown a bug in one spit of tobacco juice,
Or fan life into wilted sweet-peas with his hat,
Or stand all night watering roses, his feet blue in rubber boots.

The following student piece was done after reading the poem:

THE APPLE PICKER

He would climb up trees as high as he could go, feeling how strong each branch is as he went. He would stretch as far as he could go to pick the ripest apple. Then he would toss it down on the soft grass, or stuff it down his deep pocket, occasionally he would stop to eat one of the apples, then throw the core down to the ground. To pick the best apples he would wrap his legs around the branch, then reach with his hands so far that some people considered it dangerous. He could practically leap from branch to branch like an ape. The unripe apples he would leave, to pick on his next visit.

— Jeremy Kahn, 6th, Hunter College Elementary School, Manhattan

•**Idea 142:** Try the same exercise, but do it in the first person.

PROFESSIONAL BASEBALL FIELD

I was on the baseball field sweating. My legs and hands were trembling. The bases were loaded, and my team had two outs and the score was 7 to 6. Now I got ready to bat. The ball came in fast, then I hit the ball with all my strength, and the ball went into the air, looking like a dot in the sky, then falling out of sight. Every man on the bases ran home, and my team won 10 to 6. Then I felt people hitting me on the back, yellling with joy. Then I felt myself smiling. Then I walked to the locker room feeling very good indeed.

— Sherwin Mateen, 5th, P.S. 321, Brooklyn

•**Idea 143:** Take a walk through the neighborhood looking for people at work, and make an album of protraits of local workers working.

Writing Adventure Action

Another good source of action writing is adventure fiction. I particularly like a longish scene from James Dickey's novel *Deliverance* in which the protagonist climbs a sheer cliff at night. (Another sample, if you don't mind the gore, is a paragraph taken from James Clavell's bestseller *Shogun* on page 82 of this book.) The *Deliverance* piece is really a sort of classic of describing action and at the same time plotting out the psychological events in the narrator's consciousness. At each step of the climb the narrator experiences a new level of terror and self-control. I first read this piece lying in a tent during a rainstorm, and I remember the tension in my body as I responded to the author's minute description of physical and psychological danger. The character's calves tremble; his whole body shakes. The cliff itself seems to come alive and presses at him, and then, at a certain crisis point, stops pressing. The organization of the piece follows the character's psychological changes: first he has considerable success in his climbing, is even a little proud of his competence, then he begins to look at the climb as an intellectual problem of how best to make his next move. But the physical strain begins to be too much; he has a loss of the sense of competence and power, and he is overwhelmed by the vastness of the cliff, the moon on the river. He begins to believe that the cliff wants to get rid of him.

From DELIVERANCE

I got to the bulge and then went up over it and planted my left foot solidly on it and found a good hold on what felt like a root with my right hand. I looked down.

The top of the overhang was pale now, ten or twelve feet below. I turned and forgot about it, pulling upward, kneeing and toeing into the cliff, kicking steps into the shaly rock wherever I could, trying to position both hands and one foot before moving to a new position. Some of the time I could do this and each time my confidence increased. Often I could only get one handhold, but it was a strong one, and I scrambled and shifted around it until I could get a toe into the rock and pull up.

The problem-interest of it absorbed me at first, but I began to notice that the solutions were getting harder and harder: the cliff was starting to shudder in my face and against my chest. I became aware of the sound of my breath, whistling and humming crazily into the stone: the cliff was steepening, and I was laboring backbreakingly for every inch. My arms were tiring and my calves were not so much trembling as jumping. I knew now that not looking down or back — the famous advice to people climbing things — was going to enter into it. Panic was getting near me. Not as near as it might have been, but near. I concentrated everything I had to become ultrasensitive to the cliff, feeling it more gently than before, though I was shaking badly. I kept inching up. With each shift to a newer and higher position I felt more and more tenderness toward the wall.

Despite everything, I looked down. The river had spread flat and filled with moonlight. It took up the whole of space under me, bearing in the center of itself a long coiling image of light, a chill, bending flame. I must have been seventy-five or a hundred feet above it, hanging poised over some kind of inescapable glory, a bright pit.

I turned back into the cliff and leaned my mouth against it, feeling all the way out through my nerves and muscles exactly how I had possession of the wall at four random points in a way that held the whole thing together.

It was about this time that I thought of going back down, working along the bank and looking for an easier way up, and I let one foot down behind me into the void. There was nothing. I stood with the foot groping for a hold in the air, then pulled it back to the place on the cliff where it had been. It burrowed in like an animal, and I started up again.

I caught something—part of the rock—with my left hand and started to pull. I could not rise. I let go with my right hand and grabbed the wrist of the left, my left-hand fingers shuddering and popping with weight. I got one toe into the cliff, but that was all I could do. I looked up and held on. The wall was giving me nothing. It no longer sent back any pressure against me. Something I had come to rely on had been taken away, and that was it. I was hanging, but just barely. I concentrated all my strength into the fingers of my left hand, but they were leaving me. I was on the perpendicular part of the cliff, and unless I could get over it soon, I would just peel off the wall.

    —James Dickey

The scene in the book is much longer, but I chose just this part in order to leave things suspended, as it were, in the life-and-death situation. Most competent adventure and thriller writing depends heavily for its effect on the suspense of moments like this. Will the characters live or die? Will they overcome the opposing force or succumb to it? I like to ask students, after they've read this, if they think the climber is going to make it, and I am astounded by how often someone guesses that he won't. This is a reminder of how many of the conventions of literature have not yet been absorbed by students—in this case the convention that the "I" telling the story has lived to tell the tale. There is no necessity for this convention to have been developed—if you really believe, at least for the moment, that someone is writing about conversations and feelings and events from the past in that much precise detail, then you might also believe that a ghost can speak. It sounds wrong to us, but that is because of the convention we are used to. Early novel readers and writers were not used to this convention of a person writing the actual, "real" truth as a sort of imaginary memoir; those first novels were all in the form of letters, a realistic writing device, or else the writer would purport to have found a memoir of someone's life in an old oaken trunk. In other words, a realistic frame had to be set up for the story. Today we dispense with that and simply pretend for the moment, as we read our first-person or third-person narrative, that we are reading what actually happened, as it happened. We have developed a skill in imaginative reading. But we can't assume that all students automatically understand the conventions. Often when I read something to a class, I am asked, "Did that really happen? Are they still alive?"

Reading and writing are, in fact, so inextricably linked that I believe we are always, when we teach one, teaching the other. If we teach literature with no practice in writing, then we are teaching (wrongly) that writing is an arcane craft reserved to the Great Men. If, on the other hand, we teach writing only from Creative Writing Recipe Cards, never bringing our students to literature, then we are teaching from limited and impoverished language models.

I like the following student piece that was written after a hearing of "Climbing a Cliff" because the child takes suggestions from the professional piece yet makes her own work out of it.

•

Once, in the country, I was trying to climb up a cliff that was very slippery. I tried to climb the cliff a few times, but I just couldn't do it. The next day I went running up the cliff. I ran until I got up to the top of the cliff. There was a hole on the top of the cliff which I almost fell into. I went sliding right down again the same way I went when I got up there, but it was a little different because I was bumping into things that I couldn't stop, not even for a little while. I was trembling and got very cold with fright. Finally I got down safely. I went into my house and I told my grandmother. My heart was pounding very hard. She sent me to take a bath and go to sleep.
— Miriam Taveras, 5th, P.S. 321, Brooklyn

•

Action writing is not only, of course, found in adventure stories. The following is a nonfiction scene full of both narration and the detailed description of individual actions. Many people are familiar with this scene from the play and movie versions of *The Miracle Worker,* but the source of those dramatic moments is this portion of the letters of Annie Sullivan about her work with the young Helen Keller. I like to follow this with a class discussion about whether this is more interesting to read or to see in the dramatized version. You can take this, with more sophisticated students, into a discussion of the differences in written work and dramatized work — into the very differences between television and movies and drama and books. Is action easier to convey with live or filmed actors or through photographs or drawings or through words? What can you put into a written piece that you can't put into a movie?

•

Helen's table manners were appalling. She puts her hands in our plates and helps herself, and when the dishes are passed, she grabs them and takes out whatever she wants. This morning I would not let her put her hand in my plate. She persisted, and a contest of wills followed. Naturally the family was much disturbed, and left the room. I locked the dining room door, and proceeded to eat my breakfast, though the food almost choked me. Helen was lying on the floor, kicking and screaming and trying to pull my chair from under me. She kept this up for half an hour, then she got up to see what I was doing. I let her see that I was eating, but did not let her put her hand in the plate. She pinched me, and I slapped her every time she did it. Then she went all round the table to see who was there, and finding no one but me, she seemed bewildered. After a few minutes she came back to her place and began to eat her breakfast with her fingers. I gave her a spoon, which she threw on the floor. I forced her out of the chair and made her pick it up. Finally I succeeded in getting her back in her chair again, and held the spoon in her hand, compelling her to take up the food with it and put it in her mouth. In a few minutes she yielded and finished her breakfast peaceably. Then we had another tussle over folding her napkin. When she had finished, she threw it on the floor and ran toward the door. Finding it locked, she began to kick and scream all over again. It was another hour before I succeeded in getting her napkin folded. Then I let her out in the warm sunshine, and went up to my room and threw myself on the bed exhausted. . . .

—Annie Sullivan, from her letters
in *My Life* by Helen Keller

•**Idea 144:** Rewrite this scene from Helen's point of view.

•**Idea 145:** Or from the point of view of Helen's mother or father, eavesdropping at the door and hearing this alleged teacher wrestling with your beloved child.

•**Idea 146:** Read aloud and act out the Helen Keller piece and any of the pieces written by students. Since these are primarily action pieces (Helen Keller could not talk at the time of the incident), there should just be the movements of the actors to accompany the voice of the reader.

•**Idea 147:** After the acting out, ask the students to write in their own words what they saw. In other words, to compare the action as they saw it to the original written form.

•**Idea 148:** A wide-open assignment suggested by this piece is to describe vividly any action in which two or more people or animals have a wordless conflict. This could be done with people giving each other looks like saber cuts, or babies struggling over a block, or chameleons displaying aggressively.

•**Idea 149:** From more on writing out of the idea of conflicts, see page 107 et passim in chapter 5.

Objective Description of Action

Newspaper writing describes action as objectively as possible, with its ostensible focus not on anyone's feelings about the events, but on an accurate conveying of those events. Objective writing is in fact almost non-existent, but the tone of newspaper-style objectivity is frequently affected by writers when they want their material read as facts rather than individual opinion. It is an interesting style to imitate. It often uses the sharply delineated journalistic organization of the Five W's: When, What, Who, Where, and Why. This is one of those structures that is intrinsic to a certain style of writing and has a lot to offer beginning writers in the way of an easy form to master. I particularly like, as an example, the following opening to a nonfiction article. The piece, written in the objective Five W's style, functions as a short-short story. Also, within its narrow (and remember, *nonfiction*) limits, it uses most of the elements of fiction: description of people, place, action, and dialogue. Only the element of interior monologue is missing, as is appropriate to reportage.

From "The Black Middle Class: Making It"

Rachel Simmons, tall, 22, black, waits for a subway. The platform is nearly deserted except for a middle-aged white man leaning against a post. The man looks tired, his horn-rimmed glasses slipping down his nose. He is perhaps a clerk of some kind, wears a shirt with four ball-point pens in the pocket, a tie, a pair of worn slacks, crepe-soled shoes. Rachel doesn't pay much attention to him until two punks saunter quietly down the grimy steps onto the platform. They're in baggy pants and T-shirts, sneakers; one has on a loose leather vest with deep pockets. Rachel, though she works as a receptionist in an ad agency, can spot their thing in a second, knows for certain what's in the pockets. The two of them pivot, check out the platform, see her and gauge her for a few seconds, then settle on the scene. They move casually behind the white man, walk past him, laughing a little too loud, eyeing the curvature of the tunnel. Then they stop, turn and head back toward the man just as nonchalantly as before, as if they're enjoying themselves. Rachel takes it all in. She heads for them just as they pull the knife.

The white man is startled. One of the punks shoves him. He drops his newspaper. "Gimme the wallet." It is quick and scary, the knife a glint of steel in the low light of the tunnel. Then Rachel moves, strides quickly toward them. She yells, "Get the hell out! You're just continuing the *stereotype!*"

She spits out the syllables, advancing on them with her height, her flashing eyes. They are taken aback. They withdraw, try to summon up some reserve, show the knife. She keeps coming, mad as hell now. "Just a part of the stereotype, *fools!*" she scolds.

"Shee," one of them groans, now wary of the noise, the time elapsed, looking at Rachel and heading for the exit. "We just *robbin'* the man."

She lifts her purse, and they take off, up and out of the tunnel. The man slumps against the steel post, hugging it, not sure of what has happened. Rachel turns, smiles, towers over him and says softly, "You're all right."
— William Brashler, *The New York Times Magazine*

One student responded with this:

It was on a summer night. I was walking through the dark park on Courtland Avenue. All of a sudden I saw a young boy about 12 or 13 years old running like somebody was chasing him. Then around 12 boys in their teens came running around the corner. I was scared because I was by myself. The boy ran in the street, started screaming. The boys caught him, told him to shut up, they beat him bad. He had just got paid and the boys needed money. It was $3.00 for each. The boy wouldn't give his money

up. They pulled out a knife ready to stab him. I felt sorry for him. I was even more scared than he was. I came out so they could see me, and took out some money. They chased me. I was right next to my building. I unlocked the bottom door and ran in. They almost grabbed me. The door closed in time. The boy I guess had run; all of the other boys were after me. I went into my house and told my family. They told me to stay in for a while, the boys might still look for me. I stayed in for two weeks.
—Tammy Cole, 8th, I.S. 184, The Bronx

•**Idea 150:** Write a description of some event you have witnessed as if you were a newspaper reporter telling about it. Be sure to include the Five W's.

•**Idea 151:** Do the same thing, but make it be some tiny, ordinary event: your father taking his morning shave, a fly settling on the table and rubbing its legs together.

•**Idea 152:** Write a newspaper report on some event from history. (Teachers sometimes make class newspapers about the period of history they are studying—say colonial times. Be sure and include classified ads and advice columns and comics, even though they may be anachronistic.)

Newspaper style writing can be used with great, impassioned effect. The next selection also in the Five W's mode, is an account of the bombing of a small town called Guernica by the Fascists during the Spanish Civil War. This was the first time airplanes had been used systematically to destroy a civilian population. Today, after London, Dresden, Hiroshima/Nagasaki, and Cambodia, this destruction from the skies seems ordinary, but at the time of this writing there was a great international out-cry and Pablo Picasso was inspired to commemorate the event with his monumental painting, "Guernica." One of the things to point out to students is how powerful terrible events are when the writer *doesn't* exclaim, "Isn't this just awful? Have you ever heard anything so terrible?" Instead, the writer tries to be a sharp lens showing the thing just as it was, and in this case the facts themselves speak with full power of the horror of the bomb-ing.

The whole town of 7000 inhabitants plus 3000 refugees was slowly and systematically pounded to pieces. Over a radius of five miles round a detail of the raiders' technique was to bomb separate *caserios* or farm-houses. In the night these burned like little candles in the hills. . . .

The tactics of the bombers, which may be of interest to students of the new military science, were as follows: First, small parties of airplanes threw heavy bombs and hand grenades all over the town, choosing area after area in orderly fashion. Next came fighting machines which swooped low to machine-gun those who ran in panic from dugouts, some of which had already been penetrated by 1000 lb. bombs, which make a hole 25 ft. deep. Many of these people were killed as they ran. A large herd of sheep being brought in to the market was also wiped out. The object of this move was apparently to drive the population underground again, for next as many as 12 bombers appeared at a time dropping heavy and incendiary bombs upon the ruins. The rhythm of this bombing of an open town was, therefore, a logical one: first, hand grenades and heavy bombs to stampede the population, then machine-gunning to drive them below, next heavy and incendiary bombs to wreck the houses and burn them on top of their victims.

— George Lowther, *The New York Times*

The form of this fragment is almost a how-to piece for bombing a small town systematically. The how-to form gives it a faintly sardonic tone that overlies the objective description and is one of the reasons the piece in its entirety is considered a classic of journalism. This example is good to use along with advertisements to discuss the function of propaganda — the kind of writing meant to move people to definite attitudes and actions.

•**Idea 153:** Think about this "Guernica" piece in terms of point of view. Describe the same action from the point of view of one of the survivors rather than of a journalist who *seems* to have observed the whole thing from a great distance, almost as if from an airplane himself. Imagine how it would *feel* to be there. What would you think was happening? What would herald the beginning of the bombing? What sounds would you hear first? What sights and smells? In what order would things appear to happen to you?

•**Idea 154:** Describe these events from the point of view of one of the Fascist pilots.

•**Idea 155:** From the point of view of the sheep.

•**Idea 156:** Write your own description of some terrible action as seen from a great distance. Try to write in an objective, newspaper style.

A shot ran out across the lake. The wounded duck plummetted from the sky, to land, flapping wildly, and broke the glass-like surface of the water. The bird was not dead but the shotgun spray had broken a wing and placed a few pellets in the bird's chest. Oddly enough the bird still lived. Still beating its wings madly, it hit its own chest as if it were trying to pull the pain away without the use of hands. Then the water churned and again it was silent. A giant pike, upwards of five feet in length, had dragged the crazed bird under the water. Crunching down with its jaws to stop the flapping, it reached the bottom. The pike let the bird go and opened its huge jaws to swallow the bird whole.

— Nick Bazarini, 9th, Stuyvesant High School, Manhattan

•**Idea 157:** Describe the same action you wrote about in Idea 156, showing how you feel about it. You can either say so, or, better, let the words show how you feel.

•**Idea 158:** Write about something, seen from a distance, that is not alive but *is* in motion.

Up and down, running and leaping through the air like a deer round and round slithering on the ground like a snake. Here it comes, there's no place to hide. It blows its horn like a train, every house is wrecked. Slashing and breaking everything in sight, it passed and you could hear screams from the TORNADO.

—Erica Stoltz, 5th, P.S. 321, Brooklyn

•**Idea 159:** Write about the movement of a crowd of people.

•**Idea 160:** Collect some news photographs and try to describe vividly the thing caught in the action, supplying in words the movement that the photograph can't have.

•**Idea 161:** Try the above twice, once writing precisely and objectively, and then again with figurative language, comparing the thing to other things.

•**Idea 162:** Pretend to have been an eyewitness to some event in history, recent or current. Try to describe it from the point of view of someone who has been greatly affected by it. (For an example, see "Journal of a Plague Year" on page 138.)

•**Idea 163:** Try this with something from this week's newspaper.

•**Idea 164:** Pretend to be on a trip and describe the landscape passing you in the distance. (See the *Huckleberry Finn* selection on page 117.)

THE RIVER

Travelling, moving all the time. Cold and fast, up to six miles per hour. Green, but not polluted. The surrounding air is cold. Don't fall in! Don't fall in! Many fish abound. Brown trout with their brown background and black spots, and rainbow and brook trout with their mixed colors. They are wary, and hard to catch. This is a wild river, and will have no mercy if you accidentally fall in.

—Stephen Guerra, 5th, P.S. 321, Brooklyn

•**Idea 165:** Write about something changing: a cloud passing over the sun, a flower growing.

•**Idea 166:** Try looking at one movement in great detail, as if the motion had been slowed down by a slow-motion camera shot.*

•**Idea 167:** Try describing an event as if you were looking at it with a wide-angle camera lens.

Using Action to Show Deeper Levels of Meaning

Action can also be used to show, without telling in so many words, what is *really* going on. Perhaps the author doesn't actually know what is really going on until after the action is described; in this case the writing of the action also becomes a study or exploration of character. Action in this

---

*See also "Slow Motion Descriptive Poetry" by Ron Shapiro in *The Whole Word Catalogue 2* (McGraw-Hill/Teachers & Writers Collaborative), Zavatsky and Padgett, eds., p. 141.

78

context is intricately woven into the other elements of fiction—the gesture of a hand is part of what the person is saying. I love how much can be shown by an action—the nervous tic, the hands that grasp like talons, the incomplete caress. We have an infinite number of gestures and actions with which we express ourselves and reveal ourselves. Whole communications can take place with no words at all (look again at the Helen Keller conflict on page 73).

•**Idea 168:** Play an improvisation game in which two people both want the same chair and have to resolve this without words. Will a fight necessarily ensue? Will one become gallant and offer the chair to the other? Try this improvisation in front of the class.

•**Idea 169:** Write, and act out, how a person behaves when she has won the lottery, is in love, is tired, has received bad news, or is looking for a fight.

•**Idea 170:** Now act it out in front of the class by reading it aloud and having two students follow the instructions.

•**Idea 171:** Write a "conversation" between two people in which no words are said.

The following brief selection from an adult novel has a bit of action that reveals a great deal about a certain old woman and about her family by describing her eating habits. The narrator is watching the grandmother eat and flashing back in imagination to the grandmother's childhood and to the relationships within the family. There are many topics of discussion that could be extracted from this piece. How are the old treated by families today? What are the differences between generations?

From THE CLAMSHELL

At the end of the table, my grandmother eats. No one watches her do this. They are repelled by it. To cover her noise they keep up a counterpoint of conversation across the table. I have to glance at her.

She sits, her old eyes close to her plate, tearing at her turkey, stuffing it into her mouth with her fork. She is a savage, hungry child, self-comforting, self-pleasing, who has been hungry in a creek-side cabin forgotten by us all, eating sow-belly and cornpone when they could get it, the father away at war. The child she feeds so urgently was born in 1861. Now, taking a pickle from the Waterford glass in front of her, remembering that there is someone else, she leans over, her face covered wi th turkey grease, and presents it to her great-grandson, who takes it and squeezes it in his hand.

—Mary Lee Settle

What does the Waterford glass pickle dish tell you about the family? Why does the grandmother seem to find her most human connection with the little great-grandson? The thing I love about this fragment is the way the grandmother's eating creates in the narrator's mind this whole scenario of the grandmother's brutally poor and hungry childhood. A gesture can do this, can call up a whole past world.

•**Idea 172:** Write what might come next in the scene by Mary Lee Settle.

•**Idea 173:** Write an action in which the past seems to be revealed through present action.

•**Idea 174:** Write a scene where the actions reveal tensions.

On the stage she danced, my older sister a ballerina, dancing happily to the music as gracefully as can be. She jumped with a beautiful smile. My father sitting next to me looked so grim. He had such a straight face. I was scared. He never wanted my sister to be a dancer. I watched my sister dancing merrily and then I turned my head just to see to my father's grim face....

—Dina Pruzansky, 4th, P.S. 6, Manhattan

•**Idea 175:** Write your own dinner table scene in which family tensions are shown by the people's actions.

•**Idea 176:** Write a family dinner scene in which someone's table manners cause a conflict.

•**Idea 177:** Describe in detail a very young child eating.

•**Idea 178:** Describe an animal eating.

•**Idea 179:** Go into a restaurant or lunchroom and watch someone eat. Take notes and describe as exactly as possible how he or she does it.

•**Idea 180:** Write a description of someone with disgusting table manners.

•**Idea 181:** Now do one of a person with prissy manners. Consider these lines from Chaucer's *Canterbury Tales* describing a nun:

At meat well taught was she with-alle:
She let no morsel from her lippes falle,
Nor wet her fingers in her saucers deep;
Well could she carry a morsel and well it keep
That no drop ever fell upon her breast

•**Idea 182:** Try an imitation in verse and the old-fashioned language of the Chaucer lines.

•**Idea 183:** Secretly observe someone in this room now and write a description of every little action.

THE GIRL ACROSS THE TABLE

The girl sitting across from me puts her head in her hands and sighs. She starts erasing something vigorously. She then starts writing and turning her pencil over again. Nobody but me watches her. She's erasing again now. Now she rubs her eyes while trying to think of something to write. She looks like she's proofreading. In fact, she looks like she's getting bored with the whole thing. Well, she's not doing anything new ex-

cept tap-tap-tapping her pencil on the table. She's standing...I think she's finished...and, in that case, so am I!
— Terry Kaye, 4th, P.S. 6, Manhattan

•**Idea 184:** Describe a person's actions, showing how you feel about him or her.

•**Idea 185:** Write the description of a person doing some sport well. You might concentrate on some part of the body, the legs or torso, say.

> She is like a deer, a gazelle. Her face is strained from concentration, and her long legs reach out ahead of her as she turns the corner of the track. It is as if she is a machine, her arms and legs working together in synchronization. It all looks so easy when she runs, like it is a natural thing to do. One is unable to realize by looking at her that she had been running at top speed for so many laps. The only thing noticed is a streak of color going past and soon coming back again. Finally, her leg stretches over the line and her whole body relaxes. The tension drains out of her face, as it is replaced by a smile. It is not an ordinary "hello" smile, but a smile of pride and accomplishment.
> — Darcy Jacobs, 9th, Stuyvesant High School, Manhattan

•**Idea 186:** Have someone stand in front of the class and demonstrate a tennis swing or good form for hitting a long ball in baseball, and take down a word portrait as you watch.

•**Idea 187:** Describe the movements of a person doing something very difficult, very pleasant, very new to them, or very boring. Don't forget the movements in the face muscles.

•**Idea 188:** For an interesting idea for imitation for advanced students you might take a look at Jonathan Swift's "Directions to Servants in General."*

MORE PIECES USING ACTION BY ADULTS

From A SPACE APART

> Galatia had two water tanks set on hills on opposite sides of town. Theirs was the East Tank, and it was shimmering in the sinking sun, except for the dull ten-foot letters that spelled GALATIA WVA....

---

*In Janice Thaddeus's article called "Imitation and Independence" in *Teachers and Writers Magazine,* Vol. 12, No. 2.

Climbing was Tonie's idea, not hers. But the truth was that the familiar terror was a tonic. The hill fell away so fast that you felt you were hanging out of an airplane. It was dangerous to have Tonie behind you too, because sometimes she froze and had to be coaxed down, but Tonie was sticking with her tonight. Her hands got cold and stiff from the metal, and her stomach began to heave a little with each rung. It had been a long time since she had done anything so pure. She stopped halfway up and leaned backwards. Better to fall up into the blue than be sucked under the garbage.

"Don't do that," said Tonie.

Deliberately, because she had been nice for so many weeks and smiled at so many people, she shook the ladder until it wavered and clanged along its whole length. Tonie pressed her forehead against her rung, but didn't whimper. She's going to make it to the top this time, Lee thought, a little sorry because Tonie's courage put her under obligation to go further herself. The one thing she had never done was to step off the ladder onto the roof of the tank. There was a narrow rim along the edge of the steep dome where you could hook your heels if you kept your weight back. Making no promises to herself, and keeping her eyes off the ground, she contorted herself through the ladder supports and slid out along the roof. She was in a sweat, but leaning back, her body arched with the dome, she was not uncomfortable.

—Meredith Sue Willis

From SHOGUN

He felt, more than saw, the sword slashing for his throat and leaped backward out of his way. One Gray stabbed after him, the other halted over Mariko, sword raised. At that instant Blackthorne saw Mariko come to life. She threw herself into the unsuspecting samurai's legs, crashing him to the deck. Then, scrambling across to the dead Gray, she grabbed the sword out of his still twitching hand and leaped on the guard with a cry. The Gray had regained his feet, and, howling with rage, he came at her. She backed and slashed bravely but Blackthorne knew she was lost, the man too strong. Somehow Blackthorne avoided another death thrust from his own foe and kicked him away and threw his knife at Mariko's assailant. It struck the man in the back, causing his blow to go wild, and then Blackthorne found himself on the quarterdeck, helplessly at bay, one Gray bounding up the steps after him, the other, who had just won the forepoop fight, racing toward him along the deck. He jumped for the gunwale, and the safety of the sea but slipped on the blood-wet deck.

Mariko was staring up, white-faced, at the huge samurai who still had her cornered, swaying on his feet, his life ebbing fast but not fast enough. She hacked at him with all her force but he parried the blow, held her sword, and tore it out on her grasp. He gathered his ultimate strength, and lunged as the *ronin*-samurai burst up the gangway, over the dead Grays. One pounced on Mariko's assailant, another fired an arrow at the quarterdeck.

The arrow ripped into the Gray's back, smashing him off balance,

82

and his sword sliced past Blackthorne into the gunwale. Blackthorne tried to scramble away but the man caught him, brought him crashing to the deck, and clawed for his eyes. Another arrow hit the second Gray in the shoulder and he dropped his sword, screaming with pain and rage, tearing futilely at the shaft. A third arrow twisted him around. Blood surged out of his mouth, and choking, his eyes staring, he groped for Blackthorne and fell on him as the last Gray arrived for the kills, a short stabbing knife in his hands. He hacked downward, Blackthorne helpless, but a friendly hand caught the knife arm, then the enemy head had vanished from the neck, a fountain of blood spraying upwards. Both corpses were pulled off Blackthorne and he was hauled to his feet. Wiping the blood off his face, he dimly saw that Mariko was stretched out on the deck, *ronin*-samurai milling around her. He shook off his helpers and stumbled toward her but his knees gave out and he collapsed.

— James Clavell

From THE ADVENTURES OF HUCKLEBERRY FINN

On this second night we run between seven and eight hours with a current that was making over four mile an hour. We catched fish and talked, and we took a swim now and then to keep off sleepiness. It was kind of solemn, drifting down the big, still river, laying on our backs looking up at the stars, and we didn't ever feel like talking loud, and it warn't often that we laughed — only a little kind of low chuckle. We had mighty good weather as a general thing, and nothing ever happened to us at all — that night, nor the next, nor the next.

Every night we passed towns, some of them away up on black hillsides, nothing but just a shiny bed of lights; not a house could you see. The fifth night we passed St. Louis, and it was like the whole world lit up. In St. Petersburg they used to say there was twenty or thirty thousand people in St. Louis, but I never believed it till I see that wonderful spread of lights at two o'clock that still night. There warn't a sound there; everybody was asleep.

—Mark Twain

HOW TO TEACH METAPHOR

Listen to children speaking as they walk into the room. Jot down their phrases. One student asks to go to the bathroom. You refuse his request. He says, "This school is like a prison." A girl walks in from Levy's class and some of the boys yell out, "Hi, Chuleta." Everyone laughs.

As you're ready to begin the lesson, motivate the students by asking, "Why did everyone laugh when they heard the word/name 'Chuleta'?" They'll answer, "Because it's funny." You will persist and continue asking leading questions, such as "What is a chuleta? Why do you suppose people call her that?" Make the connection or association between her name and the word. . . .

—Anonymous teacher, I.S. 184, Bronx

From TRANSITION, a novel-in-progress

The light threw a circle over the men and the steer. Everyone was silent. They looked like figures on a stage made of dust. Mr. Laudenslager handed the revolver he'd brought to her father and he and Pablo moved to one side. The revolver too made a shadow, a small one on the ground and she thought how she could watch it all by watching just these shadows, but she was going to watch, she knew. She was spellbound.

The steer just stood there, with the rope held unnecessarily around his neck between the two men, facing her father, facing the scaffold beyond, the light glancing off the licks of white curled hair against the black at the top of his awkward shoulder bones, his nostrils grey-black from wet. He blinked. Then her father aimed squarely at his forehead and shot.

She jumped back. The same jolt blanched through them all. The noise was not the loud bang she expected. It was a muffled quick metallic and seemed inseparable from how the steer stood now in a shocked hesitation and then swayed as his legs began to fold beneath him at the knees and she could see the dark red blood seeping from the cylindrical jabbed black emptiness the bullet had thrust into his skull. It sopped the black hair of his forehead in thick flowering rivulets down towards one eye and down the white nose to the cup of one grey steaming nostril, and then his legs gave way under him and he heaved to the ground with a dull plopping and the dust rose like fine smoke around him.

"Stand away," her father shouted, as the animal rolled onto his back, as the legs spewed out, then in, the hooves flopped and clawing the air. He lurched to one side then another, his spine buckled, his legs and head brought towards one another then jerking out, she saw his hooves slide in their pawing along the ground to search a way to place them on it, to get up again, and his head twisted and lagged after his movements, his eyes wide and frantic, and dust powdered out from around his huge struggling body until finally he lay still. It did not take a very long time.

The men moved in around him. She heard her father say something. Then he knelt over the steer and cut him at the throat. A stream of brighter blood than the other burst out and continued steadily thick forming a pool in the dust to his side, until it drained to a trickle. Then her father took the same knife and slit the hide from the bursting gash in the throat all the way down the center of his belly to his hind end. He moved to the throat again and took up another knife, a curved one, and Mr. Laudenslager another, and they crouched over him on either side to begin the skinning but she couldn't see, their backs were to her, their squat shadows meshed and obscured.

The boys had moved near now. They spoke to one another, occasionally, observing. She and the other girls stood further back, just outside the light, watching the boys and their fathers and the steer.

"Can I try it, Pop?" Danny asked.

"Why I guess so. Get you a knife there."

Her brother picked up one of the several curved knives that lay together near the scaffold.

"Watch awhile." Danny knelt next to his father and watched. "You got the hang of it? Then start on down."

Danny moved away from the two men at the shoulders of the steer to start at the stomach. He was on the opposite side, and she could see what he was doing very clearly, and she wondered if she had been a boy if she would do it.

He put the point of the blade in the cut Papa had made, holding the edge of the hide taut in his left hand, and slid the blade flat under the fur. and the edge became a flap as it parted. The membranes that fastened the hide to the body of the steer were white, moist, and numerous. He flicked the knife quickly against them, working his way down the edge of the vertical cut. When he had gone down a ways, to open the hide enough to give room, he began back up from the point he'd started, flicking the knife, becoming quicker and more deft, accumulating the hide in his left hand, and when he had too much to hold, he let it fall onto the still firm coat of the steer's side.

Maggie was fascinated. It came away so easily. It suddenly looked to her as if it were formed for the purpose of skinning. It came away cleanly, the fibers barely holding it on together, snipped like her mother snipped threads of basting, parting like a zipper, and the coat of the steer that seemed the steer itself that they had named it Pinto from, became a thick hide, folding and folding away, becoming a blanket upon the ground, while what it left became a white moist hulk slightly smaller but the same shape as the steer. The steam rose off it.
—Suzanne McConnell

MORE PIECES USING ACTION BY STUDENTS

•

He was running as fast as he could. He was almost as swift as a deer. One foot up, leap off the second foot and glide on the air. Before he knew it, he was ahead of the others by at least ten yards, but he wasn't tired at all. All the other racers were panting with their tongues dribbling out of their mouths. They were drooling and you could see sweat breaking out of them. They were hardly moving at all, he thought. Their shoelaces came untied and their feet hardly lifted off the ground. He looked ahead. There was the finish line just ahead. He looked back at the faces of the other racers. Still running at the pace without any sign or feeling of being tired, he tripped. His feet went out from under and he spun in the air once and landed on his back. He closed his eyes in pain. Later he opened his eyes and he was on his back on his bedroom floor. It was all a dream. He had fallen out of his bed.
—Andrew Boorstyn, 5th, P.S. 321, Brooklyn

BASKETBALL PLAYER

He grabbed the ball, making a smacking sound on the floor as he dribbled toward the basket, running lightly toward an open space under the backboard. Sweat is running down his face. He takes his free hand to wipe it off. He springs! sending the ball neatly into the basket. He lands with a thud. He hasn't won a game for his team, but the cheers rise out of the stands. He breaks out into a smile and wipes the fresh beads of sweat from his face. He looks around frantically for the ball which has fallen into the opponents' hands. Elbowing through the crowd of players, he ran toward the player with the ball. He watched the opponents' face now, eager for him to take the shot. The opponent sprang, he was blocked. Now he ran to the other side of the court, panting. He dribbled once again, to the other side of the court, this time without so much vigor. He wasn't blocked at all, and sprang for a dunk shot. It sank. They won.
— Rebecca Schanberg, 5th, P.S. 87, Manhattan

•

A frog hopping from one place to another, his skin shining in the sun, croaking, its tongue going in and out of his mouth catching dirty flies, hawks swooping down from the air trying to catch him. He finally jumps into the pond after a while to soak his dry skin.
— Sherwin Mateen, 5th, P.S. 321, Brooklyn

•

Sweat running down his forehead,
moving boards up and down,
waiting and waiting for lunch break.
Hammers banging up and down,
forcing the nails in the boards.
Concentrating on his work in the hot sun,
Keeping busy.
— Emma Sussman, 5th, P.S. 321, Brooklyn

•

The train conductor working away with the clickety clack of the train on the track taking tickets one by one and punching holes through. Yelling everyone off and everyone on, working away with the clickety clack of the train on the track. Closing and opening the doors on the train, working like this every day, concentrating even with the clickety clack of the train on the track.
— Anton Graham, 5th, P.S. 321, Brooklyn

•

As the train pulls into Borough Hall, a handsome-looking black man steps on. Wow! This guy is sharp! He looks like a businessman from Wall Street, where I'll bet he'll get off. Look at that 3-piece suit! Leather bag! Oops, he's looking at his watch. Looks like it's gold plated. Ah, he knows what time it is now, and his hands have just settled at his sides. Oh! He's changed his mind. His hand is moving upwards. Is he looking for something in his pants pocket? Nope. His breast pocket? Nope. His shirt pocket? Nope. His hand is still moving upwards, upwards – into his nose his finger goes. I turn my head away. Oh well, nobody is perfect.

— R. Michael Lee, 9th, Stuyvesant High School, Manhattan

HOW TO MAKE A FRIEND

I was playing basketball, and I saw this boy over there sitting down on the bench, and I said, Yo, do you want to play some basketball? He said yes, so we started playing. He was beating me 20 to 22 and after the game was over, I took him to the store, but he didn't have any money, so I treated him to a pack of chips and a soda and after that we were walking down the street talking about where did you live before you moved here, and after that, he took me to his house to meet his family, and then I went home.

— Shaheed Raheem, 7th grade, J.H.S. 258, Brooklyn

•

Sitting near the gutter on the filthy sidewalk, the derelict searches through the soggy newspapers and apple cores in hope of finding some food. It is raining heavily. He searches, and upon seeing a morsel of food, he pounces on it, chewing ravenously and greedily. He is so lonely in the world, and has no one at all. Maybe something he did condemned him to this terrible misery and hopeless despair. He looks so sad. Maybe I should say something to him or give him some food. His clothes are filthy and his hands are dark and disgusting. He takes the half-eaten apple cores and sits among the pigeons and the dirty brown leaves. Winter will come soon and then what'll he do? As I wondered whether I should give him anything, he got up and crept away, off into the forbidden depths of the dark and unrelenting park.

— Anonymous, Stuyvesant High School, Manhattan

•

The beggar, having no confidence and future, is swaying in this street of this cold city. As a child of about five years approaches him, unaware of this beggar's existence, the beggar looks at the child passionately, murmuring some wonderous experience he had with his family and grandchildren. The child, still unaware of him, is stopped by him; he then gently places a quarter and all he has in the innocent looking hands of the child, and wishes all his best of him. Finally again he sways off and wanders in this cold world.

— David Lam, 11th, Stuyvesant High School, Manhattan

Chapter 4: Writing Dialogue

The human world runs on conversation. Compromises are made in the halls of Congress; business deals are put together over martinis at lunch; lovers decide to embark on marriage as they sit on a ledge overlooking a mountain vista. We talk constantly, even to inanimate objects and our pets. We talk to babies long before they understand us, immerse them in language, and they begin to learn. We chat and argue, curse and cajole: everything happens to the tune of human conversation. Mme. de Staël, the nineteenth-century woman of letters, considered conversation an art form:

> [In France] words are not merely, as they are in all other countries, a means to communicate ideas, feelings, and needs, but an instrument one likes to play and which revives the spirit, just as does music in some nations, and strong liquors in others. It is a certain way in which people act upon one another, a quick give-and-take of pleasure, a way of speaking as soon as one thinks, of rejoicing in oneself in the immediate present, of being applauded without making an effort, of displaying one's intelligence by every nuance of intonation, gesture, and look — in short, the ability to produce at will a kind of electricity which, emitting a shower of sparks, relieves the excess of liveliness in some and rouses others from their painful apathy.

I love the way Mme. de Staël seems actually to believe in salutary effects to our health from conversation, as if it were a sport. In her day, conversation was considered a lively art, to be cultivated and mastered. People vied for invitations to the house of a great conversationalist, and would later discuss whether or not the talker had been in good form that night. They considered conversation an entertainment and, to some extent, a performance. Today, with less self-consciousness than in Mme. de Staël's time, we also enjoy conversation and entertain ourselves with it. It is the medium through which we navigate in our relationships with other human beings.

For this reason if for no other, conversation would have an important place in fiction writing. No moment is more revealing and intense in novels and stories than the moment at which the people begin to talk. Dialogue in fiction (and interviews in nonfiction) give people a chance to speak in their own voices, to present themselves in the way they want to be seen. In the previous chapters we have given attention to the indirect revelation of character through gesture, appearance, even setting. In dialogue we hear the way people want to present themselves even as we simultaneously make indirect inferences from the manner in which they do it. What stories do they have to tell? How do they approach others? How do they react to the others' approaches? Is the speaking style terse or elaborate? Do they talk a lot, or only rarely? Is their talk more of a barrier between them and others than an avenue of communication? Sometimes the words in a dialogue almost disappear: there is a sense in which the conflict between Helen Keller and Annie Sullivan on page 73 is a dialogue even though it has no direct quotations and one of the actors has not yet learned language.

The novelist Anthony Burgess once said that he begins every new book by writing pages and pages of dialogue — no settings, no descriptions, just the words. He hears the people talking in his mind and writes what they say. He later discards the major part of this material, but it has served its purposes; he has worked out his characterizations and plots through dialogue. Writing dialogue is for him a technique for thinking, a way to plan his novel. In my work also I find dialogue to be central. I don't always *begin* with it, but over and over again I find that the climax of a scene I have written will be the moment when the people begin to talk. Sometimes I do write the dialogue first, and then around it build the rest of the story: how the people look, what they are thinking. After this stage, I often discover that the dialogue has to be changed, but that doesn't matter because it has acted as a structure for my writing.

This was what I was thinking one afternoon when I said to a class of fifth graders, "Conversation is the *spine* of a story." I was more or less visualizing a backbone to hang things on, but just to check that I was communicating what I wanted to, I added, "You all know what a spine is, don't you?"

"Sure," called out one boy. "It's what holds you up."

"No," said another voice. "It's where the nerves run back and forth to your brain."

Of course, I thought. Just so. I was amazed and delighted at the completion of my image. It is the skeleton that holds the rest of the thing up, and it is the channel through which flow the energy, the impulses, and the information.

I find, then, that dialogue writing is one of the most natural points at which to begin writing with students. There are possible yearlong projects using dialogue, in which you can expand pieces of student writing to other media. I particularly like dialogue for the way it organizes a piece of writing and suggests a method of rewriting (that is, the fleshing out of the dialogue-skeleton). I considered beginning this book with the chapter on dialogue because of the ease with which young students and students who are behind their grade level can slip into writing it, but as I thought over the structure for this book I also realized that dialogue (along with the subject of the next chapter, monologue) is probably the most quintessentially *fictional* of the elements in this book. Dialogue certainly appears all the time in nonfiction (interviews, dramatizations of scenes, reconstructed conversations in biography, etc.), but the relationships between people, the inherent drama and conflict and connecting that occur in dialogue, are at the heart of the fiction writer's art. Dialogue is at once natural and familiar to young children and the functionally illiterate and at the same time a field for the most subtle and delicate fictional techniques. It is at the heart of fiction writing because it is like the greatest novels — highly wrought and artistically formed, yet intensely, inevitably, familiar.

Observing and Remembering Conversations

Dialogue is an especially good way to start those students writing who lack confidence in themselves as writers because it is something that needs no extended explanation or introduction. Everyone knows what a conversation is, and even if the words "conversation" and "dialogue" are unfamiliar to them, they still know what it means when two people are talking. The simplest assignment is one that students who are used to failing at writing will find amazingly possible:

•**Idea 189:** Record an actual conversation you have heard. It can be as simple as "Hi, Joe" and "Hi, Frank." The only rule is that it be an actual conversation you have overheard.

ARGUE

Your mama, says the boy to the other. There's a big crowd around them. Boy: When you were born, your mama died when she saw you! Other: When you were born, your mama had a waist 200,000 inches. Boy slugs other. Man comes. Man: Break it up, break it up. Crowd: Blankedy Bleep Bleep. For a little while it goes on. Man: Which one of you started it? Boy: He did. Other: Bull crap. He started. The boys go around the corner and fight.

— Anonymous

•**Idea 190:** Write a conversation that once happened between you and one of your parents or some other adult.

•**Idea 191:** Write a conversation you overheard between some people older than you.

•**Idea 192:** Write a conversation you have heard between some young children you know.

•**Idea 193:** Do the same exercise, but make up a conversation.

Both observation exercises and remembered or reconstructed conversations are important to try. In one case you are trying to capture something as it is happening — the raw material of how people talk — and in the other you are doing some editing, probably remembering the most important part of the conversation, some of the high points rather than every little repetition and throat clearing. If your students try to write realistic-sounding conversation, they need to recognize the difference between *actual* transcribed conversation, which is wordy and somehow flat sounding, and well-made invented conversation which *sounds* natural but is probably much briefer and more pointed than real life conversation would be.

•**Idea 194:** Working in a group, with or without an adult's help, write a conversation. Try to have it feel like something that could really happen in your school. You can use conversation form or you can write it like a play, in dialogue form.

Fiction dialogue form:

"When you were born, your mama died when she saw you!" said one boy.

The other boy said, "When you were born, your mama had a waist 200,000 inches."

Play dialogue form:

BOY: When you were born, your mama died when she saw you!
OTHER BOY: When you were born, your mama had a waist 200,000 inches.

•**Idea 195:** The following fragment of a love story with dialogue is by a group of seventh grade girls in the South Bronx. Finish this story. (You can make any changes you want.)

DAVID AND MARIA

Maria is a girl who is tall, has light skin, medium size, black hair, has like a switch to her walk, nice smile. She is shy and when she gets around her boyfriend, she stutters. She wears tight pants. David is tall, black hair, dark brown eyes, and has dimples when he smiles.

One day in a crowded hallway in the school, students are screaming and running back and forth. People are talking.

"Did you hear what happened to me today?"

"Are we going to play football tomorrow?"

"My boyfriend kissed me!"

David says, in a voice trying to get over the crowd, "Hey, Maria! Come over here!"

Maria says, "What is it, Davey?"

They go dashing through the crowd trying to get to each other. Finally they reach each other.

David says, "Meet you after school under the train station?"

Maria says, "Okay, sugarplum."

Then he takes her by the hand to a corner where nobody is. He looks at her lips and she looks at his and slowly they come together. Then suddenly, Mr. Miller, an old-fashioned, mean teacher with a potbelly taps David on the shoulder.

Clearing his throat Mr. Miller says, "Don't you think you two should be getting upstairs now? David, I'll speak to you after class."

David and Maria give each other a look.

•**Idea 196:** Now try spying. Take your notebook and station yourself somewhere in the school or out of it, and quietly write down exactly what people say as best you can. Some good places for this are lunchrooms, bathrooms, offices, but any place will do. Younger children love this, and even older students like it if they can do it on their own time, surreptitiously, perhaps on a bus or grocery check-out line.

Here is what a seventh grade teacher from New Jersey observed in her classroom:

— Vinnie, you got a good grade.
— I did? What did I get?
— It's a good grade. Go look.
— I got a 97? I got a 97? I got a 97? Hey Eddie, I got a 97. Do you think it's a mistake?
— No, why should it be a mistake?
— Because *I* got a *97!*

•**Idea 197:** Spy in a public place near your school every day for a week at about the same time. Make a class collection that includes typical conversations in your neighborhood. After reading your class collection aloud, try to draw some conclusions about typical conversations. Do people joke a lot? What do they seem to talk about most? Members of the opposite sex? Teachers? What do adults talk about, as opposed to students?

•**Idea 198:** Try this with a tape recorder.

•**Idea 199:** Tape record some people talking in your class and at the same time write it down. How are the two versions different? How could you make the written one more interesting?

•**Idea 200:** How would you make the taped version more interesting? (Sound effects? Intonation?)

•**Idea 201:** Choose one of your observed or remembered conversations. Extend it. That is, set the scene: describe the place and the people. Tell how they said things and what they did with their hands, what expressions were on their faces.

•**Idea 202:** Take this same extended, or fleshed-out conversation and add even more material to it. Make up what happens next, and perhaps the next day and/or the day before.

•**Idea 203:** Don't forget to include the "how" things are said. For an exercise in putting in the "how," write the following conversation, filling in as much as you can to make it more interesting. You can do anything you want to it as long as you keep the skeleton of the following words:

It's been a long time.
Yes, a long time.
Is this it?
I guess it is.

One student wrote:

THE LOVE STORY

Boy—"It's been a long time since I've seen you," in a low voice.
Girl—"Yes, a long time. It's been funny without you," in a high voice.
Boy—"Is this it or isn't it?" in a low voice.
Girl—"I guess it is, my sweetheart," in a high and happy voice.
Boy—"I guess it's time to go to California," in a sad voice.
Girl—"I've been lonely at night in bed," in a disgusted voice.
Boy—"Me too, to be exact," in a sad voice.
Girl—"Why did you leave me when I was going to have the kid?" in a mad voice.
Boy—"OK, I have to leave," in a sad voice.
Girl—"Stay with me," in a sad voice.
Boy—"OK, I will stay with you all my life," in a happy voice.
—Yvonne Montijo, 5th, P.S. 321, Brooklyn

A small group from a teacher education class at Medgar Evers College wrote this from the skeleton story:

They were meeting again at the Rockland County Station. It was deserted and late at night. He was wearing a white fox coat, and he had a wide, deep scar on his right cheek. "It's been a long time, baby."

"Yes, a long time," she said in a scared voice, even though she was dressed like summertime, wearing a floral blouse under her coat and a wide-brimmed summer hat. "Is this it?"

He said, "If you're looking for the best, I guess it is."

They exchanged a brown paper package for a Lord & Taylor bag....

•**Idea 204:** The opposite exercise would be to hand out a sheet describing *how* things are said and have everyone fill in the words said:

"_____," he said gently, touching the cat on the tip of its nose.

She grabbed the cat away, and snarled, "_____!"

•**Idea 205:** Take one of your real life conversations and act it out as a play. Decide if you need to fictionalize it at all to make it more dramatic. Feel free to rearrange and change things.

Using Dialogue in Plays and Other Media

One of the wonderful things about dialogue — especially with younger children, but also with any group that would benefit from an extended project growing out of their writing — is that you can use it in other media. You can actually plan your dialogue lessons as a sort of springboard to putting on plays, making video or radio dramas, or even making comic books. Children get a lot of satisfaction from reading aloud what they have written. As you share writing — a natural part of many teachers' writing programs — you are already moving into another medium, the medium of public speaking and dramatic reading, which requires skills different from writing. Children who are not necessarily the best writers will often be the class favorites when it comes to oral presentation. A step beyond reading aloud is the reading aloud with pantomime: the writer or someone else reads the piece while other students act it out as it is read. This involves an extra person, and gives the actors a chance to concentrate on gesture and movement rather than memorization. The next stage, of course, is to go through the process of memorizing lines and putting together props and acting out the play or playlet for the class and perhaps other classes. Short plays with a few characters and one or two showy but simple props give wonderful dramatic satisfaction and can be done as a sort of in-school guerilla theater that improves performing skills and prepares a class for a big year-end production, if your tastes run that way. I prefer an assembly of short pieces written and acted by various members of the class to one big play written by professionals, but any dramatic production is wonderful for getting a class to pull together by using everyone's skills.

Dramatic media can also be stimulating for writing in the opposite direction. That is, have students write *after the fact* of the presentation. A simple way to improve listening skills is to have the students write their own version of one of their own members' plays after it is presented. Encourage them, if you try this, to include any gestures or ad-libbed bits that were part of the performance. To a great extent a play is a group effort, and many of the greatest playwrights have always revised their work after it was already in rehearsal. Shakespeare supposedly wrote many of his parts to fit the particular talents of the members of his company. Everything is grist for the writer's mill, perhaps especially limitations.

•**Idea 206:** Make a group play. The method for doing this requires a scribe (probably an adult, to write fast enough and know to get down little asides and to include interesting bits of business). To begin you can work as a go-round, having everyone contribute one line or one character, and once things get moving, you can be more open about it.

I did the following play with a third grade class—the group was chosen by chance, and we had a total of somewhat less than an hour in which we not only planned and scribbled down this play but also practiced and performed it for the class!

THE REAL UNCLE FRED
A Mystery Play

(One morning MELISSA *woke up. She stretched.)*

MELISSA: I want to wear my bracelet to school.

(When she goes to the dresser, she looks on top and finds that it isn't there.)

MELISSA: Jumping jelly beans! My million dollar bracelet is missing! I better call my mother, sister and Uncle Fred! Mommy, Mommy! My bracelet's missing! Janet, my bracelet is missing! Uncle Fred! My bracelet is missing!

MOTHER: I'm going to punish you if you don't find that bracelet.

MELISSA: I put it on the dresser last night!

JANET: So call the cops.

(MOTHER *goes off to do that.)*

MELISSA: Holy Tomato! Janet must have done it because she's the only girl in the family who likes wearing bracelets except me.

UNCLE FRED: That little girl wouldn't steal a bracelet.

JANET: Thanks for believing me.

UNCLE FRED: All youse better go to school.

MELISSA & JANET: No way!!

(Enter MOTHER *and* DETECTIVE CAROL.)

MOTHER: Here's the detective, Detective Carol.

DETECTIVE CAROL: Where did you put it last?

MELISSA: Jumping Jack Rabbits! I put it on my dresser and it's not there!

(UNCLE FRED *gives a strange look.)*

DETECTIVE CAROL: Where is his room?

MOTHER: It better not be you, Fred.

UNCLE FRED: It ain't me, woman!

DETECTIVE CAROL: I think it's him because he gave a strange look at Melissa.

JANET: Uncle Fred doesn't really look like Uncle Fred. He looks phoney.

MOTHER: He does look sort of phoney.

DETECTIVE CAROL: The only way we can find out is if he takes us to his room.

UNCLE FRED: It's not in my room! I'm no phoney!

(They all go in UNCLE FRED's *room. They find the bracelet.)*

UNCLE FRED: Zikes!

(He goes running out of the room and offstage. A loud thumping is heard.)

DETECTIVE CAROL: There is a knocking at the closet door!

JANET: Let's look in there.

(Out comes the real UNCLE FRED.*)*

REAL UNCLE FRED: It's about time.

DETECTIVE CAROL: What happened?

REAL UNCLE FRED: That phoney Uncle Fred locked me in.

DETECTIVE CAROL: Now we know who stole Melissa's bracelet.

> —Phaedra Becker, Janis Cakars, Jordana Erlich, Jessica Hanlon, Michael Montoya, and Celeste Salerno, 3rd grade, P.S. 321, Brooklyn

•**Idea 207:** Read the selection on page 116 from an adult play, Federico García Lorca's *Blood Wedding,* and write your own continuation of it.

•**Idea 208:** Do this, but put the play into the form of a story, describing the people, etc.

•**Idea 209:** Try writing in conversation/story form one episode of your favorite television program. Make it as vivid and interesting as any other piece of your writing, and don't assume that the reader knows the personalities of the characters.

•**Idea 210:** Do the same thing with a movie or a play. When I was a child I used to do this all the time. Whenever my family came back from the movies, I would rush in and immediately act out or write my own version. I did this with favorite books too; it is a way of claiming something important for your own and tailoring it to your own needs.

•**Idea 211:** Do the same assignment—writing the story of a play or movie or television show—but make substantial changes in it. If it is set in the past, move it to the present, or change the sex of the major characters.

•**Idea 212:** Try some of your favorite pieces of dialogue writing as radio plays. Put them on tape recorders, writing in and inventing your own sound effects: feet walking, fists smacked into palms for fights, etc. Radio dramas can be very effective as productions because they cut down the number of variables and allow more focusing; everything is done in words and sounds. For the moment the actors can forget facial expressions, gestures, facing the audience, etc.

•**Idea 213:** Do some short interviews, using either a tape recorder or note pad. Ask other students about favorite hobbies, or perhaps talk to local business people and workers. After collecting the words, do a little editing to make sure it sounds interesting and natural.

•**Idea 214:** Try interviewing one another in writing. Write the question and have your partner write an answer. Or do a simultaneous interview this way.

•**Idea 215:** Have a conversation in this way, without using your voices, only writing. (A variant of the ever-popular art of sneaking notes to your friend in school.)

•**Idea 216:** Take any dialogue of the ones you've written — remembered, made-up, taken from a television show — and do it as a comic book. You might collaborate with someone else, one person giving the plot and dialogue, the other doing the drawings.

•**Idea 217:** Another interesting form is the *fotonovela,* in which dialogue balloons are used in much the same way they are in comics, but instead of drawings, the figures are black-and-white photographs of actors. In the professional *fotonovelas* the stories are often based on melodramatic soap-opera-style plots, even featuring stars of Spanish soap operas as actors, but in the classroom any good story and an instamatic camera could result in an interesting project. (For a more complete description of such a project, see my article "The Fotonovela and the Marriage of Narrative and Art" in *Teachers & Writers Magazine,* Vol. 8, No. 1.)

•**Idea 218:** A standard creative writing assignment is to take a comic from the newspaper or from a comic book and white-out the balloons. You then xerox copies and have students write their own dialogue. Some years ago Phillip Lopate had the diabolic idea of doing this with Chinese comic books which our students assumed, incorrectly, read in the same direction that books do in English. They had to make all sorts of explanations for the action that was happening in bizarre, reverse order!

If the idea of dialogue being used to write comic books appeals to you, be sure and see the abovementioned issue of *Teachers & Writers Magazine,* Vol. 8 No. 1, which is devoted to that subject.

•**Idea 219:** Another standard creative writing assignment is for students to write from the teacher's collection of magazine pictures. An assignment I like better is for the teacher to collect pictures of two people in some sort of interaction and ask the class to write the conversation they are having. Here are two examples of writing that came from that assignment:

The mother is saying to her daughter, Do you love your brother?

The daughter is saying to her mother, Yes Mommy. I love my brother and you.

Make sure you don't drop him.

The sister is saying to her mother, Mommy, do you love me like you do Brother?

Yes, of course. I love both of y'all. Now, let's go to sleep.

—Latonya Williams, 3rd, P.S. 321, Brooklyn

PICKING OUT LINT

"Hold still," said the old man to the old woman. "You have a lot of lint in your hair."

"No!" said the woman in a loud voice. "Please hurry, I have some unfinished work to do."

"But you don't want to leave here with yellow lint in your hair, do you?"

"OK, I'll stay a few more minutes."

The man was picking a lot of lint from the woman's hair. Then the man said, "I am finished. I am finished."

The woman said, "Thank you, you are very kind to women."

"That's my job."

"Bye," said the woman.

—Sean Jones, 5th, P.S. 321, Brooklyn

Using Dialogue to Contrast Characters

Conversation is, of course, an ideal place to explore, reveal, and develop character. Styles of talking can be used to exemplify deep differences between two characters' inner qualities or between their relative conditions. Their different opinions and beliefs can be demonstrated as can indeed the very states of their respective souls. One person is a fast talker and one is deliberate. One wants to get to the heart of things, and one wants to avoid it. For example, in the following scene from Dashiell Hammet (part of which has already been quoted in the chapter on describing people, p. 45), we see the Fat Man and Sam Spade talking together. The Fat Man chatters in an oily, elaborate, flattering manner, accompanied by all sorts of actions — drinking, offering cigars, laughing. This is, of course, a whole scene with much more than dialogue included, but the focus is on contrasting the two men through the style of their discourse.

From THE MALTESE FALCON

The fat man raised his glass and held it against a window's light. He nodded approvingly at the bubbles running up in it. He said: "Well, sir, here's to plain speaking and clear understanding."

99

They drank and lowered their glasses.

The fat man looked shrewdly at Spade and asked: "You're a close-mouthed man?"

Spade shook his head. "I like to talk."

"Better and better!" the fat man exclaimed. "I distrust a close-mouthed man. He generally picks the wrong time to talk and says the wrong things. Talking's something you can't do judiciously unless you keep in practice." He beamed over his glass. "We'll get along, sir, that we will." He set his glass on the table and held the box of Coronas del Ritz out to Spade. "A cigar, sir."

Spade took a cigar, trimmed the end of it, and lighted it. Meanwhile, the fat man pulled another green plush chair around to face Spade's within convenient distance and placed a smoking-stand within reach of both chairs. Then he took his glass from the table, took a cigar from the box, and lowered himself into his chair. His bulbs stopped jouncing and settled into flabby rest. He sighed comfortably and said, "Now, sir, we'll talk if you like. And I'll tell you right out that I'm a man who likes talking to a man that likes to talk."

"Swell. Will we talk about the black bird?"

The fat man laughed and his bulbs rode up and down on his laughter. "Will we?" he asked, and, "We will," he replied. His pink face was shiny with delight. "You're the man for me, sir, a man cut along my own lines. No beating around the bush, but right to the point. 'Will we talk about the black bird?' We will. I like that, sir. I like that way of doing business. Let us talk about the black bird by all means, but first, sir, answer me a question, please, though maybe an unnecessary one, so we'll understand each other from the beginning...."

— Dashiel Hammett

Notice that although the Fat Man uses far more words than Spade, he is trying hard not to say much, and Spade, in fact, cuts straight through to the point of the conversation — the black bird. A lot of talking can mean many things, then. Notice also the way it is Spade who sets up the discussion as an antagonistic one. He contradicts whatever the Fat Man says. If the Fat Man calls him close-mouthed, he insists that he is a big talker, even though all the evidence of the passage points to his being in fact a close-mouthed man, just as the Fat Man says.

•**Idea 220:** Continue the conversation between the Fat Man and Spade. What happens next? If you know the movie, that's okay. Write the rest of the scene anyhow. Then get the novel and compare the way you completed the scene to the way Dashiell Hammett did.

•**Idea 221:** Have two people talking, one with a secret and the other trying to find out what it is.

•**Idea 222:** Invent a detective and a villain or enemy and write a typical conversation between them, showing their styles.

•**Idea 223:** Write a conversation in which two people are highly contrasted in their speaking styles. Perhaps one is a snob and one is proud of his working-class roots. Maybe one is a grammar nut and the other likes to use slang. One has an accent and the other is prejudiced against foreigners.

•

Setting: A busy subway during rush hour.

Junky of very low class bumps into a very solemn man of a very rich family on his way home. He is rather grouchy in a proper way. The junky has his Walkman radio on and a ripped leather jacket and dirty Adidas sneakers. He thinks he's cool and *bad!* "Excuse me, but I think you had better watch where you are going, young man, this is a perfectly new suit and I do not intend to have *your* slimy hands all over it!" The solemn man said this roughly in a slight English accent.

"Yo man I did not touch you, anyways will you shut up, this is my favorite song, you know man? I really dig it." The junky started to walk away, but stopped as if he remembered something. "Hey man, I just noticed, my name is Joe and it is not 'Young Man.'" He said this sarcastically. "My hands are not dirty, and if you want to fight about it, I'm down."

"Why I never! I think I *will* call the police. I have never put up with such nonsense. Good day, *Joe!*"

"Eh, man, anytime, anytime." They both walk in different directions and forget all about it.

—Maya Newton, 5th, P.S. 321, Brooklyn

•

One day a friendly neighbor came over to a new couple's house to welcome them into the neighborhood. She knocked on the door, and the grumpy husband answered.

"What do you want?" he exclaimed meanly. She straightened up her back knowing well that this would be a tough man to turn into a friendly neighbor.

"I just wanted to welcome you and your wife to the neighborhood," she said in a worried voice.

"My wife isn't home right now, so you can go home and she'll visit you when she feels like it."

"Oh, I'm very sorry if I disturbed you," she said in a disappointed voice.

"Yeah, well you should see we don't want you people coming around and bothering us by welcoming us into a neighborhood we ain't welcome in."

"This happens to be a very friendly neighborhood and you are as welcome as anyone else and I'm sorry if you feel you're not!"

"Yeah, well. . . ."

"Yeah, well what? I tried to be friendly by coming over and instead I get this!"

"Oh, so you think you're so great, well I think you all stink."

"And I think you stink!" She walked away as quickly as possible and angrily. She would never try to be the first friendly person on the block ever again.

—Amanda Belskie, 5th, P.S. 321, Brooklyn

101

I like the way, in Amanda's piece, the woman speaker actually goes through a change—perhaps an unfortunate one, but a genuine change for all that. She becomes irascible and aggressive—more like the mean neighbor, in fact.

•**Idea 224:** Do what Amanda did: write a conversation in which two people are very different, but one changes and becomes more like the other. Perhaps the nasty one could become nice, or vice versa. Or the one who uses good grammar could begin to fall into slang.

•**Idea 225:** Write one of these contrasted conversations with just the people's words, and then, perhaps on a different day, add the setting and a physical description of the individuals. Try to weave it all together, putting in the *how* things were said and what people were doing as they spoke. Perhaps the nervous person paces around the room, etc.

•**Idea 226:** Write a dialogue in which one person takes the opposite position on everything the other says, completely contradicting everything.

•**Idea 227:** Write a conversation in which one person is furious and the other is trying to calm that one down.

•**Idea 228:** Choose a partner, and separately invent and describe a character. Then read each other's descriptions and together write a dialogue in which the probably oddly assorted characters interact.

RED DRAGON (SINBAD THE CHAOTIC)

I'm a red Chaotic evil Dragon who takes innocent people, eats them, and then takes all their money. I have spikes in a line down my back and a whole bunch at my tail to hit people with. I have 100,000 gold pieces worth of treasure (which I stole). I breathe red hot breath which kills. I have armor that can only be pierced by a totally gold arrow.

JOHN WALTINMIER

I'm a 26-year-old New Yorker who now lives in downtown Brooklyn. I am an ex-con. I was sent to prison in 1959 for trying to mug an old lady of her hair comb, and some lip gloss. She hit me over the head with her handbag, and knocked me out. I have purple and green hair, and my eyes are silver. My toes are square and my ears are crooked.

DIALOGUE BETWEEN JOHN WALTINMIER AND
SINBAD THE CHAOTIC

(SINBAD *flies down and starts walking down the street. He starts following* JOHN.)

JOHN: Whew! Boy it's hot around here.
SINBAD: Ahh! Dinner has arrived.
JOHN: *(Turns.)* How ya doin', Red? I haven't seen you since my last nightmare.
SINBAD: Make one move and I'll have you broiled.

JOHN: Hey, have you used Scope lately?

SINBAD: No, but after I burn you, you could fit into a Scope bottle!

JOHN: Hey man, let's be friends. By the way, you got a light?

SINBAD: Sure, Pimpsqueak! *(He breathes.)*

JOHN: Hey man, you better turn down your thermostat!

SINBAD: What did you say? *(Snorting.)*

JOHN: Oh, just forget it. See you in my next nightmare, Red. *(He opens the door and begins to walk.)*

SINBAD: *(Angrily.)* You insulted me! *(He hurls his claws at John, then starts to run after him. Pretending to have hit the door, he falls down and says wearily)* Never trust a human.

—Alexander Barret and Jeremy Nessoff, 5th, P.S. 321, Brooklyn

•**Idea 229:** Act out the results of this writing assignment, as is pretty obvious above that Alexander and Jeremy did.

•**Idea 230:** Do it in comic book form. This is especially successful if you use outlandish characters as the above boys did, drawing on Dungeons and Dragons or other fantasy materials.

•**Idea 231:** Write a conversation in which two people are working at cross purposes. One wants, say, to get something cheaply, and the other is trying to sell an expensive version of the item. The following is an interesting adult example of this idea from a novel called *The Dunne Family* by James T. Farrell in which the item being dickered over is a coffin for Dick Dunne's mother! Notice that there are not only two speaking voices, but also two interior monologue voices during the course of the conversation. Dick Dunne speaks first:

From THE DUNNE FAMILY

"Holy Saints, Mr. Duffy, you've made the wrong estimation of me!"

They were standing before an ornate mahogany coffin with silver trim. It was a fifteen-hundred-dollar coffin. "I was merely attempting to give you an idea of the range of coffins we offer. I was not trying to sell you this number."

"I gotcha, Mr. Duffy." Dick said, thinking that here was a smooth article if he had ever seen one.

—Smooth or not, I've got your number, Dick thought.

"We intend to give Mother a dignified burial, but also an economical one, Mr. Duffy."

"I understand perfectly, Mr. Dunne."

—A good face for playing poker, Dick thought.

"I think what you want, Mr. Dunne, is my seven-hundred-and fifty-dollar funeral."

"We're wasting time, Mr. Duffy," Dick said.

"My time is at your disposal, Mr. Dunne, and I do not consider it a waste of time to pursue your particular needs in this sad hour when your mother has passed on up to Heaven."

Dick scarcely listened.

"Don't tell me, Mr.Duffy, that you cannot provide a decent and dignified funeral for less than seven hundred and fifty dollars," Dick said.

"Why certainly we can," Mr. Duffy said, undaunted.

"Well, tell me about it, if you please."

"You know what a funeral includes, don't you?" Mr. Duffy asked.

"I would assume that I do."

"The main item, of course, is the casket," Mr. Duffy explained. He went on:

"Now in my seven-hundred-and-fifty-dollar funeral, Mr. Dunne."

—Much too high, Dick thought.

"I'll show you what the casket is like from the catalogue," Mr. Duffy said.

"Mr. Duffy?"

"Yes, Mr. Dunne?"

"You say you have a seven-hundred-and-fifty-dollar funeral and that the casket for this costs . . . ?"

"Five hundred dollars."

Dick shook his head.

"That's too expensive, Mr. Duffy."

"Well!" Mr. Duffy exclaimed.

Dick waited for him to go on.

"I do not overprice my funerals, Mr. Dunne."

"I'm certain you don't, Mr. Duffy, or I wouldn't be here."

"My funerals, let me explain, are dignified. Duffy funerals are known in the locale as class funerals."

"Yes, I know. You have a fine reputation."

"Thank you, Mr. Dunne. I'm glad to know that you've heard of Duffy funerals."

"Oh yes, I've heard about Duffy funerals."

"When I give funeral services, Mr. Dunne. . ." he began.

—You add the hot air at no extra charge, Dick thought.

". . .I must take the reputation of Duffy Funerals into consideration. My funerals are not costly, no more than anything that is class is costly," Mr. Duffy said.

—Larry should hear this bunkum, Dick thought.

"You're a business man yourself, Mr. Dunne. That's why I know that you can understand what I'm talking about. As you must know, my line is not strictly business, although quite naturally, it has, as it must, its business aspects. My line is primarily a service. It is essentially as much of a service as that of a doctor."

"I know all that, Mr. Duffy, but if you'll pardon me, we have to make the burial arrangements for my mother, may God have mercy on her soul."

"Why, yes, Mr. Dunne, I was just coming to that, the arrangements for the departure of your beloved mother, may her soul rest in peace."

—Coming to it the long way around, Dick thought.

"Now Mr. Duffy, I'd like a funeral that will have the class of Duffy Funerals but at a more reasonable price. Five hundred dollars for a coffin is too high."

"If you think so, Mr. Dunne, but just let me say this. What's needed is a coffin that is durable. And it stands to reason that to get more durability in a coffin, you must go up in price to a reasonable extent."

He paused.

"What price did you have in mind, Mr. Dunne?"

"I'll tell you, Mr. Duffy. I'd like a dignified Duffy funeral for, oh, I'd say two hundred and fifty dollars."

Mr. Duffy did not bat an eyelash. There was, however, a slight flush in his cheeks.

"I can give you a funeral for two hundred and fifty dollars, but of course it's different from my—"

"Let's settle here and now, Mr. Duffy, and you elucidate for me the class funeral for my mother, may God have mercy on her soul, for two hundred and fifty dollars."

A man lives and learns, Mr. Duffy was thinking. He would never have taken Mr. Richard Dunne for a cheapskate.

He outlined in detail what the two-hundred-and-fifty-dollar funeral included. He would settle everything now. He had already taken up too much of his time with this little cheapskate.

—James T. Farrell

•**Idea 232:** Write a conversation in which one or both parties is thinking something very different from what they are saying. This is a wonderful way to show hypocrisy.

•**Idea 233:** Write a conversation in which two people are having an argument over something entirely inappropriate to the situation: what a sick man is going to leave them in his will, or their high salaries in front of someone who just got fired.

•**Idea 234:** Try a conversation in which there is someone in a weaker position and someone in a stronger position.

•

I had received the note during lunch. It said to go directly to the principal's office after school. I thought about it absently all afternoon. I approached his office with dread.

"Good afternoon," he said. "I want to speak to you about something very important." His tone deadened; I felt sick. "You know, we take pride in most of our students, great pride." He said this with a terrible, piercing emphasis on the "most." I thought I might vomit. "I noticed you the first month of your freshman year," he said, pointing his pencil down at me. "You looked like such a nice boy. Smart and studious." The butterflies in my stomach turned into great swooping condors. "And now that you have won this scholarship..." he said with a sly smile. The weight lifted. I sat back and breathed heavily.

—Gabe Wasserman, 10th, Stuyvesant High School, Manhattan

•**Idea 235:** Try one in which the weaker is clever enough to trick the stronger.

•**Idea 236:** Also look at the piece called "First Day of School" on page 173 in which a student and teacher are at cross purposes.

•**Idea 237:** Write a conversation in which one person is trying to convince another of something.

Using Dialogue to Reveal What Is Going on inside Characters

Dialogue, then, can be used to reveal characters by contrasting the way they talk. It reveals things directly about characters. In the following sample one of the characters does all the talking and tells her own story. In fact, the piece has so much of one person's voice that it borders on being a monologue, but closer inspection shows the narrator, for all her silence, to be quite an active participant in the conversation through gesture and inner observation. The narrator (and the reader) infers some things about the speaker that she might rather have had left unguessed.

From THE CLAMSHELL

She is so tall, standing above me, that I almost run up the wooden steps until she is small again. She takes my hand and leads me up into the rose drawingroom, yellowed in the sun, the fire morning-white. She sits me down beside her. She glances up at the painting by habit to reassure herself. I don't think she even knows she does it.

"I'm glad Annie brought you here," she says, more softly than I can believe. She pats my hand, then moves her dry fingers over my palm. "Once I had a cascade of hair, a waterfall. When I had it cut, I cried all day over my awful little stubbly head. Don't think I don't know why I warned you like that this morning. You see, I married—a second time. I was forty, he was thirty, an ex-student who'd stayed in Charlottesville." Her low morning-room voice moves easy as silk over the facts of the matter, "Some of them do, you know. Oh, they like the life and just stay, sink into it. People said he married me for my money. I don't believe that. We really loved each other." This admission is as easy as the rest. "I gave him everything he wanted. He had an awful accident, cleaning his shotgun after a day's hunting."

106

I hold her hand tighter, but she doesn't know it. Her own is dead.

"I almost died," she says, quite factually.

Her eyes retract beyond the space recognized as safety between herself and what she sees — not coldly, for that would be reaction, but to someplace behind anger or tears, a rejection of us all [. . . .]

She gives my hand a little slap.

"You come back, you hear?" The Southern girl peeps through the lady voice and she has put me away as neatly as she would a magazine. She leaves me without telling me why she is going.

— Mary Lee Settle

The piece is told in the present tense to increase the reader's sense of immediacy. One wonders, as the narrator doesn't say, but must wonder too, what really happened in the gun-cleaning accident of the young husband. The tone that is created is at once mysterious and intimately revealing, not atypical of those moments in real life when people reveal themselves to us.

•**Idea 238:** Write a conversation in which one person does all the talking.

•**Idea 239:** Write a conversation in which the narrator receives a story from the other person.

•

She brought me up into her small loft apartment. Everything was dark and gloomy. "I have to talk to you!" I could tell fear, anger, and a tidal wave of sadness were coming on. Before she could speak again, tears rolled from her face like rain over a cemetery in a horror picture. "They killed him, I j--just s--aw him a few hours (sniffle) ago and now he's gone." I couldn't help but feel sad, but I knew I must be strong so she could have someone to lean on. "I brought you here cause you're the only one I can talk to." I knew the whole story, and it was easier for me to understand, as she knew. "I told him not to do it, I told him, God help me, why couldn't he listen?" She broke down in tears again; her hands covered her face as though the darkness would take her as it had taken him. "I should have stopped him; I let him go. It's my fault. I don't deserve to live." She trudged towards the window, I didn't move so as not to break her thought.

— Anonymous, 10th, Stuyvesant High School, Manhattan

Using Dialogue to Write about Conflict

A dialogue scene with conflict at the heart of it has elicited some of the best pieces of writing I have ever had from students. I think this is probably because nothing is more fundamental to human experience and human creativity than conflict and struggle. We live in conflict every day of our lives; from our earliest infancy we want things we can't have. We are constantly engaged in struggles with other people that sometimes result in great destruction and sometimes in fruitful deepening of understanding. Conflict occurs between nations, between individuals, and within individuals. Students can easily brainstorm dozens of conflict situations that could be used as starters for writing assignments.

The universality and multiplicity of conflict is one of the reasons I like to use it for writing. Another reason is that I truly think conflict is behind much of what we call "creativity." It was memories of certain interesting and partialy unresolved conflicts in my childhood that were the source material for my first novel. I think, too, of the food expert who recently had to go on a low-sodium diet. He had a conflict because he not only loves to eat, but also makes his living by testing recipes and judging foods and restaurants. How did he solve this conflict? He invented high cuisine for low-sodium dieters. Consider too a great basketball player as he goes to the basket; much of the beauty of his achievement—his "moves"—comes from how he gets by the opposing players. In all these cases, the resolution of conflict requires inventiveness.

•**Idea 240:** The broadest possible assignment is simply to write or make up a conversation with a conflict in it.

•**Idea 241:** Do the same thing, but have the conversation within one person.

•**Idea 242:** Express in dialogue an extremely silly conflict.

•**Idea 243:** As a class, brainstorm as many conflict situations as you can think of and keep the list available for people to use for writing ideas.

•**Idea 244:** Give the list to another class and see if they can write the conflicts up or add to the list.

One delightful way of exploring conflict through dialogue is to use inanimate speakers rather than human beings. This works well with young children, but can free the imagination of older students also. If the conflict is between an ax and a tree, there may be a willingness to explore feelings of terror that would be repressed if the conflict were between a big person and a small one. As a stimulus for this assignment, I like to use a wonderful poem by May Swenson called "Bleeding."

BLEEDING

Stop bleeding   said the knife.
I would if I   could said the cut.
Stop bleeding   you make me messy with this blood.
I'm sorry   said the cut.
Stop or   I will sink in farther said the knife.
Don't   said the cut.
The   knife did not say it couldn't help it but
it   sank in farther.
If   only you didn't bleed said the knife I wouldn't
have   to do this.
I know   said the cut I bleed too easily I hate

that I   can't help it I wish I were a knife like
you and   didn't have to bleed.
Well   and meanwhile stop bleeding will you said the knife.
Yes you   are a mess and sinking in deeper said the cut I
will have   to stop.
Have you   stopped by now said the knife.
I've almost   stopped I think.
Why must you   bleed in the first place said the knife.
For the same   reason that you must do what you
must do said   the cut.
I can't stand   bleeding said the knife and sank in farther.
I hate it too said   the cut I know it isn't you it's
me you're lucky to be   a knife you ought to be glad about that.
Too many cuts around   said the knife they're
messy I don't know how   they stand themselves.
They don't said the cut.
You're bleeding again.
No I've stopped said the cut   see you are coming out now the
blood is drying it will rub   off you'll be shiny again and clean.
If only cuts wouldn't bleed   so much said the knife coming
out a little.
But then knives might become dull said the cut.
Aren't you still bleeding a little said the knife.
I hope not said the cut.
I feel you are just a little.
Maybe just a little but I can   stop now.
I feel a little wetness still   said the knife sinking in a
little but then coming out   a little.
Just a little maybe just enough   said the cut.
That's enough now stop now do   you feel better now said the knife.
I feel I have to bleed to   feel I   think said the cut
I don't I don't have to   feel said   the knife drying now
becoming shiny.

This poem is at once easy to understand and quite subtle. Young children are amused by it (or amused by the fun of finding it gross!) and they enjoy the literary game of figuring out why it is arranged in the particular way that it is. Some say the peculiar blanks are an image of blood flowing; others say it is the cut itself. I particularly like to begin a discussion by asking the class whether they would prefer to be the cut or the knife. A considerable majority of students would prefer to be the knife on the grounds they don't like to be hurt. But there is always a variety of responses: some say they would rather be the cut because it doesn't hurt anyone. Others say they don't like the cut because it's such a whiner. Once someone even said he would prefer to be the cut because it can heal but the knife will always remain the same. What is the difference between the two characters, I like to ask, reverting to my interests as a fiction writer. Is one bad and one good? I personally don't think so, finding the two rather complementary in their relationship, like people in a bad marriage who find some satisfaction in how they hurt and humiliate one another. At some point I try to bring the discussion around to the line where the cut says it has to bleed to feel, and the knife says it doesn't have to feel. There's no moral to the story, but lots of material for discussion.

Before asking students to write, I usually do a quick brainstorming of other pairs of objects (or, occasionally, qualities). I had assumed the objects would be things like baseballs and baseball bats, but from the first time I ever did this lesson, I got all kinds of pairs that didn't seem to me to have any natural animosity at all — shoes and socks, bulbs and sockets, etc. When the students wrote, though, it turned out that there is competition and conflict everywhere in the world as they see it — everything from lips and lipstick to bacon and eggs. You get the feeling it's a rough world out there, in the medicine chest as well as the street. The obvious truth is, of course, that the arguments and fights and discussions that come out of this assignment are human ones. And children seem to know more about what is going on in the spaces between people than adults give them credit for.

•**Idea 245:** The assignment is to write your own prose or poetry dialogue between two things having a conflict.

STORYTIME

WIFE: Breakfast is ready.
HUSBAND: These eggs! All the yellow stuff is getting on my bacon!
EGGS: I'm sorry I'm sliming on you but what has to be done must be done.
BACON: Don't lie. I know you want me to have yellow clothing. So just break it.
EGGS: Ouch, watch out, Bacon. My slime will get on you. Just think of it as "The Flood."
BACON: Really now. Don't cut up with me. I'm too skinny to get cut up. Ugh! Slime. Ugh! Slime.
EGGS: Get under me. It will be great.
BACON: Okay, but, just but, if you do anything nasty, I will bite your rear.
EGGS: Okay, come on under.
BACON: I can't breathe. I'm going to be Kibbles and Bits!
EGGS: Bacon, oh Bacon, ouch! You, you bit me on my rear!
BACON: Let me get out from under you.
EGGS: There's a little of me left. I say good-bye. Let's be friends again.
BACON: Okay, I'll see you in the old man's belly!
— Russell Jordan, 5th, P.S. 124, Queens

EAR AND SOUND

"Why do you ring and echo through my tunnels?" questioned the ear.

"That is what I am. I don't mean to annoy you, I mean to make you float!" shouted the sound.

"You did it again! How do you make your noises? I can only hear and listen, for that is what I am," the ear said.

"Well, I must continue to 'feed' you the things that you must learn. Please listen, do not talk!" said the sound.

"Why must I listen, I must be able to do more."

"You hear, and I talk. I think!" said the sound.

"No, I hear and you make sounds, not talk, you make noises," corrected the ear.

"Nonsense sounds, noises, nothing that makes sense," said the sound.

"Yes, now let me listen to your sounds so I can send messages to the brain so that body can react to you," said the ear.

"Then you must be quiet! But what sounds do you want to hear?"

"Nonsense sounds. Whatever comes," answered the ear.

"Nonsense, nonsense," sounded the sound.
— Kristy McNutt, 5th, P.S. 321, Brooklyn

•**Idea 246:** Try this exercise with two nations like the U.S. and the U.S.S.R. or the Sioux Indians and the U.S. Cavalry. See if nations, if they could talk, could do any better at solving their problems than people.

•**Idea 247:** Have a dialogue between abstractions such as Love and Hate, Happiness and Sadness, Greed and Generosity, etc.

•**Idea 248:** Letters can be a form of conversation too. Write a letter to a food you hate and have it write back.

•**Idea 249:** Write a letter to any object that you like or don't like — a baseball, a pair of tight designer jeans, old shoes, etc. — and have the object write back.

•**Idea 250:** Try a dialogue between plants and animals.

•

Oh please don't gnaw, said the tree to the beaver.
Well how do you think I make a living? (The beaver says in a very low voice.) I sell houses to all my friends, and nibble on the bits.
Oh yes, I know that, but I am a tree, a sycamore tree, that has beautiful white leaves that dance with the wind, and in the fall my leaves turn orange, yellow, brown, and red.
Yes, said the beaver, chuckling. I know, but what about me? For I get all my food for repayment of the houses.
Then all you heard was the howl of the first sycamore tree.
Then the beaver went to the next tree, and the same thing happened.
Finally, three trees after the sycamore, of nibbling on and taking the wood away, he just had one more tree which was the father of all the sycamores. And he got angry and said, You, you dirty beaver. I don't believe it! Why, our leaves are beautiful and in the fall turn orange, yellow, brown, and red. Furthermore, you don't know how it feels to be a tree. To stand still all your life and get old and tired. Bu — bu — but —
And before the beaver could say anything, you heard the cry of the syca-

more tree and the beaver, because a lumberjack cut down the tree which fell on the beaver. A wise owl on an oak tree said, Now the beaver knows how it feels.

—Gaby Sherrow, 4th, P.S. 87, Manhattan

Often students use these things in the Talking Things exercises as stand-ins for real people and real-life conflicts. In fact, it is often family life that is being explored in the conflict writing. One of my all-time favorite and most successful lessons deals directly with conflict in family life, using a selection from literature as the stimulus. The piece is a paragraph from Tillie Olsen's novel *Yonnondio: From the Thirties*. She took the title from a Walt Whitman poem which explains that the word is Iroquois for "lament for the aboriginal peoples."

The success of this assignment may result from its direct exposition of serious economic and social ills that beset families. Even students from stable homes, affluent homes, and polite homes are affected by this piece — because there is no home without tension and conflict. I am not trying, in this lesson, to get students to reveal all; I am not their therapist and have no intention of using their writing to make a diagnosis about their individual or family neuroses. What I am after is to show that writing can be about anything and everything; I want them to feel free to use elves, dwarves, and wizards from Dungeons and Dragons in their writing (if D & D is an enthusiasm of theirs), and I want them to feel free to write about deep-seated family malaises, if those are important to them. I would never assign as an exercise to write about the death of a loved one, but I would certainly bring in a poem about someone's grandmother dying and then ask them to write anything it reminded them of. For some children the following selection from *Yonnondio* leads to a writing about two teenaged sisters arguing over who gets to wear a shared necklace. For others it is a chance to write, perhaps in fictional form, about real family tragedy. In writing, when it is functioning at its best, *all things human are welcome*.

....No one greeted him at the gate — the dark walls of the kitchen enclosed on him like a smothering grave. Anna did not raise her head.

In the other room the baby kept squalling and squalling and Ben was piping an out-of-tune song to quiet her. There was a sour smell of wet diapers and burned pots in the air.

"Dinner ready?" he asked heavily.

"No, not yet."

Silence. Not a word from either.

"Say, can't you stop that damn brat's squallin? A guy wants a little rest once in a while."

No answer.

"Aw, this kitchen stinks. I'm going out on the porch. And shut that brat up, she's driving me nuts, you hear?" You hear, he reiterated to himself, stumbling down the steps, you hear, you hear. Driving me nuts.

—Tillie Olsen

112

I find this to be an extraordinary combination of fictional elements. The brief setting is full of sense impressions: the sound of the son's song, the baby's screams, the smells of diapers and burned pots, the sight of the woman with her head down. In these few lines we also have interior monologue working along with the dialogue, and there is a wonderful contrast between the characters as revealed through their two speaking styles — the man's aggressive talkativeness and the woman's deeply depressed taciturnity. There is a powerful image of enclosure in the figure of dark walls coming in "like a smothering grave." There is even a little grammar lesson in the two spellings of "squalling" and "squallin," one in the narration and one in the man's dialect, within a direct quotation.

I deeply admire the way this passage works, its expert fictional technique within a tiny span, but there is something much deeper than technique in it, or else it would not touch students of so many different ages and stations in life. Many students suggest immediately that there is something economic behind this family's problem: the subtitle of the novel is, in fact, "From the Thirties," so the teacher at least can associate it with the Great Depression. Poverty permeates the scene. Many students are certain that the man has just lost his job and comes home angry and unable to find a way to tell about it. Others assume he is on his way out to get drunk.

The exchange between the man and the woman, too, seems familiar to students. Everyone is aware of struggles between people who love; we are also living in a time when struggles are resulting in divorces. Children from quiet families where voices are never raised often seem relieved to read about (and perhaps write about) a family where the tensions are out in the open. Children from families with plenty of noise recognize the man's shouts as familiar.

•**Idea 251:** One assignment that works well with this is to write what came before and/or next in this story. Here are two examples of students' responses.

•

You hear, he reiterated to himself, stomping down the steps, you hear, you hear. Driving me nuts. I can't take it here no more. First I lose my job, then I have to come home with this house smelling the way it do. Then on top of all that I have to hear this baby cry all the time. Don't you think a person gets tired of this all the time?

So what do you think I do? Do you think I sit on my butt all day long and relax and have a maid wait on me? *No!* I don't. I be in here working my *hardest.* I try to keep this house running.

Well, it don't look like you doing a darn thing in this house. I'm leaving. (As he walks to the door.)

Where are you going?

Out.

She said, Wait, don't leave. You know you need me and I need

113

you. We could work something out between us. I think we can patch things up. Let's give it a try.

OK, he tells her. You know I love you and I don't know how I could stay mad at you, because I need you.

All of a sudden the phone starts to ring. Hello, is Mr. Johnson there?

Yes he is.

Well, can I speak to him? Hello, this is Mr. Jones, your boss. Hey man, you got your old job back.

Thanks man, thanks a lot. Hey Helen! Guess what? I got my job back. I knew that things would work out for us.

—Leashawn Peaks, 7th, I.S. 218, Brooklyn

BEFORE THE STORY. IN A WORK BUILDING.

"Johnson, Johnson, where are you?"

"Leroy, I'm over here, now what the hell do you want?"

"Listen, I'm the head of this company, and you're fired."

"What!?"

"I said you're fired."

"Why?"

"Why! Because I said so. You don't know how to talk to a boss nor work well without taking a break every ten minutes. You are also crazy and steal things."

"Steal! Steal!"

"Yes, you're a crackpot."

"Oh Lord, I can't believe this."

"Just get out."

"O.K., I'm going. Sheesh."

—Dorian Elton, 5th, P.S. 321, Brooklyn

•**Idea 252:** The other assignment that goes with this piece is simply to write a conflict of your own. It can be either true or invented, and be among any people you want. Most students will still choose the family situation, though.

•

He walked in the door at 8:00 A.M. Mother was sitting on the couch. . .she said nothing. He said nothing. . .he went to his room. As he approached the door knob she said, "Come here, boy." He said, "Yes, Mama." She said, "Do you know what time it is?" He said, "Yes, Mama." She said, "Damn you do. You walk in here at 8:00 in the morning and expect me not to wait for you." "Mama, I'm sixteen and not a little boy anymore." "I don't care if you were 21 you don't walk in my house at no 8:00. You either shape up or ship out." "I guess I'll have to ship out."

He gave her a kiss, said good-bye, and walked out the door.

She ran to the door to grab him, but he pulled away. Mama said,

"Come here, boy," with tears in her eyes. She started crying. When he saw this he came back. He said, "Mama, I don't want to see you cry, I'll stay." "But you'll have to make a promise," they both said at the same time. "Yours first," he said. "O.K.," Mama said. "You'll never walk in here again after 4:00." "There you go again," he said. "Just joking," Mama said. "Now yours." "Don't cry in front of me again." "O.K.," she said, hugging him so hard he almost cried himself.

— Ashaki Rucker, 5th, P.S. 87, Manhattan

MORE DIALOGUES BY ADULTS

From ALLEGRA MAUD GOLDMAN

But I was nervous that first day. There were about twenty-five kids in the class, and it was too many people in one room. Mrs. Mendelssohn assigned us to desks in alphabetical order. I was in the third row.

"The first thing we are going to learn today is clasroom etiquette," Mrs. Mendelssohn said. "Who knows what etiquette means?"

No one said anything, so I said, "Etiquette is knowing which fork to use and who goes through the door first."

Mrs. Mendelssohn looked at the cards on her desk so she would figure out who I was and then she said, "Thank you, Allegra. Etiquette is also raising your hand for permission to speak. Let's try it again. Who knows what etiquette means?"

I felt I had done my share so I looked out of the window at Bedford Avenue and the houses across the street and wondered how my mother was enjoying her first day with absolutely no children in the house. Meanwhile, nobody was raising his hand.

"Allegra?"

I looked at Mrs. Mendelssohn.

"Raise your hand, Allegra," she said patiently.

I raised my hand.

"Yes, Allegra?"

"Yes what? I said.

"Give me the answer to the question you raised your hand to answer," she said.

"I raised my hand because you told me to."

"Don't argue. Just answer the question."

"Etiquette is raising your hand," I said.

There was more about hands, because when we had gotten that all

straightened out, Mrs. Mendelssohn taught us how to fold them and place them on the edge of the desk and how to sit quietly at attention. I tried to stay awake.
— Edith Konecky

From SENSE AND SENSIBILITY

Conversation, however, was not wanted, for Sir John was very chatty, and Lady Middleton had taken the wise precaution of bringing with her their eldest child, a fine little boy about six years old, by which means there was one subject always to be recurred to by the ladies in case of extremity, for they had to inqure his name and age, admire his beauty, and ask him questions, which his mother answered for him, while he hung about her, and held down his head, to the great surprise of her ladyship, who wondered at his being so shy before company, as he could make noise enough at home. On every formal visit a child ought to be of the party by way of provision for discourse. In the present case it took up ten minutes to determine whether the boy were most like his father or mother, and in what particular he resembled either; for of course everybody differed, and everybody was astonished at the opinion of the others.
— Jane Austen

From BLOOD WEDDING

(A room painted yellow)

BRIDEGROOM: *(Entering)* Mother.
MOTHER: What?
BRIDEGROOM: I'm going.
(He starts to go .)
MOTHER: Wait.
BRIDEGROOM: You want something?
MOTHER: Your breakfast, son.
BRIDEGROOM: Forget it, I'll eat grapes. Give me the knife.
MOTHER: What for?
BRIDEGROOM: *(Laughing)* To cut the grapes with.
MOTHER: *(Muttering as she looks for the knife)* Knives, knives, cursed be all knives and the scoundrel who invented them.
BRIDEGROOM: Let's talk about something else.
MOTHER: And guns and pistols and the smallest little knife — and even hoes and pitchforks.
BRIDEGROOM: All right.
MOTHER: Everything that can slice a man's body. A handsome man, full of young life, who goes out to the vineyards or to his own olive groves — his own because he inherited them...
BRIDEGROOM: *(Lowering his head)* Be quiet.
— Federico García Lorca

From HUCKLEBERRY FINN

I got to feeling so mean and so miserable I most wished I was dead. I fidgeted up and down the raft, abusing myself to myself, and Jim was fidgeting up and down past me . . . Jim talked out loud all the time while I was talking to myself. He was saying how the first thing he would do when he got to a free state he would go to saving up money and never spend a single cent, and when he got enough money he would buy his wife, which was owned on a farm close to where Miss Watson lived; and they then would both work to buy the two children, and if their masters wouldn't sell them, they'd get an Ab'litionist to go and steal them.

It most froze me to hear such talk. He wouldn't ever dared to talk such talk in his life before. Just see what a difference it made in him the minute he judged he was about free. It was according to the old saying, "Give a nigger an inch and he'll take an ell." Thinks I, this is what comes of my not thinking. Here was this nigger, which I had as good as helped to run away, coming right out flatfooted and saying he would steal his children—children that belonged to a man I didn't even know; a man that hadn't ever done me no harm.

I was sorry to hear Jim say that, it was such a lowering of him. My conscience got to stirring me up hotter than ever, until at last I says to it, "Let up on me—it ain't too late yet—I'll paddle ashore at first light and tell." I felt easy and happy and light as a feather right off. All my troubles was gone. I went to looking out sharp for a light, and sort of singing to myself. By and by one showed. Jim sings out:

"We's safe, Huck, we's safe! Jump and crack yo' heels! Dat's de good ole Cairo at las', I jis knows it!"

I says:

"I'll take the canoe and go and see, Jim. It mightn't be, you know."

He jumped and got the canoe ready, and put his old coat in the bottom for me to set on, and give me the paddle; and as I shoved off, he says:

"Pooty soon I'll be a-shoutin' for joy, en I'll say, it's all on accounts o' Huck; I's a free man, en I couldn't ever ben free ef it hadn't ben for Huck; you's de bes' fren' Jim ever had en you's de *only* fren' ole Jim's got now."

I was paddling off, all in a sweat to tell on him; but when he says this, it seemed to kind of take the tuck all out of me. I went along slow then, and I warn't right down certain whether I was glad I started or whether I warn't. When I was fifty yards off, Jim says:

"Dah you goes, de ole true Huck; de on'y white genlman dat ever kep' his promise to ole Jim."

Well, I just felt sick. But, I says, I *got* to do it—I can't get *out* of it. Right then along comes a skiff with two men in it with guns, and they stopped and I stopped. One of them says:

"What's that yonder?"

"A piece of raft," I says.

"Do you belong on it?"

"Yes, sir."

"How many men's on it?"

"Only one, sir."

"Well, there's five niggers run off tonight up yonder, above the head of the bend. Is your man white or black?"

I didn't answer up promptly. I tried to, but the words wouldn't come. I tried for a second or two to brace up and out with it, but I warn't man enough—hadn't the spunk of a rabbit. I seen I was weakening: so I just give up trying and up and says:

"He's white."

"I reckon we'll go and see for ourselves."

"I wish you would," says I, "because it's pap that's there, and maybe you'd help me tow the raft ashore where the light is. He's sick—and so is mam and Mary Ann."

"Oh the devil! We're in a hurry, boy, but I s'pose we've got to. Come buckle to your paddle and let's get going."

I buckled to my paddle, and they laid to their oars. When we had made a stroke or two, I says,

"Pap'll be mighty much obliged to you, I can tell you. Everybody goes away when I want them to help me tow the raft ashore, and I can't do it by myself."

"Well that's infernal mean. Odd, too. Say, boy, what's the matter with your father?"

"It's the—a—the—well, it ain't anything much."

They stopped pulling. It warn't but a mighty little ways to the raft now. One says:

"Boy, that's a lie. What *is* the matter with your pap? Answer up square now, and it'll be better for you."

"I will, sir, I will, honest—but don't leave us, please. It's the—Gentlemen, if you'll only pull ahead, and let me heave you the headline, you won't have to come a-near the raft—please do."

"Set her back, John, set her back!" says one. They backed water. "Keep away, boy, keep to looard. Confound it, I just expect the wind had blowed it to us. Your pap's got the smallpox, and you know it precious well. Why didn't you come out and say so? Do you want to spread it all over?"

"Well," says I, a-blubbering, "I've told everybody before, and they just went away and left us."

"Poor devil, there's something in that. We are right down sorry for you, but we—well, hang it, we don't want the smallpox, you see. Look here, I'll tell you what to do. Don't you try to land by yourself, or you'll smash everything to pieces. You float along down about twenty miles, and you'll come to a town on the left hand side of the river. It will be long after sunup then, and when you ask for help you tell them your folks are all down with chills and fever. Don't be a fool again, and let people guess what is the matter. Now we're trying to do you a kindness; so you just put twenty miles between us, that's a good boy. It wouldn't do any good to land yonder where the light is—it's only a woodyard. Say, I reckon your father's poor, and I'm bound to say he's in pretty hard luck. Here, I'll put a twenty-dollar gold piece on this board, and you get it when it floats by. I feel mighty mean to leave you; but my kingdom! it won't do to fool with smallpox, don't you see?"

118

"Hold on, Parker," says the man. "Here's a twenty to put on the board for me. Good-by, boy, you do as Mr. Parker told you, and you'll be all right."

"That's so my boy, good-by, good-by. If you see any runaway niggers you get help and nab them and you can make some money by it."

"Good-by, sir," says I. "I won't let no runaway niggers get by me if I can help it."

They went off and I got aboard the raft, feeling bad and low, because I knowed very well I had done wrong, and I see it warn't no use for me to try to learn to do right — a body that don't get *started* right when he's little ain't got no show — when the pinch comes there ain't nothing to back him up and keep him to his work, and so he gets beat. Then I thought a minute, and says to myself, hold on; spose you'd a done right and give Jim up, would you felt better than what you do now? Now, says I, I'd feel bad — I'd feel the same way I do now. Well, then, says I, what's the use you learning to do right when it's troublesome to do right and ain't no trouble to do wrong, and the wages is just the same? I was stuck. I couldn't answer that. So I reckoned I wouldn't bother no more about it, but after this always do whichever came handiest at the time.

— Mark Twain

From A SPACE APART

Their voices seemed to have been discussing her for hours. Sometimes they would take a detour and discuss her sister, but they always came back to her. She sat in the centermost circle of the rag rug beside Rastus Smith the dog and turned his ears inside out. He groaned and kicked his hind legs. Their voices had unrolled through lunch, then out of the kitchen into the den. Her father sat in his reclining chair with a newspaper on his lap. Her mother, barefoot, looked out the window at the side of the hill. It was Easter vacation, and Tonie had been up there with the dog all morning. She wanted to leap over her mother now and race through the glass, take up the side of the hill again, only this time she and Rastus Smith wouldn't come down; they would hide out permanently. The wild girl and her dog.

"Every year," said her father. "Every Easter you do a play, no matter what I say."

Her mother's toes were half buried in the rug. "This is so simple, honey, no props, nothing."

"Nothing but Lee."

They were talking about the Easter play her mother had made up for her sister Lee. Tonie went to rehearsals sometimes, on her father's hospital nights or when he had meetings. She wrapped herself in the velvet curtains around the baptistry or lay in the dry tin tub itself and listened to Lee practice saying over and over, "He lives! The one who forgave even me, Mary Magdalene! He lives!"

"John," said her mother. "You should see Lee. She is so good — "

"I suppose I should be thankful you aren't building towers and trap doors in the sanctuary this time."

"I never put a trap door in the sanctuary. You'd understand what I'm so excited about if you'd just come to a rehearsal once."

"How can I come to a rehearsal? I have to cook dinner for Tonie."

Tonie listened closely for a while and decided they were mostly joking. Just so they stayed on Lee and the play. She didn't mind when her father cooked: they had nice quiet dinners, reading while they ate, *Life* magazine for him, comics for her, and for dessert, big bowlfuls of ice cream. There was an unspoken rule that he never started in on her when it was just the two of them having dinner together.

As if he were reading her mind, her father suddenly said, "And as if the play wasn't enough, there's Tonie. Nothing is ever simple with Tonie."

She thought, It wouldn't be hard to live up on the hill with Rastus Smith except for learning to eat groundhog because that was the only thing he could ever catch.

Her mother said, "Tonie just tries to be honest." The bare feet came toward her and the dog: the soles were yellowish and there were veins across the tops. They rolled Rastus Smith's loose skin back and forth across his ribs. He grunted and looked mournful, then moved to the patch of sun under the window.

Tonie was left alone in the bull's-eye of the throw rug. They all concentrated on Tonie. She muttered, "You told me never to tell lies."

Her father said to her mother, "Are you her coach? Whose side are you on?" He had a beautiful deep voice; you could hear every word he spoke.

"You said never lie."

"Stop repeating that!" His fingers flew up in the air; no one was joking anymore. "What does that have to do with your getting baptized?"

"Oh John, you understand very well what she means."

She wanted her mother to stay out of it. It made too many to watch. Her mother suddenly squatted and laid her hands on Tonie's shoulders, then her neck, and rubbed the skin on her cheeks and twisted her ears the way she did to Rastus. "Don't, Mama, leave me alone."

"Oh dear," said her mother. "I can't keep up with them. Now Lee's my best friend and Tonie can't stand me to touch her. You used to be such a little nuzzler, Tonie."

Her father did not tease, and she didn't look at his face, but there were these huge spaces between his fingers as he gripped the chair. "She still has to explain to me why she doesn't want to get baptized."

Her words squirted out: "I do too want to get baptized."

"You see?" said her mother.

"I don't see anything."

"I want to get baptized but I don't want to promise!"

"She understands exactly. She doesn't want to promise to go and sin no more when she figures it's impossible. I think she's ever sensitive."

He wasn't looking at her, she saw, but at her mother. And one finger, the forefinger on his right hand, began to tap. I'm making him nervous, she thought. She wished he would yell at her and get it over with. Get to the spanking even.

"Vera," he said, "I cannot deal with both of you at once."

"But she's right, John. She doesn't want to make a promise she knows she's going to break—it seems so reasonable."

"It is not reasonable. Eight other children are ready to promise. Including my sister's son. Why is no one else balking? Why is it only Tonie who refuses to recite the declaration of faith? And what about all the dozens of other children I have baptized over the years, including Lee? Why have none of them found the declaration of faith so pernicious?"

"I don't mean she's really *right*. Just that her motives are good."

Tonie did a thing with the insides of her ears; she made a pressure that blocked off some of the noise and unfocused her eyes. She made her father into a smear, made his gray suit stick to a green reclining chair, and she couldn't see his finger tapping anymore.

He leaped to his feet. "What's she doing? Stop jiggling, Tonie! I refuse to lose my temper over this nonsense."

Her mother tried to hug her, but Tonie ran out of the house after her father, chased him as far as the sidewalk in front.

She yelled, "I can explain!"

He stopped, he turned. "Tonie," he said "we won't have this. We'll talk about it later when you and I have both calmed down."

—Meredith Sue Willis

MORE DIALOGUES BY STUDENTS

•

We sit there, all gathered round the story teller. Grandfather was now telling of his exploits as a young man in his twenties. "And people came from all over the country just to taste our beer and listen to my piano playing." I see his beard disappear, his gray hair all gone. I can go back through time into his story as he must be doing. "Then came the war. I realized I must leave, my life was in danger. The boat sailed into the harbor, we all watched as the green lady with the torch signalled peace and tranquility to us." His vivid details lit up our faces. Possessed by his charisma, we begged him to continue. "I set up a little furniture store, long hours. I was torn between the thoughts of my real home and the new life that was given to me here. I met your grandmother one day. That seemed to change everything." Time suddenly came back to the present as Mom called us to dinner....

—Anonymous sophomore, Stuvesant High, Manhattan

•

    The large man was shaking the small child to the point where there was no love between them. That man is the child's father, believe it or not, but the child never had any intentions of feeling love for him. The room was large with a rather pleasant atmosphere. A large bookcase covered one wall and the door was on the far side of the room. The child cries surprisingly quietly. The father was mumbling curses the boy hadn't even heard of. The door burst open and into the room dashed a pretty woman. "You leave that child alone, what in hell could have that poor child done to deserve such treatment?!" "You mind your business," yelled the father, shaking his fist. "I'm his mother. It is my business," declared the lady," and I demand to know what he's done." "Well, the little brat put soap in my coffee and I've got half a mind to murder him," the man said. "You put him down, I'll settle this with you," said the boy's mother. The child was released and put to bed. From his bed he could hear them screaming. "I hate them both," thought the child.

    —Molly Chatain, 5th, P.S. 87, Manhattan

•

GRANDMOTHER: Do you think that William is safe? It's quite dark out and — God forbid — if he goes in the street after a lost ball he might be run over! Please let us call him in?
LADY: William is careful, so please let me do the worrying.
GRANDMOTHER: One misstep and he could go to heaven!
LADY: Mother, listen, we care fine about the boy!!! We just give him more fun than we had. Hint, hint.
GRANDMOTHER: May you end up in hell if the child is killed. Don't look at me.
MAN: Listen here. If you don't stop this — this idiotic worrying, you can *leave!*
GRANDMOTHER: *(timidly)* I was only trying to help.
LADY: You really want to help?
GRANDMOTHER: Yes.
LADY AND MAN: Then go wash the dishes!

    —Sarah Gray, 5th, P.S. 321, Brooklyn

THE BROTHER AND SISTER

    He was tired. He was walking up the stairs. When he finally reached the top, he just looked around.

    The walls were still pink. The floor was brown.

    The corridor was long with five doors.

    Suddenly he heard a noise coming from his room. He ran. He opened the door. There on the floor was his curious sister Elda.

    "What are you doing in here, you little brat!!?" he asked.

    "Nothing, you square-headed gorilla!" yelled Elda.

    "What happened to my room?" he asked, "and what is my hamster doing out of his cage?" and with that, he shoved his little sister out of the way and put his hamster back in the huge 4' by 3' cage he built with plants in the corners.

Then he picked up a sign that said

ALL HANDS OFF!!!
Authorized Personnel
ONLY!!!
UNAUTHORIZED PERSONNEL
WILL BE SEVERELY
PUNISHED!!!!

He turned around and saw a hill of his stuff and suddenly he turned red all over with anger and attacked.

—Renier Maiguel, 6th, P.S. 124, Queens

STUDENT HAS NO HOMEWORK

(TEACHER *collecting homework, but when reaching* CHERYL . . .)

TEACHER: Cheryl, where is your homework?
CHERYL: Oh, I don't have it today.
TEACHER: Why not?
CHERYL: Because it's not here.
TEACHER: Well, did you do it?
CHERYL: No, because yesterday me and my mother were going to the store. She was walking on her hands and got hit by a car.
TEACHER: Do you expect me to believe that?
CHERYL: Yes, because it's true.

(Just then the principal comes in.)

PRINCIPAL: What's going on?
TEACHER: Cheryl didn't bring in her homework. She claims her mother got hit by a car.

*(*CHERYL *and the class begin to laugh.)*

PRINCIPAL: Well, Cheryl, is she hurt?
CHERYL: Of course. Now she has no fingers on one hand, three toes, no feet, one eye, two pupils, half a nose and one ear.
TEACHER: Cheryl, that's impossible. She would have been dead.
CHERYL: Well, don't complain to me. It's not my fault she got hit.

(The class screams "IT'S TRUE!")

PRINCIPAL: Well, who do you stay with?
CHERYL: The rats and roaches.
TEACHER: I'm awfully sorry.
CHERYL: Makes me. . .no, never mind.
TEACHER: *(Forgets about homework.)* Cheryl, I'll let you slide.

—Yvetta Simmons, 8th, I.S. 184, Bronx

DECEIT

MOTHER: Who's that coming in the door?
FATHER: It's me, honey.
MOTHER: I'm afraid I have some news. Sit down please.
FATHER: Okay.
MOTHER: I'm divorcing you.
FATHER: What you talkin' 'bout, girl?
MOTHER: I'm talking about Janet.
FATHER: My bigmouth secretary must 'a been runnin' her mouth off again. I'm gonna kick her butt.
MOTHER: I've already arranged the divorce. It's taking place in two weeks.
FATHER: But I can explain. . . .
MOTHER: Well I'm not listening.
FATHER: *(Walks out. Slam goes the door.)*
MOTHER: You can come out, Steve.
STEVE: You know, that was a great way to get rid of him.

— Yohance Prince, 4th, P.S. 124, Queens

WAKING UP

"Jeremiah, are you awake?" said Zach at 6:00 in the morning.

"I am now, Zach. What d'ya want?" I said angrily.

"Can you come upstairs with me?" said Zach meekly.

"I don't move from this pillow for another hour and a half," I said calmly.

"Please," Zach said while throwing a block at me.

"O.K.!" I screamed, tumbling out of bed.

"I love you, Jeremiah," he said while butting me in the stomach with his head.

— Jeremiah Greenblatt, 5th, P.S. 321, Brooklyn

Chapter 5: Writing Monologue

In fiction and on stage, characters reveal themselves through monologue. In real life many people explore and evaluate themselves through journal writing. In all of these cases the instrument for expression is what we call "voice" — the "sound" of personality and mood coming through the written word. We all have, of course, more than a single style — in speaking aloud as in writing. Sometimes we write formally, sometimes we use precise and linear language (as we, say, fill out a form). Sometimes we let ourselves go and swell with pomposity and righteous indignation as we write a letter of protest. We write to a friend and use a cheerful voice full of colloquialisms and private jokes. As a fiction writer, I might write a story in my grandmother's dialect, which is not the way I speak but is familiar to me. We play many roles in our lives, but we also have many different parts of our real selves. The establishing of the appropriate voice in a piece of writing is perhaps the most essential part of writing, and the most difficult to explain. A private journal is a good place to try out voices; I suppose this is one reason diaries and journals are especially popular with adolescents who are the ones among us who are most intensely trying on roles. In our diaries we can, on alternate pages, be distraught with unrequited passion and dripping with sarcasm at the stupidity we see around us.

All the outlines and topic sentences in the world will fail to breathe life into a piece of writing if it doesn't have authentic voice. The paper or report may be adequate; it will probably get a passing grade, but no one will enjoy reading it. It will lack the wholeness of personality; it will sound like so many boilerplated fragments rather than like the thoughts of a real human being. In some writers, the voice is the organizing principle of the work: not preplanning and subheading, but the psychological order and rhythms of the voice. Some writers actually "hear" voices as they write — have the sensation of eavesdropping on a conversation or receiving dictation from a storyteller. So when you sit down to write and begin to hear voices, be happy: welcome the mystery, and be sure to get it all down!

In fiction and drama there are many types of monologue. Sometimes the voice seems to be aware of its audience and addresses it directly — makes an impassioned plea for understanding, perhaps. This is the soliloquy of drama, the monologue in fiction. Other times the reader has the illusion of overhearing a character's actual thoughts; this is interior monologue. In stream of consciousness, the character appears to be not so much thinking as immersed in the immediate experience of the senses.

The aim of this chapter is for students to try out many of these types of monologue — everything from journal keeping and fiction diaries to stream of consciousness itself — in a way that will ultimately help them master the art of writing in their own voices.

The Mind in Flux

There is a technique called *freewriting* or *directed freewriting* (see Ideas 1 and 2 in this book) in which the writer puts down her or his thoughts for a limited period of time. Certain assumptions about the human mind underlie all the material in this chapter, so I think a class discussion of how the mind works can be a good way to get started here. It is important, for example, for students to realize that the mind does not naturally make logical essays or even full sentences. It does not naturally, in fact, move in a straight line at all, but jumps from one topic and one free association to another for long periods of time before settling in on the subject at hand. This is not a *failure* of the mind but the way it works. The business of the mind is thinking, but not necessarily in linear, logical order.

I like a discussion about "How do you think?" with younger children especially, but it is an interesting question to ask anyone. Do you think in pictures or words or some combination of the two? Do you see whole scenes in your mind clearly like a movie, or do things flit by like ghosts? When does the one happen and when does the other happen? What is your mind doing as you do other things? As you sit in school, work, walk, talk to friends, play a sport? Do you ever hear voices? Have debates with yourself? With your mother telling you to do or not do something? Do you give yourself little peptalks? There are some good topics here for expository writing, and it was, in fact, a certain spirit of experimentation that led early twentieth-century fiction writers like James Joyce and Virginia Woolf to try to capture the actual flow of experience—not to describe it or imitate it, but to reconstruct it—in stream of consciousness.

126

•**Idea 253:** The assignment, then, is freewriting: Write down whatever is going through your mind, without censoring it or changing it. It doesn't have to make sense. Some students, especialy those who are generally successful at doing assignments, get a little huffy about this.

•

I really don't understand the assignment, but I better do it. I wonder what Eric is writing? His paper says, "Look over there..." I wonder what I should write? Think fast. O god my ear is hurting again. Man oh man what can I write. This is *not* very fun.
　　　　　—Geeta Tate, 6th, Hunter College Elementary
　　　　　School, Manhattan

•

My mind is thinking the same as my stomach. Food! 15 minutes before lunch and I'm starved. I want to eat my paper. My mind went blank. But I am still starved. I have a lunch group so I am going to my friend's house. I wonder what we're having, but I don't care unless it's tomato soup. I hate it. I hope we have Spaghettios. I love them. But I don't really care. All I care is that I eat.
　　　　　—Nell Maloney, 3rd, P.S. 321, Brooklyn

Geeta's piece is typical, not trusting the teacher to have really meant what she said, challenging a little by saying this is not fun, observing what's going on around her for lack of anything better to do. Even the return of the earache rings true: if she had been comfortable with the assignment she would never have remembered her pain. Nell focusses on something rather more pleasant, but equally honest, and that is her desire for lunch. When she explains what her lunch group is, though, Nell is clearly writing for the teacher.

Some students will write pieces that make far less sense than Nell's or Geeta's. They may see colors, or hear a list of words, or have a sort of waking dream.

•

I can't think of anything. I see a green wall with a yellow circle at the bottom. Now it is red blinking on and off. Now it is half black half red. It's all red again. Now I see a black head. It's turning into a red wall with a flashlight. Now it has a white line down it. Now one eye is red and one line on the bottom. Now it has a black line. Now the whole thing is turning white. Now it is half white, half black. Now it's black. The top of it is two colors, left side orange, right side red.
　　　　　—Peter King, 3rd, P.S. 321, Brooklyn

I often use this freewriting technique before starting a day of writing;

127

I do it in my journal, usually without a clock in front of me, but with the same idea of keeping the flow going, not pausing to censor or think ahead, just to find out what is on my mind. Writing this way a while seems to clear my mind for the more structured work I have planned. Without finding out what was really on my mind, and giving that an outlet, I might have had much more trouble concentrating on my other work. Freewriting also acts as a pump primer, getting words to begin to flow. This last function of the freewriting technique is far from its least important one.

At first many adults, including teachers, can't let go in freewriting. They force themselves to keep to complete sentences and clear meanings, but they do get at some subjects on their minds, anyhow.

•

This room is full of energy and ideas, people are trying to put things on paper. I hear wiggling and scratching and I like Norma's leather boots and Sue's too, and Carmen's concentrated navy blue and bells very annoying while wiggly children sit in the auditorium poking each other and drawn in by Mohammed Ali. They call this stream of consciousness, layers of the brain running along continuous themes. The mind never really turns off it continually runs things in and out of focus. A giggle of nervousness, a newspaper, an airplane goes by as do noises of breathing and Sue stands and bells ring and coffee is ready and people are looking down and the pencils are moving. The energy of thought continuous flow. Where are the others. This is a necessary experience for us.
—Anonymous teacher

•

Today was a very good day. The students were anxious about the reading test so was I. The reason I say it was good is that there were few interruptions. Students listened, they asked questions, responded to directions and completed their work. I wish everyday could be as smooth as this one. There were few if any disciplinary problems. I even enjoyed my lunch for once. A day like today is also enriched by the beautiful weather, a bit cool but bearable.
—Anonymous teacher

•Idea 254: Try five or ten minutes of timed freewriting every day for a week. Do it with your class and discuss whether it gets harder or easier. Is there any general change in the sort of things you write about, or do you seem to fall into a pattern?

•Idea 255: Before beginning freewriting, close your eyes for fifteen seconds and follow your minds without writing. Then, after an initial chance to observe the mind without writing, begin to write. Can you capture some of what went running through your mind before you wrote?

•Idea 256: Another approach is not to *listen* to yourself, but to *talk* to yourself. This is an exercise for establishing your voice, discovering how you are most comfortable. The following example reminds me of a similar desperate voice in *my* head complaining about school!

•

It's almost report card time again. Every time report cards come, the atmosphere in school changes. Tests. . .tests. . .they seem to come in endless numbers. That's all I think about right now. . .tests and more tests. And the one today wasn't even announced. It's really quite unfair. Too many tests! There's no time — I come home so late (4:45) and have so much to do! I don't watch T.V. anymore — almost at all — and still there's no time. I always feel I'm rushing. . .hurrying trying to save precious time . . .What is the point of having time if not to enjoy it? It's a little like swimming underwater, when you can't come up for a breath of air. You have your eyes open, searching for the place where you can take a breath — you know it's there, somewhere — but you can't see it — it's out of sight. And you need the breath right now. If only you knew where it was, you could hold out a little longer. But it doesn't seem you'll ever breathe again.

— Doris Iarovici, 10th, Stuyvesant High School, Manhattan

•**Idea 257:** Another approach is to have conversations with yourself. We do this all the time, and for some reason the idea seems to hit a lot of students right.

•

"Amy," I said to myself in a firm voice, "Begging your mother for a hamster won't do any good, it just may make her *not* want to get a hamster." "I know," I said in a timid voice. "But it may do some good," I said hopefully. "Take your chances," I said to myself. "I will," I said in a firm voice, "even though it probably won't work." "But I'm still going to try," I said hopefully.

— Amy Stern, 3rd, P.S. 6, Manhattan

•**Idea 258:** Some high school students know about scientific theories of the left-hemisphere/right-hemisphere division of the brain. The left hemisphere is supposed to be the logical, linear side, the one that directs language and the right hand if you're a righty. The right brain, however, appears to control many of the subconscious and unconscious processes, the dreams and intuitive graspings of connections. Try a discussion between the two hemispheres of your brain.

•**Idea 259:** Or, set up some other binary division such as: introspective versus gregarious, angry versus calm, selfish versus unselfish, practical versus impractical, boastful versus modest, shy versus bold, etc.

•

Isn't it wonderful to be mysterious and incomprehensible? I mean, the power one feels at times, why it's almost invigorating! That wicked look on your face can give anybody a shudder. Besides, what good would your friendliness do? You just get taken advantage of, and suffer useless pain. But with this cynical attitude, you can still have lots of fun and laugh at people. Yes. It's best to be silent and somber for you'll never suffer again.

Ah, the warmth of friendship, so nice and comforting, what more can one ask for? The love of a friend, the soothing of one's soul, how it touches my heart. This is the better way, because you'll win many friends and valued respect. So, be brave, open up, and let your love flow and you'll be happy you did. Sharing of all the good times is really worthwhile.

—Ronald Wong, 10th, Stuyvesant High School,
Manhattan

•**Idea 260:** Try also some of the exercises in Chapter 2 on pages 37-40, especially the one based on the poem, "Self-Portrait as a Bear" on page 39.

•**Idea 261:** Still another variation on this is the scolding voice versus the congratulating voice. Write for five minutes in a scolding tone and then, at a signal, switch to a praising tone for another five. If possible, try both to scold and praise yourself for the same quality or behavior.

•

Cleto, you have to learn to be awake on the train as you ride home. Don't you know that the F train hasn't got all the glass dividers it used to? You have that bad habit of putting your hand up against them. Didn't you know there was no glass where that man was sitting? Sure, say it was a mistake, but you slapped the guy in the side of the face.

Boy, Cleto, you did that guy a favor. He was snoozing off. Who knows what would have happened to him. You may have saved him from being robbed or missing his station because he was asleep. He may have been badly beaten if it wasn't for you waking him up and making him aware of what was around him in the subway car....

—Anacleto Trigo, 10th, Stuyvesant High School,
Manhattan

•**Idea 262:** Try writing to yourself in any voice (grouchy, say) and then, at a signal from the teacher, switching to an entirely different mood. You might use any of the pairs in the inner debate exercise above.

Writing Journals and Diaries

If I were to become a regular, full-time classroom teacher tomorrow, I think the first thing I would do would be to beg, borrow, or steal enough blank notebooks for every student to use for a journal. As all the present research is showing, regular, frequent practice of writing is the one absolute essential for mastery. Writing is like bicycling: there is no lecture, no preparation, that teaches how to do it. You have to learn by doing. There are hints and helps that can be given along the way, of course, but they are all meaningless unless the student is actively engaged in the process of writing. The beauty of journal-keeping is that it is a place to practice, to try things out. If it is going well, there is also far too much material for the teacher to correct, so it becomes a place for practice without correction. One technique is to ask every week or two for the students to choose one section of the journal and expand it or prepare it in some other way to turn in as a composition that *will* be checked in the usual way. This is, in fact, the way real writers work; the vast majority of the material that they put on paper never reaches the eyes of a reader: why should children, who need even more practice, have every sentence and word-doodle of theirs scrutinized for errors? I make many, many false starts and out-and-out errors of grammar in my writing. I hope to catch most of them, or that my editor will catch most of them, before you read my work. The point here is not that every word a child writes is so precious it can't be criticized or changed. On the contrary, I would like to see classrooms as places with an atmosphere where writing is almost as ordinary as talking — where much of it is waste, and certain portions are prepared as final products for general perusal. Diary-keeping works into this process admirably.

Everything can go into a diary. My own journals go back, with gaps, to my tenth year. There is everything in them: reports of major events, copies of letters I sent, ideas for stories, a sketch of a skirt I would like to make if I ever get time to go back to sewing. There are responses to books and movies, and complaints about life and comments on people. There are descriptions of incidents and places and people and drafts of essays expressing my opinion on various subjects. There are dreams and incidents so painful I can hardly bear to read them even now. There are poems by me, and copies of poems by Emily Dickenson and Theodore Roethke. I have a separate set of diaries of teaching experiences that I have used in the past to glean for articles and also to think through problems and successes. Diaries are also, of course, an accepted form of *belles lettres*. Diaries are often published — and in some cases the diaries are more famous than whatever other work the writer did. Other diaries are read less for their literary value than as records of historical periods and great events. They have enormous immediacy and vitality from having been written as the events were happening. Even when diaries are published, they remain flowing and fairly formless, because their purpose is not to follow a pattern (say, thesis statement, exemplification, restatement of thesis) but to chart the ever-unfolding *present* of a life.

•**Idea 263:** It sounds almost silly, but one of the best ways to get a journal project going in a classroom is to provide blank books. These can be any ordinary spiral bound or composition notebooks, or the elaborate and more expensive blank books covered in attractive fabrics that are displayed on turning racks in so many bookstores these days.

•**Idea 264:** One teacher I know has her students cut construction paper and notebook paper in the shape of a head, and the students make their own self-portraits on the outside and then put their thoughts on the pages inside.

•**Idea 265:** You might want to try out various types of diaries — probably in the same book, but it might be worth trying several little books to get a feel for the different types:

Commonplace book — Very popular a hundred years ago. You write down sayings and passages from your reading that appeal to you. Today you might include lines from songs, things you heard on television, etc.

Scrapbook — This includes newsclippings and matchbooks, etc., that represent events in your life, along with writing.

Sketchbook — Instead of writing in a journal, draw what you saw or what happened to you.

Dream Book — Write your dreams every morning.

•**Idea 266:** Go to a good bookstore or library and look through books of published diaries.

•**Idea 267:** Read the diaries of famous people (Queen Victoria) and diaries that made their writers famous (Anne Frank). Take a look too at some of the diaries from the distant past — by people like Jonathan Swift or Samuel Pepys, or eleventh-century Japanese court ladies like Lady Murasaki Shikibu and Sei Shonogan (see page 136).

•**Idea 268:** We already had one selection from the childhood diary of Anaïs Nin. (See page 10). Here is the diary entry of her initial impressions of New York.

From LINOTTE: THE EARLY DIARY OF ANAÏS NIN
AUGUST 11, 1914

We were all dressed and on deck. It was 2 o'clock and one could vaguely see a city, but very far away. The sea was gray and heavy. How different from the beautiful sea of Spain! I was anxious to arrive, but I was sad. I felt a chill around my heart and I was seeing things all wrong. Suddenly we were wrapped in a thick fog. A torrential rain bean to fall, thunder rumbled, lightning flashes lit the heavy black sky. The people promptly took refuge in the lounge. None of the Spanish passengers had ever seen weather like that, so the frightened women wept, the men prayed in low tones. We were not afraid, Maman had seen many other storms and her calmness reassured us. We were the first to go back up on the wet deck. But the fog continued and we waited. It was 4 o'clock when the ship began to move again, slowly, as though she approached the great city with fear. Now, leaning on the railing, I couldn't hear anything. My eyes were fixed on the lights that drew closer. I saw the tall buildings. I heard the whistling of the engine. I saw a great deal of movement. Huge buildings went by in front of me. I hated those buildings in advance because they hid what I loved most — flowers, birds, fields, liberty. Maman came up to me and took me for a walk, whispering in my ear the wonderful things that I was going to see, but although I admire New York for its progress, I hate it. I find it superficial. I saw it was an ugly prison. Maman was still walking, but seeing that I wasn't paying the slightest attention, she didn't talk to me anymore, but her eyes looked worried. My head felt heavy, my heart seemed full enough to burst. I felt sad and unhappy. I envy those who never leave their native land. I wanted to cry my eyes out. Maman went away again and again I leaned on the railing and filled my lungs with the pure evening air. It was growing dark, we were arriving and I had to come out of my sad reverie. I cast a last glance around me at this last bit of Spain, which seemed to have wanted to accompany me this far, to remind me of my promise that I would return. Inside myself I answered, Oh, yes, I shall return to Spain. . . . .

— Anaïs Nin

•**Idea 269:** Write a diary entry for your first visit to a strange place. (This may have to be a memory.)

•**Idea 270:** Find out when your relatives first came to this country. Imagine you are a young person arriving at that time and make up a fictional diary entry for your first impressions of the New World.

•**Idea 271:** Make a diary of any special trip or experience of yours. The following is an excerpt from a girl's long diary of her hospital stay:

WEDNESDAY, JANUARY 21

Today I have Anaphylactoid Purpura and my doctor. Dr. Wethers, said that I should go to the hospital for five days. I am in St. Luke's Hospital now, in Room 5738. We took the elevator to the seventh floor. At the desk we were looking for somebody to show us my room. Miss Chiu showed us my room. She took my blood pressure and my temperature.

My bed is near the window, and when I look out I see St. John's Cathedral in the snow and the sky is very very gray. In the nighttime I'm going to be sleeping here.

I've got a companion who is 12 years old and I wonder what her name is. She is asleep and her mother is half-asleep. I'll find out later when she wakes up.

Miss Chiu took me out to see how tall I was. 51 inches. Miss Chiu asked me what I like to eat. I said, "Everything."

Mommy is writing because my hand is swollen.

I asked what the side bar-guard rails were for and Mommy pulled it up to show me how it was done. But she couldn't get it down! Finally Daddy figured out how to get it down. Thank goodness!

* * *

It's very modern here, and it's very nice — but there's no place like home.

Now it's supper time. I'm having a tray in bed: a cheese sandwich, fruit cocktail with cottage cheese, milk, lemonade, and vanilla ice cream.

* * *

Dr. Cooke came in after that and gave me an examination. My stomach still hurts. My hand is still swollen. And my rash is still all over my legs and arms. I'm tired and I think I'll go to sleep early.

—Hilary Gelber, *Seventeen Days in St. Fluke's Hospital*

●

Another common type of diary that moves out of literature and into science is the observation diary. Many scientific researchers keep logs of their observations, and out of this data later work their ideas into articles. This is the basic act of looking around you and trying to put what you see into words. There is a quality of meditation that shows up in some of the best writing of this sort. Much of the material in Henry David Thoreau's *Walden* has this quality of meditation growing out of observation. He did a lot of sitting and looking, and when I ask students to make themselves quiet and bring their senses to bear on examining a thing and describing it, I often have the model in my mind of Thoreau looking at leaves, at the sky, at water (as in the selection on page 28) or at mice, as in the following selection:

From WALDEN

The mice which haunted my house were not the common ones, which are said to have been introduced into the country, but a wild native kind not found in the village. I sent one to a distinguished naturalist, and it interested him much. When I was building, one of these had its nest underneath the house, and before I had laid the second floor, and swept out the shavings, would come out regularly at lunch time and pick up the crumbs at my feet. It probably had never seen a man before; and it soon became quite familiar, and would run over my shoes and up my clothes. It could readily ascend the sides of the room by short impulses, like a squirrel, which it resembled in its motions. At length, as I leaned with my elbow on the bench one day, it ran up my clothes, and along my sleeve, and round and round the paper which held my dinner, while I kept the latter close, and dodged and played bo-peep with it and when I at last held still a piece of cheese between my thumb and finger, it came and nibbled it, sitting in my hand, and afterward cleaned its face and paws, like a fly, and walked away.

—Henry David Thoreau

Another example that elaborates and takes scientific observation into literature is the following piece by surgeon-essayist Richard Selzer.

134

SKIN

Gaze upon the skin as I have, through a microscope brightly, and tremble at the wisdom of God, for here is a magic tissue to suit all seasons. Two layers compose the skin — the superficial epidermis, and, deeper, the dermis. Between is a plane of pure energy where the life-force is in a full gallop. Identical cells spring full-grown here, each as tall and columnar as its brother, to form an unbroken line over the body. No sooner are these cells formed than they move toward the surface, whether drawn to the open air by some protoplasmic hunger or pushed outward by the birth of still newer cells behind. In migration, skin cells flatten, first to cubes, then plates. Twenty-six days later the plates are no more than attenuated wisps of keratin meshed together to guard against forces that would damage the skin by shearing or compression. Here they lie, having lost all semblance of living cellularity, until they are shed from the body in a continuous dismal rain. Thus into the valley of death this number marches in well-stepped soldiery, gallant, summoned to a sacrifice beyond its ken. But . . . let the skin be cut or burned, and the brigade breaks into a charge, fanning out laterally across the wound, racing to seal off the defect. The margins are shored up; healing earthworks are raised, and guerrilla squads of invading bacteria are isolated and mopped up. The reserves too are called to the colors and the rate of mitosis increases throughout the injured area. Hurrah for stratified squamous epithelium!

> — Richard Selzer in *Mortal Lessons, Notes on the Art of Surgery*

Some students responded:

BLOOD

Pumped through the body by an irresistible force, it contains three ranks. The red nurses, white maids, and the policeman platelets. The minute an artery is punctured, tiny platelets try to stop the rioters from escaping through the skin. The white cells do the cleaning job. And the red cells nourish the body. Then they go to the cleaners and return to the heart to start the cycle over again. Their only means of transportation are the narrow streets, Artery Avenue and Vein Lane. . . .

> — Susan Kleinman, 6th, Hunter College Elementary School, Manhattan

SOUND

Starting from the deep blackness of the pharynx, reverberating, moving upwards, always upwards, through the throat, into the mouth. Flipped by the tongue toward the lips, someone's big mouth opens, allowing the sound to pass through. Through the air, like a bird soaring—

Then into someone's ear, through to the drum, and, being heard, ending the long journey.

> — Matthew Levie, 5th, Hunter College Elementary School Manhattan

Another superficially simple technique using diaries is that of lists. I would have thought lists too dull if I had not a few years ago discovered *The Pillow Book* of Sei Shonogan. Sei Shonogan is interesting for many reasons, not the least of which is that people are still reading her diary which was written around 990 A.D. in Japan in a language that has to be studied or translated even for contemporary Japanese readers. This "pillow book" is a collection of observations and reminiscences and character sketches that the lady kept in a box under or in her pillow. The titles of her lists are so provocative that they tend to elicit poems or poetic paragraphs from students.

THINGS THAT HAVE LOST THEIR POWER

A large boat which is high and dry in a creek at ebb-tide.
A woman who has taken off her false hair to comb the short hair that remains.
A large tree that has been blown down in a gale and lies on its side with its roots in the air.
The retreating figure of a sumo wrestler who has been defeated in a match.
A man of no importance reprimanding an attendant.
An old man who removes his hat, uncovering his scanty topknot.
A woman, who is angry with her husband about some trifling matter, leaves home and goes somewhere to hide. She is certain that he will rush about looking for her; but he does nothing of the kind and shows the most infuriating indifference. Since she cannot stay away forever, she swallows her pride and returns.
> —Sei Shonogan in *The Pillow Book,* translated by
> Ivan Morris

PLEASING THINGS

Finding a large number of tales that one has not read before. Or acquiring the second volume of a tale whose first volume one has enjoyed. But often it is a disappointment.
Someone has torn up a letter and thrown it away. Picking up the pieces, one finds that many of them can be fitted together.
One has had a very upsetting dream and wonders what it can mean. In great anxiety one consults a dream-interpreter, who informs one that it has no special significance.

. . . .

I realize that it is very sinful of me, but I cannot help being pleased when someone I dislike has a bad experience.
It is a great pleasure when the ornamental comb that one has ordered turns out to be pretty.
Entering the Empress's room and finding that ladies-in-waiting are crowded around her in a tight group, I go next to a pillar which is at some

distance from where she is sitting. What a delight it is when Her Majesty summons me to her side so that all the others have to make way!
— Sei Shonogan in *The Pillow Book,* translated by Ivan Morris

Here are some other lists from *The Pillow Book:*

Rare things
Things that make one's heart beat faster
Elegant things
Unsuitable things
Things that cannot be captured
Embarrassing things
Things that give a hot feeling
Awkward things
Shameful things
Things without merit
Things that fall from the sky

THINGS THAT CANNOT BE CAPTURED

Large colorless rings appear in the water.
Looking at the colors of the warm summer forest.
Oh so small snow flakes so soft and cold.
A bald eagle so graceful yet shy.
Waiting by an archway by an old stone church.
I am sitting by a lake watching the rowboats.
— Erica Stoltz, 4th, P.S. 321, Brooklyn

•**Idea 272:** Using one of Sei Shonogan's lists, or one of your own, write a pillow book style entry.

Writing Fiction Diaries

Diary entry novels and stories used to be very common — the books would be prefaced with the disclaimer that the author was actually not the author but the editor of these pages found in an old chest or whatever. The idea was that you couldn't merely write a story but had to have a possible real life situation out of which these documents — these diary pages or letters — might have been generated. It is fun sometimes to try writing a story through the device of fictional diaries — you get the illusion of immediacy and freshness and you try to imagine what this character you have invented would write in a diary. In elementary school I kept a "fiction diary" in which I, my best friend, and my little sister were the main characters. Mostly we travelled and got into danger (wearing our clever identical outfits), and the fictional Sue thought up brilliant ways to save us.

•**Idea 273:** Take a real diary entry, something that actually happened to you, and use it as the beginning of a fiction story.

•**Idea 274:** Write your own fiction diary. Remember the convention that the diary-writer is writing shortly after the actual events and no more knows what will happen next than we do in real life.

•**Idea 275:** Do the same kind of story, but make it in letters instead of diary entries.

•**Idea 276:** Do it with a friend or partner, taking different characters, and advancing the story by writing the next letter in the series.

Daniel Defoe wrote a number of fictional diaries and memoirs, including his famous *Robinson Crusoe*. He never exactly lies, but he writes his books as if he were the character or the eyewitness to the events he is writing about. In fact his books, especially *Journal of the Plague Year,* were based on research and hearsay. His object was to have a fair number of readers mistake what he had written for the truth. *Journal of the Plague Year* purports to be the journal of a man who lived through the years of the hideous bubonic plague in London.

From JOURNAL OF THE PLAGUE YEAR

It is scarce credible what dreadful cases happened in particular families every day. People in the rage of the distemper, or in the torment of their swellings, which was indeed intolerable, running out of their own government, raving and distracted, and oftentimes laying violent hands upon themselves, throwing themselves out at their windows, shooting themselves &c.; mothers murthering their own children in their lunacy, some dying of meer grief as a passion, some of meer fright and surprize without any infection at all, others frighted into idiotism and foolish distractions, some into despair and lunacy, others into melancholy madness.

The pain of the swelling was in particular very violent, and to some intolerable; the physicians and surgeons may be said to have tortured many poor creatures even to death. The swellings in some grew hard, and they applied violent drawing-plaisters or poultices to break them, and if these did not do they cut and scarified them in a terrible manner. In some those swellings were made hard partly by the force of the distemper and partly by their being too violently drawn, and were so hard that no instrument could cut them, and then they burnt them with causticks, so that many died raving mad with the torment, and some in the very operation. In these distresses, some, for want of help to hold them down in their beds, or to look to them, laid hands upon themselves as above. Some broke out into the streets, perhaps naked and would run directly down to the river, if they were not stopped by the watch-men or other officers, and plunge themselves into the water wherever they found it.

It often pierced my very soul to hear the groans and cries of those who were thus tormented, but of the two this was counted for the most promising particular in the whole infection, for, if these swellings could be

brought to a head, and to break and run, or, as the surgeons call it, to digest, the patient generally recovered....
— Daniel Defoe

•**Idea 277**: Write about some disaster (volcano, avalanche, tidal wave, nuclear plant meltdown, etc.) as if you yourself were an eyewitness to it. Make sure you know enough about the disaster to have some convincing details. (For some reason — probably the natural delight of human young in gore and grossness — this assignment is one of my nearly-never-fail ones. A lot of kids like to write these.)

EXTRACT FROM THE U.S.S. THRESHER'S
FIRST MATE'S DIARY

The alarm just went off, and the crew is running from station to station. We are rapidly sinking. We're 910 feet below the surface. I can hear groans from the hull as it strains from the pressure. I imagine that I can see the hull beginning to implode. The sub is pitching and we're taking on a list to port. The radio is out, and the technicians are frantically trying to repair it.

I can smell an electrical fire from aft. The chief engineer is shouting for more power. Some idiot is shutting down the reactor — something about the flood-water. I try to tell him to open the auxiliary valves, but he won't listen.

The bulkhead doors are swinging shut and I am trapped. The pressure on the hull is mounting. I know I will not survive. I try not to panic, but it is no use. Suddenly I am pounding on the bulkhead door. It won't open. The water is coming in now. It is freezing. People are shouting. I.....
— David Parichy, 6th, Hunter College Elementary
School, Manhattan

•

I have to hide in my cellar while bombs blow up; windows crash, people keep falling down and blood gushes down like a waterfall to where I am hiding. Usually I throw my father's tools and things and so far I've killed 30 people; everytime I throw something I vomit in a corner....I wonder what is happening outside....All of a sudden a bomb drops in. I scurry up the stairs but it's too late my arm is broken and so is my leg; more blood comes, but this time it is out of me. My mother comes rushing toward me. We get to shelter, after a long journey on a boat, there is still more war, but this time it's calmer, and a lot of people are dead. All of a sudden everything is dim. I hear a crash and I bump myself real hard. I wake up and I find it was only a dream, but still, what my cousin set up the night before (of a Fisher-Price set) looked like the war I had just been in and now that I have fallen on it, I have made it come to an end.
— Phoebe Potts, 4th, P.S. 321, Brooklyn

139

•**Idea 278:** Another, less violent, assignment would be to skip the idea of disasters and simply have diary entries from other times and places, perhaps from a period in history you are studying in class.

•**Idea 279:** Write the fictional diary of the first settler on a distant planet. It may be quite earthlike or not at all.

•**Idea 280:** Write the diary of an average person on an average day in the future.

DECEMBER 4, 4322

Dear Diary,

Today I got a brand new hypercycle. Now for some bad news, I stole it. Yes! That's right. I stole it. Right out of Wing Wong's hyper repairs window. It's the newest model.

It all started when my old-fashioned Concorde (You know what that is. It's a method of travel in, what century was it, I think it was either in the 19th or the 20th century. Wait, it was the 20th century.) broke down in front of Wing Wong's. I took it in. Mr. Wong said he wouldn't repair it because it was not hyper powered. So, I looked in the green pages. Couldn't believe it, not one place serviced antiques. So, to get revenge, I stole the new hypercycle.

DECEMBER 5, 4322

Dear Diary,

I have some good news and some bad news. First, the good news. I will never have to worry about being caught for stealing a hypercycle. Now, the bad news, the reason I won't be caught is I've already been caught! Believe it or not! I left it double parked last night and when a police officer was going to put a ticket on it, he noticed it was a stolen car. Now, I have to serve a jail sentence and pay a fine for double parking. What a bummer!

DECEMBER 6, 4322

Dear Diary,

Well, I have some good news and some bad news. First the good news. I've escaped from prison with my hypercycle. Now, the bad news, in doing so, I broke the cycle and have to bring it for repairs at Wing Wong's. Not again!

—Adam Horowitz, 5th, P.S. 87, Manhattan

The following excerpt from literature is from a story that tries to chart the development of madness in a person. While few of us will ever suffer insanity, there is a moment in everyone's life when we wonder, "Is this really happening? Am I crazy?"

The sample is from Nikolai Gogol. The man first hears a little dog talking and gradually becomes convinced that he is the king of Spain, and that these people who come to get him are taking him to his kingdom.

From DIARY OF A MADMAN

Year 2000, April 43

This is a day of great jubilation. Spain has a king. They've found him. *I am the King.* I discovered it today. It all came in a flash. It's incredible to me now that I could have imagined that I was a civil service clerk. How could such a crazy idea ever have entered my head? Thank God no one thought of slapping me into a lunatic asylum. Now I see everything clearly, as clearly as if it lay in the palm of my hand. But what was happening to me before? Then things loomed at me out of a fog. Now, I believe that all troubles stem from the misconception that human brains are located in the head. They are not; human brains are blown in by the winds from somewhere around the Caspian Sea. . . .

January of the same year which
happened after Februarius

I still can't make out what sort of place Spain is. The customs and the etiquette at the Court are quite incredible. I don't see, I don't grasp it, I don't understand at all! Today, they shaved my head, although I shouted with all my might that I did not want to become a monk. But then they began to drip cold water on my head and everything went blank. Never have I been through such hell. I just can't understand the point of this peculiar custom, so stupid, so senseless. And the irresponsibility of the kings who never got around to having this custom outlawed is quite beyond me.
— Nikolai Gogol

•**Idea 281:** Write a diary of a mad person. In the two following examples by fourth graders there are some interesting variations on the original. Joanna seems to think that being insane would impair your spelling and cause puns while Adam seems to connect dreams and insanity.

THE FUNNY FARM
MEN-TALLY

Joanna A.
120/91/29000

dar, Diary!
      i Am diing from LiVinG! i Pray to my deVil to cil mee. i Pray to my God cil meee! i taLk to my hand if it screems at Mee, i screemm at my conslurp when he dAncEs i KICK Myself if i tAlk to mySelf i wear my beeaney to sleeepp.
      i Am going home to the Nut house.
                                        Hi!
P.Q.S. =i love KILLing the peoople

141

Killing & love
Killer
— Joanna Abbott, 4th, P.S. 321, Brooklyn

•

One day when I was walking through the park I heard a dog say my name.
I turned and looked at the dog. Then all of a sudden I started to get like a
dog. I was barking at the dog's owner and the dog barked at me and then
all of a sudden I was on a bench. I had dreamed the whole thing. But then I
looked down and there was the dog whispering my name.
— Adam Steele, 4th P.S. 321, Brooklyn

Monologue and Character Development

The fiction diary and journal of a madman ideas focus the writing
more on experience and event than on character. It should be obvious that
something as intimate as the thoughts of a person must be an important way
to explore character. One way monologue explores and develops characters
is through the speech—the justification or vindication—that a person
makes in his or her own behalf. This sort of speech can be found often in
nineteenth-century novels. An example of monologue I like to use is from
Mary Shelley's *Frankenstein*. The monster has learned human speech, and
in fact speaks well (unlike his representations in the movies). He mastered
language by hiding in the home of some well-educated but poor people and
slipping in and reading their books, and for a while even having conversations with an old blind man. By the time of this passage, however, he has run
a long, grim race with Dr. Frankenstein, who has died. An interesting point
about this speech is that although the monster is confessing to terrible
crimes, we tend to feel sympathy for him. This is the point, of course, of
making an impassioned speech explaining yourself; you want another
human being to understand you, to accept what you are, or this version of
you that you are telling. When writing in a character's voice a good writer
almost always feels sympathy for the character. That is how you write first
person. You pretend to be inside the heads of the characters you are
writing—you try to see with their eyes, hear with their ears. Of course you
become sympathetic—you become, in some small way, for a moment,
another person. First person narrative and monologue most often fail when
the author has not sunk deep enough into character; you can't write a
monologue from someone else's point of view if you remain yourself feeling
contempt or condescension or even admiration for the other one. Good fiction writers lose themselves on purpose or inadvertently in their characters.

[THE WRETCH SPEAKS]

"But it is true that I am a wretch. I have murdered the lovely and the
helpless; I have strangled the innocent as they slept and grasped to death

his throat who never injured me or any other living thing. I have devoted my creator, the select specimen of all that is worthy of love and admiration among men, to misery; I have pursued him even to that irremediable ruin. There he lies, white and cold in death..."
—Mary Shelley, *Frankenstein*

•**Idea 282:** Continue Frankenstein's monster's speech in the same style and tone, or write what came immediately before.

•**Idea 283:** Write a flowery speech justifying, or confessing to, something you have done that you should not have. This can be serious or funny. But try to do it in the style of the confession of Frankenstein's monster. ("It is true that I stole your pearl necklace, but....")

•**Idea 284:** Write the speech of the ghost of one of the monster's victims. What is that person's point of view? Or the point of view of a member of the victim's family.

•**Idea 285:** Write the speech of someone who is unusually ugly or beautiful.

YUCK'S FACE

Hi, I'm Yuck, the world's ugliest dog. I get out of big problems just by lifting my house. I'm an orphan because when I was born I was so ugly that my father and mother ran away from me. My face got ruined when my mother got into a fight with her trainer. Some of her bones cracked, and when she walked around the bones would jiggle and hit my face. Some of them were sharp. They scratched my face real bad. They bought a small dog house for me, now I am so ugly that I have to wear it on my head.
—George Valentine, 5th, P.S. 321, Brooklyn

•**Idea 286:** If you haven't done them yet, try some of the Inside/Outside portrait ideas from Chapter 2, starting at page 41. It is fun to take any of the outside, or physical, descriptions of people or animals and write a monologue to go with the outside. Similarly, you can take any of the monologues you've written or the samples from literature and by other students and write physical descriptions to go with them.

•

Another popular kind of imaginative writing is to imagine the thoughts, the secret desires, the dreams of *things*. I think these assignments are successful for some of the same reasons as the dialogue between two things, described in Chapter 6. The selection I use as an example of an object's monologue is taken from a short story by John Cheever. It has some of the self-vindication of the monologues in the last section, but it is also amusing. Young children, and even teenagers in a playful mood, love to animate the inanimate, to give things without tongues the opportunity to speak their piece. This selection even has the faintest tinge of the off-color about it — the fly of a man's pants is mentioned! — and this seems to bring up all sorts of disgusting and silly ideas that kids usually reserve for out of the classroom. You may prefer that they stay there, but I tend to like the vigor that comes out of this kind of writing. Part of the fun is the universality of the way body organs *do* seem to have minds of their own, or at least wills: the stomach growls inopportunely, the hair won't lie down smoothly. Our bodies are always talking to us anyhow: why not a speech, or (as the stomach says) a cry from the heart?

From "Three Stories"

The subject today will be the metaphysics of obesity and I am the belly of a man named Lawrence Farnsworth. I am the body cavity between his diaphragm and his pelvic floor, and I possess his viscera. I know you won't believe me, but if you'll buy a *cri de coeur,* why not a *cri de ventre?* I play as large a part in his affairs as any other lights and vitals, and while I can't act independently he too is at the mercy of such disparate forces in his environment as money and starlight. We were born in the Middle West and he was educated in Chicago. He was on the track team (pole vault) and later on the diving team, two sports that made my existence dangerous and obscure. I did not discover myself until he was in his forties, when I was recognized by his doctor and his tailor. He stubbornly refused to grant me my rights and continued for almost a year to wear clothes that confined me harshly and caused me such soreness and pain. My one compensation was that I could unzip his fly at will. . . .

— John Cheever, *The Complete Stories*

•**Idea 287:** The writing assignment is to pick a part of the body and have it speak. It helps to have a list of organs on the board so everyone doesn't choose brains and heart — younger children may not realize that skin is an organ, for example. Also, make sure that everyone understands that the piece is to sound as if the organ were speaking.

•

I'm the liver of a teenager and he drinks so much that he can't even walk down the steps. He drinks too too much. He drinks things that he's not supposed to. He started drinking when he was at the age of thirteen, and his parents didn't know what to do with him. So they took him to the doctor and the doctor said that I'm getting burned up. So everyone was so scared. But he didn't know what they were talking about because he was so drunk. He drank so much that he can't even walk down the steps. In a couple more drinks, I would be dead. Then after a while Bill realized what was happening and went back to the hospital and the doctor gave him some pills and I got well.

— Donna Bryant, 5th, P.S. 321, Brooklyn

Hi. I'm the right eye of David Bethridge. If it weren't for me, he wouldn't be here now, seeing (ha ha) as I've saved his life many times.

He never paid up, though, so I changed the distance from my lens to my surface and now he has to wear glasses. I guess I showed him. I see some very interesting things with David. Why the other day I saw the most beautiful brown eye you ever saw. And David got me real close so I could get a good look and exchange platitutdes till he closed me.

God I hate it when he closes me. I gave him a tic in his cheek to make up for it. Power must be spread evenly, you know. . . .
— David Bethridge, 10th, Stuyvesant High School,
Manhattan

•**Idea 288:** Another assignment is to continue the John Cheever piece, as this high school student did:

". . . I can't actually do this by myself, but with my ally the bladder we will have this Farnsworth on his knees to us yet. The small intestine was considering pulling out of the alliance, but when his worthless friend the appendix pledged loyalty to the brain and subsequently became inflamed and was removed, he. . . ."

•**Idea 289:** Write the monologue of some object that you know well—your wallet or your toothbrush—and write its complaint.

•**Idea 290:** Write a monologue of your favorite chair or your bed.

•**Idea 291:** Write a monologue of the corner around your school or block where students hang out.

•**Idea 292:** Write a monologue of any object that could tell something about people if it could talk.

•

A direct way of using monologue to explore character is to write what I call "Introductions." In these pieces fictional characters tell about themselves, just as people meeting in a group for the first time often begin with a go-round. The purpose of a go-round is to give the students an opportunity to say a few words about who they are, and why they are in this meeting. Much more is revealed, of course, than the simple information about name and hometown. One person will manage to crack a couple of jokes; another will giggle with nervousness; a third will make inappropriate apologies; a fourth will attempt to take charge and direct the ideas of the others. Introductions sometimes happen on long train or plane trips when we sit beside someone who tells us all about himself or herself in great detail—a life story with all its joy and tragedy. In other words, the Monologue Introduction has its sources in everyday life. Fictionally, it can be very gripping as the reader is drawn into the personality and speaking style (voice again) of the character.

The samples from literature that I use to present the idea of Introductions are the opening lines of three adult, first-person novels. In a sense each of these novels is one long monologue, as the speaker tells his or her story, but as the novels go on, there are many characters and events; it is these Introductions that establish the characters who are speaking. The author has in each case made important and conscious choices about how to make this first impression, what details to reveal. Is the reader to like this speaker? Trust him? Admire her? How are we to visualize the character, or is that important? In one case the speaker carefully details his height and physical appearance. In the other two those concrete physical descriptions are ignored and other things — present psychological situation, past events — are emphasized.

I usually use these three selections together with older students, but there is no reason they can't be separated, or the openings to other novels used instead.

From THE DWARF

I am twenty-six inches tall, shapely and well proportioned, my head perhaps a trifle too large. My hair is not black like the others, but reddish, very stiff and thick, drawn back from my temples and the broad but not especially lofty brow. My face is beardless, but otherwise just like that of other men. My eyebrows meet. My bodily strength is considerable, particularly if I am annoyed. When the wrestling match was arranged between Jehosophat and myself I forced him onto his back after twenty minutes and strangled him. Since then I have been the only dwarf in this court.

— Pär Lagerkvist

Pär Lagerkvist's dwarf is not a subtle character; he immediately confronts us, the readers, with his stature and facial features. He demands to be taken personally. He appears to be a concrete and straightforward character. He postulates that his strength is considerable, and then, as a demonstration of this, tells how he strangled another dwarf in a public gladiatorial conflict. Questions arise: what kind of place is this court where there are public wrestling matches to the death? (Younger and less sophisticated students often have to be told that this is a royal court rather than a judge's court or basketball one.) What is the dwarf's actual status in this court? He boasts of his accomplishments, but is there really much value to the honor of being the only dwarf in such a place? I often ask students if they like this dwarf, and if they would want him for a friend. Most are doubtful about his violent propensities, but I'll always remember one short seventh grader in the South Bronx who said he would definitely like to go around with this dwarf because he sounds like he knows how to protect himself.

146

The second Introduction is the most ordinary sounding of the three. It is a character that many of us tend to identify with — a young person who has had to overcome difficulties. A sign of this identification is that boys tend to think the character is a "he" on first hearing while girls tend to think it is a "she." The idea of being poor seems to grip everyone's imagination. Students are particularly struck by the idea of having to sleep in the same room as their parents, and also of a child having to work (as a chambermaid) to earn a living. After many readings I have come to think there is a certain tone of self-pity in the paragraph, but the appeal remains in what appears to be the set-up for a modern Cinderella story.

From "Boston Adventure"

Because we were very poor and could not buy another bed, I used to sleep on a pallet made of old coats and comforters in the same room with my mother and father. When I played wishing games or said, "Star light star bright" my first wish always was that I might have a room of my own, and the first one I imagined was Miss Pride's at the Hotel Barstow which I sometimes had to clean when my mother, the chambermaid, was not feeling well.
— Jean Stafford

Most young people, rich or poor, seem to have imagined themselves as heroes of their own dramas in which they are orphans, lost, making their own way. I don't know the psychological basis of this — and I doubt that it holds true for deeply deprived children, those with no functioning family structure — but for the children who do have families, there seems to be some great satisfaction in playing through the fantasy of loss and recovery. One eighth grader from the Bedford-Stuyvesant section of Brooklyn wrote this imitation of the Jean Stafford Introduction:

When I was poor I used to sleep on the bare floor. I had no shoes, just some raggedy pants and one blouse. My brother worked to help my mother, but he only made a little money. My mother worked in a grocery store packing bags. And that was no money. We made it a little. We had little food. We had a house with four small rooms.

When she had written this much, she showed it to me, and I asked, as I almost invariably do, for more details. "What kind of food did they eat? Tell me more about the girl," I said. So she finished the piece this way:

The food we ate was very cheap, we ate grits and corn every day. But the rich people ate steaks and beef and a lot of expensive foods. Their children went to school with pretty dresses and nice suits. Me and my brother and my mother had to make it alone. My father died and that was terrible. We were making it good when my father was alive (he worked on a train).

147

When I was 10 I got a job cleaning at a pretty white house that sat in town. I helped a little bit, but that was not that much, and now I pray to God that my mother had money.
— Felicia Mack, 8th, J.H.S. 258, Brooklyn

I don't know anything about Felicia's own circumstances, but she seems to have a good practical, working knowledge of how a family facing dire economic straits goes about trying to "make it." Her character is in some ways like the one in the excerpt from "Boston Adventure," except that Felicia's girl seems to have stronger ties to her family, and instead of ending her piece with a wish on a star, she makes a prayer to God.

The last of the three Introductions is *not* from the H.G. Wells story and television show (although *that* invisible man would make for an interesting writing assignment too). This excerpt is from Ralph Ellison's *Invisible Man,* a novel about being a black man in twentieth-century America. The issue that often touches students here is not the one of race (which I don't bring up unless one of them picks up on it) but of not being seen, for whatever reason. This must be an experience as frequent among affluent fourth graders as among young black men in the 1940s. I don't mean to suggest that the importance is equal — the kid who is ignored by his parents' cocktail guests and the educated black man who can't get a job — but only that there is some similar ground in the experience. Everyone who has gone away to school, away from the comfort of friends and families, has experienced some touch of this. Anyone who has been too young or too old or not dressed right or not assertive enough or of the wrong ethnic group has felt it. Whatever the reason, whether it is a petty one or one that represents terrible inequities in the social system, the experience is of people looking through you. In this situation, some people are so adrift that they panic, feel something like insanity. Others will take any action to get themselves noticed.

From INVISIBLE MAN

I am an invisible man. No, I am not a spook like those who haunted Edgar Allen Poe; nor am I one of your Hollywood movie ectoplasms. I am a man of substance, of flesh and bone, fiber and liquids — and I might even be said to possess a mind. I am invisible, understand, simply because people refuse to see me. Like the bodiless heads you see sometimes in circus sideshows, it is as though I have been surrounded by mirrors of hard, distorting glass. When they approach me they see only my surroundings, themselves or figments of their imagination — indeed, everything and anything except me.
— Ralph Ellison

•**Idea 293:** The basic writing assignment is to write an Introduction for a character not like yourself. It may help some students to make a brainstorming list on the board of some people they might pretend to be: a blind person, a fighter, a rich person, etc.

•**Idea 294:** The other essential assignment is to continue any one of the Introductions above in the same voice and style. What does the character say or do next?

•**Idea 295:** Think of a time you have felt invisible. Were you the only child at an all-adult party? In a new town? Tell in the first person how it felt.

•**Idea 296:** Write an Introduction-monologue for a person who is very lonely.

•**Idea 297:** Write an Introduction for a handicapped person.

THE MAN IN THE WHEELCHAIR

Why do all the kids laugh at me and all the grown-ups stare? Why do the teenagers throw rocks at me? Why doesn't anybody care or talk to me? Why do all the doctors say I'm fine when they know I'm going to die in about 9 months? Why do the muggers push me down and take my money and my wheels? Why do the mothers pull back their kids when I go by? Why do all the dogs bark at me when I go near? I'm only 62. Why should I die? Maybe I'll cry.
— Jason Frix, 5th, P.S. 87, Manhattan

•**Idea 298:** Write an Introduction for a person who is admired and envied by everyone but is secretly unhappy.

•**Idea 299:** Write an Introduction for a person who seems hopelessly ill or poor but is actually pretty content with life.

•**Idea 300:** Write an Introduction for a person with a secret, or a secret identity.

•**Idea 301:** Think of some real person you have noticed on the street or in a store, someone you don't know personally, and do his or her Introduction.

•**Idea 302:** Write an Introduction for yourself or someone else at the age of two years, then at your present age, then in the future.

•**Idea 303:** Write an Introduction for some famous person from history: Napoleon, Jeanne d'Arc.

•**Idea 304:** Do it for a sports figure.

•**Idea 305:** Do it for some television character — that is, not the actor but the character.

•**Idea 306:** Now do an Introduction to the actor who plays the character.

•**Idea 307:** Write the Introduction for a terrible criminal.

•**Idea 308:** Cut a collection of faces from magazines, some beautiful, some ugly, some in-between. Choose one from the pile and write an Introduction for it.

●

This play is so stupid. I hate this dress and this hat is itchy. These earrings hurt my ears, and I'll probably forget my lines. My sister will make fun of me and so will everyone else. I wish I didn't have to keep this stupid fake smile on my face. Oh, I'm scared. I don't want to do this. Oh no, it's my turn to go on stage. Everyone will see me. I wish I would break a leg. The teacher's getting mad. I have to go.

—Fiona Pechukas, 4th, P.S. 321, Brooklyn

MAN BY THE FIRE

I feel hot. This fire is going to burn my hands. My fingers are getting swollen and blistered by the pan's tremendous heat. If I move my hand, I will have nothing to eat. This raw cactus has to be cooked for a few years. This stone I'm sitting on is getting soft. I can't switch hands because my hand is glued to the pan. I've been on this rock now for, oh, I don't know how many years. My beard has caught on fire 54,321 times. That's why my beard is red.

—Rachel Thomas, 4th, P.S. 321, Brooklyn

●**Idea 309:** After doing several Introductions, choose your favorite and make a tape recording of it.

●**Idea 310:** Try illustrating or making a mask of your character.

●**Idea 311:** Make a presentation for another class by playing the tapes and showing the masks.

Writing Interior Monologue

Another type of monologue is the one in which the person is not speaking to someone, but speaking (or even just feeling) to herself or himself. The author's illusion is of eavesdropping into the most intimate and presumably truthful levels of another person's consciousness. This stream of consciousness appears to be similar to the freewriting described at the beginning of this chapter; both imitate the flow of the mind. The literary stream of consciousness, however, is not an automatic or unconscious outpouring of thoughts but a work constructed of them. The term, originally psychological, was coined by William James in his *Principles of Psychology* (1890). He defined it as "the flow of inner experience."

Some of the early literary experimenters with interior monologue and stream of consciousness included Henry James (brother of William), Virgina Woolf, Marcel Proust, Dorothy Richardson, and James Joyce (although they were not the first to try writing within a character's mind—see for example the piece by Tolstoy in the anthology at the end of this chapter). Some of these writers saw what they were doing as a technique parallelling to some degree the developments in painting that are called impressionism. The impressionist painters tried to capture the appearance of the actual world by laying bits of pure color side by side rather than mixing green, say, with gray and yellow and using that to represent grass. The idea was to break down the sense experience into its atomic parts and let the mind of the viewer put it back together again. The earliest, most experimental phase of interior monologue and stream of consciousness writing tried to do this too, but from the inside: to break down the texture of human experience and thought — to try for psychological accuracy as the world comes filtering through our senses.

Today these techniques appear less as an experiment and more often as a resource for fiction writers to use in forming the art work they want. I generally use interior monologue for showing moment-to-moment change in a character. You can, of course, also use it to further plot by letting a character make observations, and often several purposes can be served at once as the character tells his or her feelings about another character by, say, describing the room that other character lives in. An important quality of this technique is that it focusses on the present moment and is limited to the inner perceptions of one individual. The voice speaking and experiencing is not that of some Olympian who pontificates about the affairs of men but rather is one woman's or one man's own personal voice speaking from the center of one life.

James Joyce's *Ulysses* is the granddaddy of all stream of consciousness writing. Notice in the following excerpt from it that although there are a few points of conventional narration that orient the reader, the main thrust is the untidy, ordinary reality of household objects and mundane thoughts that take us through our morning rituals.

> Another slice of bread and butter: three four, right. She didn't like her plate full. Right. He turned from the tray, lifted the kettle off the hob and sat it sideways on the fire. It sat there, dull and squat, its spout stuck out. Cup of tea soon. Good. Mouth dry. The cat walked stiffly round a leg of the table with tail on high.

A man, Leopold Bloom, is preparing breakfast for himself and his wife. He is seeing things, he is hungry. Later he will think about what he will have for lunch, and his cat will meow. The ordinary has a place of honor in stream of consciousness.

•**Idea 312:** Write the thoughts of a person (not necessarily yourself) at a perfectly ordinary moment — getting up, having breakfast, etc.

•

> Ho hum! Time to get up? Oh, just a few more minutes, please? Aw, come on. Okay, I'll get up. What should I do first. What? You say my breath smells? Well obviously, I just woke up. Time to go brush my teeth, take my toothbrush, brrr. Good, finished, now to put on my clothes. Why does my mother have to put out my clothes for me? She treats me like a baby. Now to pack my books. Boy did I have a lot of homework last

night. There, all I have to do is get my lunch. Hmm, what do I have? Yuk, tuna fish. Oh well, get my coat, put on my hat. Put my gloves on and go.
  — Lee Rush, 6th, P.S. 6, Manhattan

•**Idea 313:** Write the inner thoughts of someone getting up in the morning and include their dream from the night before.

•**Idea 314:** Write the inner thoughts of a famous person, not at some high point of his or her career, but on an ordinary day.

•**Idea 315:** Write the thoughts of someone as something minor but irritating happens to him or her: an airconditioner drips on her head; he steps on something disgusting; a filling falls out of her tooth.

•**Idea 316:** Write the thoughts of someone active—swimming, playing soccer, dancing, sawing wood.

•**Idea 317:** An interesting variation on the above exercise combines drawing with writing. Take a piece of long paper (8½ by 14 inch mimeo paper is fine) and fold it into four vertical sections. Draw a person in an activity—a sport, a dance, climbing on a chair to reach something—but break the action into its parts so that the person steps, say, into the batter's box in the first frame, then gets the bat into position, then gives a practice swing, then makes (or fails to make) contact with the ball, etc. Save space at the bottom of each panel to write the stream of consciousness thoughts of the character at each stage, so you get the character worrying, hoping, exulting as the ball goes into the stands, etc.

•**Idea 318:** Write two separate stream of consciousnesses, perhaps for a boy and a girl who like each other and sit on opposite sides of a classroom.

•**Idea 319:** Write a dialogue (perhaps between a powerful and less powerful person) and then write the actual thoughts of the people as the dialogue is taking place. They may be thinking things very different from the ones they are saying! There is a *Mad* magazine series called "The Shadow Knows" in which two characters are engaged in some conflict situation, and behind them are their shadows, which show the real them—the cat has the shadow of a roaring lion, the slim little boy is actually a muscle man, etc.

•**Idea 320:** Sit with a partner. Write first your own thoughts and then try to guess what the other person was thinking, and write his or her thoughts.

Stream of consciousness, then, has as one of its uses the exploration of the ordinary. It also, in our time, serves another function. Language in the late twentieth century has become, as a general rule, pared down, lacking in elaboration. Simplicity is considered a virtue in our diction, and indeed, our spoken as well as our written language tends to be far less elaborate, with fewer subordinate clauses, than language 150 years ago. This change has its good and its bad sides. The best writing today (nonfiction as well as imaginative) has a clarity and a lack of bombast—writers polish and hone each phrase. The negative side of our clarity and simplicity is that a certain beauty of amplitude and expansion is lost, as is the precision that comes from complex sentences with their intricate relationships of antecedent and modifier. The danger, of course, is that a loss of complexity in language is concurrent with oversimplification in thinking. In fiction writing, at least, and in some forms of personal narrative and "new" journalism, stream of consciousness writing has become the place for complex thought and poetic insight. The technique is one of rhythm and juxtaposition. That is, one idea is laid next to another, and they reflect mutually, increasing reverberations of meaning. Symbols of manifold meaning often appear in stream of consciousness, as do leaps into spiritual as well as psychological truth. All of this work is written, too, from the perspective of one individual, who may be wise, but is not all-seeing—an approach appropriate to the twentieth century where one of our great lessons has been that there are many ways of life, many points of view.

In the following difficult but stunningly beautiful passage from Virginia Woolf's novel *To the Lighthouse,* the flashing light of the lighthouse becomes an image that centers the character's experience of life in a moment of solitude. This passage is not in the first person, but it is still a paragon of stream of consciousness writing.

> Beneath it is all dark, it is all spreading, it is unfathomably deep; but now and again we rise to the surface and that is what you see us by. Her horizon seemed to her limitless. There were all the places she had not seen; the Indian plains; she felt herself pushing aside the thick leather curtain of a church in Rome. This core of darkness could go anywhere, for no one saw it. They could not stop it, she thought, exulting. There was freedom, there was peace, there was, most welcome of all, a summoning together, a resting on a platform of stability. Not as oneself did one find rest ever, in her experience (she accomplished here something dexterous with her needles) but as the wedge of darkness. Losing personality, one lost the fret, the hurry, the stir; and there rose to her lips always some exclamation of triumph over life when things came together in this peace, this rest, this eternity; and pausing there she looked out to meet that stroke of the Lighthouse, the long steady stroke, the last of the three, which was her stroke, for watching them in this mood always at this hour one could not help attaching oneself to one thing, especially of the things one saw; and this thing, the long steady stroke was her stroke.

This is not, of course, easy reading, and I wouldn't use it with young children. But with older students it can set the mood for experimenting. I explain that to understand every word is not the point, but rather to absorb the tone, the rhythm of the piece. Like the Joyce breakfast scene, this passage is grounded in the outer world. The lighthouse is described, and it is also mentioned that the woman is knitting. (In parenthesis she does "something dexterous with her needles.") All that is happening outwardly is that a woman is knitting while a lighthouse flashes. She is doing so much more though; she is connecting herself with something she calls a "core of darkness" — something beyond or below personality. She is seeking a peace, something almost mystical.

•**Idea 321:** Perhaps the best way to use the Virginia Woolf passage is to read it aloud with the class at least twice, get a few reactions to it, and then have the students write one of their own.

•

> Day by day, night by night monotony overpowers me. School is no fun. Holidays are no fun. Vacations aren't either. Courses are taught by teachers to improve your knowledge, but it really seems useless to me. Day-dream was once a possible solution. Still, all the wild fantasies are used up, and the face of your teacher reappears. On Fridays there is only little excitement. This school is not coming again for two more days. But there is nothing to do. Only to watch gloom surround you. Sometimes, a hole or a crack appears in this unhappy atmosphere, but it is quickly covered up. You try to think about yourself, your whole life. The past — gloomy, the present — stinky, and the future — school, work, and boredom. Maybe death is the greatest pleasure for me.
> — Anonymous sophomore, Stuyvesant High School, Manhattan

•**Idea 322:** Continue Virginia Woolf's piece. Have someone come into the room and interrupt the thinker. What does she think next?

•**Idea 323:** Try having another person watch the flash of a lighthouse and write that person's stream of consciousness. Perhaps it is a young person who wants to get away from home, or someone who has just suffered a loss.

•

> How am I thought of?
> Indeed, who thinks of me?
> A passing thought,
> Or do they care?
> Do I leave an impression
> Which transcends school,
> or does it die with the day?
> Is my only gateway into people's minds verbal?
> Or do I creep in
> During a quiet moment of reflection?
> And if I manage to creep in,
> Do I emerge unscathed?
> — Anonymous sophomore, Stuyvesant High School, Manhattan

MORE MONOLGUES BY ADULTS

From SEVASTOPOL SKETCHES

"Who will it hit — Mikhaylov or me? Or both of us? And if me, whereabouts? If it's the head, then I'm done for; but if it's the leg, they'll cut it off, and I'll certainly ask for chloroform and I may survive. But maybe only Mikhaylov will be hit, then I'll be able to tell how we were walking side by side, and he was killed and I was splashed with blood. No, it's nearer me. . .it'll be me." Then he remembered the twelve roubles he owed Mikhaylov, remembered also a debt in Petersburg which should have been paid long ago; a gypsy song he had sung the night before came into his head; the woman he loved appeared in his imagination wearing a bonnet with lilac ribbons; he remembered a man who had insulted him five years ago and whom he had not yet paid back; and yet — inseparable from these and thousands of other memories — the awareness of the moment. "But perhaps it won't explode," he thought, and with a desperate resolve tried to open his eyes. But at that moment a red fire pierced his eyes through his still closed eyelids and something struck him in the middle of the chest with a terrible crash; he started to run, stumbled over a sword under his feet and fell on his side.

"Thank God, I'm only bruised," was his first thought, and he tried to touch his chest with his hand, but his arms seemed fastened to his sides and his head seemed to be squeezed in a vice. Soldiers flitted past him and he counted them unconsciously: "one, two, three soldiers, and an officer with his greatcoat tucked up," he thought: then lightning flashed before his eyes and he thought — are they firing from a mortar or a cannon? A cannon probably, there's another shot, and there's some more soldiers — five, six, seven soldiers passing by. He suddenly became terrified they would trample on him; he wanted to cry out that he was wounded, but his mouth was so dry that his tongue stuck to the roof of his mouth and a terrible thirst tormented him. He felt how wet he was about the chest, and this sensation of wetness made him think of water and he even wanted to drink what it was that made him feel wet. "I probably hit myself when I fell and made myself bleed," he thought, and as he began to give way more and more to the fear that the soldiers who were still flitting past would trample on him, he gathered up all his strength and tried to shout "Take me with you," but instead gave such a dreadful groan that he was terrified to hear himself. Then some red fires began to dance before his eyes and it seemed to him that the soldiers were putting stones on top of him; the fires danced less and less, the stones they were putting on him pressed harder and harder. He made an effort to move the stones away, stretched himself, and no longer saw or heard or thought or felt a thing. He had been killed on the spot by a bomb-splinter in the middle of his chest.

— Leo Tolstoy

From "Sermon of the Younger Monica"

As a child I stole no pears. I was the pear that was stolen. I am here now, my children, to declare that we are all pears hanging by a fragile stem above our destruction. The sun shines, we are watered, we flower and come to fruition. Then the Vandals cut us down. They took Hippo where the Bishop died. They will take Carthage as well. In some days in some places you would not know this, that the Vandals always come. I didn't know it in the flush of my health and youth, but in this city at this time, you know it. What I am here to tell you is the other part.
      —Meredith Sue Willis

From "Kangaroo"

And here come these droves of mosquitoes out of nowhere. And me the only living thing in sight. I don't know what they do the rest of the time. If it weren't for me coming along like a bloody good Samaritan they'd probably have died. They're like torpedoes, never seen anything like them. The ones we have back in Sydney are real babies, cowards, compared with these ones. I had my shirt on, although it was stifling, but I didn't want to get my back burned. But the mosquitoes know how to bite through a shirt even. I must be anemic by this time, they drank so much.
      —Glenda Adams, *Lies and Stories*

From TO THE LIGHTHOUSE

Dear, dear, Mrs. Ramsay said to herself, how did they produce this incongruous daughter? this tomboy Minta, with a hole in her stocking? How did she exist in that portentous atmosphere where the maid was always removing in a dust-pan the sand that the parrot had scattered, and conversation was almost entirely reduced to the exploits — interesting perhaps but limited after all — of that bird? Naturally one had to ask her to lunch, tea, dinner, finally to stay with them up at Finlay, which had resulted in some friction with the Owl, her mother, and more calling, and more conversation, and more sand, and really at the end of it, she had told enough lies about parrots to last her a lifetime (so she had said to her husband that night, coming back from the party). However, Minta came...
Yes, she came, Mrs. Ramsay thought, suspecting some thorn in the tangle of this thought; and disengaging it found it to be this: a woman had once accused her of "robbing her of her daughter's affections"; something Mrs. Doyle had said made her remember that charge again. Wishing to dominate, wishing to interfere, making people do what she wished — that was the charge against her, and she thought it most unjust. How could she help being "like that" to look at? No one could accuse her of taking pains to impress. She was often ashamed of her own shabbiness. Nor was she domineering, nor was she tyrannical. It was more true about hospitals and drains and the dairy. About things like that she did feel passionate, and would, if she had the chance, have liked to take people by the scruff of their necks and make them see. No hospital on the whole island. It was a

disgrace. Milk delivered at your door in London positively brown with dirt. It should be made illegal. A model dairy and a hospital up here—those two things she would have liked to do, herself. But how? With all these children? When they were older, then perhaps she would have time; when they were all at school.

—Virginia Woolf

MORE MONOLOGUES BY STUDENTS

THE BEAUTIFUL OCEAN

I see the water when I look out the classroom window. It looks so peaceful. I wish I was on the boardwalk listening to the breakers. I can hear loud and clear but I'm about two or three miles away from the beach. I feel the breeze blowing and the sun shining on my face. I wish today wasn't a full day because I would just run down to the beach and lie in the sun listening to the ocean breakers. That sound makes me feel calm, free, and alone. I like that. No bratty brother or sister. I'm all by myself. No one can find me at the beach. I wish I could stay but it's a school day and I have to work all day long. I just wish I lived near the beach. Seeing the birds fly over the ocean. The calm peaceful waters catch my attention. I wish, I just wish I lived near the beach. Then I could go there everyday, when the sun is out. It just wouldn't be fun without the sun, a breeze, and the ocean. That's the kind of day I like. To me it may be fun, but to someone else it might be boring. I don't really care. I have my feelings and they have theirs. That's all I could say. The ocean. There's no place else like it. It really leaves me breathless.

—Pamela Taylor, 5th, P.S. 183, Queens

OLD LADY

I wonder when they'll be here. It's been so long since they came. I read the book he wrote, but it didn't mention me. Maybe they forgot. Three days ago they called to say yes. I don't know what to think. It's a clear day. Not too much traffic. Soon I have to go and rest. I got all dressed up for nothing. They said they'd be here at 3:00. It's 4:30 now. I can't guess what happened. Will they ever come? If they don't get here by 5:00 I'll call home. Oh, I wish they would come. Is it? Could it be? My son! My grandchildren! You're here, finally!

—Nell Maloney, 4th, P.S. 321, Brooklyn

157

•

I am tall and dark and everyone thinks I'm a mystery man.
I walk like a rhino and talk with a roar.
Once I killed a man, dead to the floor.
My eyes are oval and half shut.
My beard grows long.
And now I work as a lumber man.
My back is hunched and round and I'm growing old.
The muscles are big, my ax is sharp.
And now I killed another man.
And now I'm in court and I'll go to the electric chair.
 —Noel Garcia, 7th, I.S. 184, Bronx

•

I had the eye of a bird and my hobby was ballet. I wore a pink ribbon around my neck and never ever took it off. Today I wore a velours shirt, its color was light black. I was told at 16 I would become a lawyer, but my mother said I was too sweet for that kind of job. My mom's description of me was a sweet girl with a heart-shaped face.
 —Cecile Meunier, 4th, P.S. 6, Manhattan

A SECRET PORTRAIT

I think I have shining
bones. And blood like
melted wax. And a
brain very very very
very round. And eye
balls very round.
And I have a bone
city inside of
me.
 —Brian Ertel, 2nd, P.S. 321, Brooklyn

•

I am a circus oyster. I work for quite low wages. The ringmaster pays me three dollars a week so I buy a bag of goldfish crackers. Oh how I dream about joining Ringling Brothers and Barnum & Bailey Circus.
 But still here I am in my old tank with all of my memories like when I was put in the tank and the circus dog was in the tank. He pounced on me but my hard shell protected me. Then when I regained my color I said to him things that are unprintable.
 But here I am stuck here just making a living.
 —Oliver Mann, 5th, P.S. 321, Brooklyn

FRANKENSTEIN FEELINGS
THE WAY I BE FEELING

The way I be feeling and be killing people because they make me scared and be very mean. That's why I'm bad. When I'm good is when I'm

158

next to a child. I be very grateful to that person, and be so happy that I have a friend. And I love to help kids when a kitten is in a tree, but when I come to communicate with others, they just run, and that gets me very unhappy. And that's why I kill people. And be friends with others.

—Ferlie Lyons, 5th, P.S. 321, Brooklyn

•

I sit silently in this droll classroom completing my English assignment. I despise English so I grow restless, anxiously awaiting the 11:20 period of gym. Finally the time comes, I put my books away with no hesitation. As usual the teacher announces ladies on line then gentlemen on line or vice versa. I feel a sense of temporary relief as I walk through the prison-like hallways arriving at the gymnasium. All my other thoughts leave me at this time—hallelujah!

—Martin Signore, 6th, P.S. 6, Manhattan

•

The nerve of her! Constantly forcing me into tight, hard shoes. As if this isn't enough she does not help me by putting her whole weight on her feet (the way she should). Instead she performs strange antics with only me to support her. This goes on at least three times a week for two hours. After these periods of torture, I am covered with huge bleeding blisters and calluses. Instead of listening to the messages of pain that I send to her stupid brain, she continues doing this without a thought for me. One of these days I am going to refuse to put up with this anymore. Unfortunately right now I am being overpowered by her desires.

—Francesca Levine, 10th, Stuyvesant High School, Manhattan

•

Hi, I'm a stomach. And boy if you were me you wouldn't like all the nasty foods they give you. Carrots peas mashed potatoes some people even eat their skin off their cuts. And you know that's disgusting. Like my brother sometimes he cuts his toenails and eats them.

—Kalvin Bethel, 5th, P.S. 321, Brooklyn

LANDSCAPE INSIDE ME

I would have a cotton field with lots of soft cotton to keep me together. I picked soft cotton to keep me warm and soft. All you have to do is tippytoe across the soft, sweet-smelling cotton with bright white mountains of all kinds of soft lovable animals. When the animals play, they do it very gently and softly. When they walk they seem to be floating. They glide across the soft bright white mountains. When I walk I have a gliding flow to it, and when I run, I float on air. It's so lovely and brighter white inside me sometimes I feel like jumping inside myself and playing with the gentle animals.

—Dara Robinson, 6th, Hunter College Elementary
School, Manhattan

•

Well, that was nice of her. She told him I talk too much. I don't talk too much—I control my speech. I'm the one who lets others talk. She's the one who can't keep quiet. Maybe sometimes I get real excited about something and go on and on, but how often does that happen? Certainly not enough to call me a blabbermouth. Ha! Talks too much. Blabbermouth suits her more than me. She spends too much time listening only to herself. I respect other people's right to talk instead of always interrupting. People like listening to me...I think...don't they? No one has ever said anything before...If she doesn't want to listen, she doesn't have to. She can go off and talk to herself. She has the gall to say I talk too much when no one can get a word in edgewise with her for an hour. No one will listen to what she says about me—they all know she's the loudmouth.

—Ben Pesner, 10th, Stuyvesant High School, Manhattan

•

Now is the time. My legs are heavy and butterflies fly about my stomach. I hear my name called out over the loud-speaker and the echo repeats in my mind.

I walk towards the podium but am distracted by the soft whispers of the audience. When I reach the seemingly far away destination, I turn to the audience and begin my speech.

I finish flawlessly and have a strong feeling of pride. Thank God it's over!

—Michel Weiss, 6th, P.S. 6, Manhattan

160

Chapter 6: Creating Structure

The Shape of Fiction

I almost never begin my own fiction writing with a plot. I sometimes begin with a situation or a conflict, but more often I begin with fragments. Sometimes it is a thing I have seen (a house, a dog) or overheard (perhaps a snatch of conversation or a passage of music). Always it is something in which I feel meaning hidden, a sort of mystery. It is this hiddenness and mystery that carry me through the great effort of writing, along with the game of What If? and What might happen then? I always try to establish a voice, either a particular tone of my own voice or, if the piece is a first person narrative, an invented voice. I am always experimenting, figuring it out as I go, adding more ideas and fragments.

At some point I begin to see that the fragments are tending to lead toward a particular action or outcome; this is when the plot of the story starts to form for me. But that moment when I see the outline of the plot is far less important to me than another moment, the one at which I see what I call the *shape* of the work, its overall pattern or form, the whole of it. I may be reading or musing, perhaps as I sit on the subway, when I have a sudden, almost tactile vision of what the work I am engaged on is like. I have, briefly, a sense of it as a whole, of its form, its shape.

Nevertheless, I feel strongly that it is not necessary for every piece of writing to have a completed form. There is nothing wrong with writing fragments. There is no necessity for finishing everything — especially with children. I myself have files full of incomplete drafts and fragments. An essential freedom for writing well is the freedom to try things out, to say things on paper that may never be polished, typed, and exposed to the world. You can try things in fragments that you might never try in a piece of formal, finished writing. In my own writing, my unpublished fragments and prose poems are more experimental than my short stories, and the short stories freer in technique and subject matter than my novels. Many children are freed by being told they aren't supposed to finish today—that today's writing assignment is just a beginning or a fragment. In other words, the freedom not to finish can itself be a vital learning tool in writing.

Sometimes too, a fragment is not unfinished at all, but complete as it stands. Perhaps it has a very strong shape already—it may not be a story, but an anecdote or vignette. It might be the perfect length for what it is (and this is often true of an intense passage of, say, description by a young child), or else a piece of work whose main energy has been spent and has nowhere else to go.

When I was a child I made up my own book imprint, Black Horsey Books. I would spend hours folding and cutting the paper, stapling it into book form, painstakingly drawing the Black Horsey emblem in the corner, doing elaborate calligraphy and art work for the cover and then, after maybe a table of contents and a first chapter, I would run out of energy and quit. I might come back a few days later, but more likely I would have an idea for a new project. The stories I used in those books didn't really grip me. The point of the Black Horsey Books was to make a book, not write a story. A few times my mother asked me why I didn't finish them, and I would be temporarily embarrassed and declare of course I would finish, but the truth is that those book fragments *were* complete. I had taken them as far as they needed to go. Formal completion, it seems to me, is an adult concept that comes to children gradually. The type of writing discussed in this book need not be finished, at least not all the time. A child who writes *only* fragments may need a conference with the teacher where the array of fragments is spread out and the teacher says, "Look at all this work you've done this term. I'm going to give you a special assignment to choose any one of these pieces and finish it." For most children, though, a pile of beginnings and fragments is a great wealth, something I'm delighted to see.

Plot

There are, of course, ways to analyze, discuss directly, and write stories by using the elements of plot. Books on fiction writing often begin with just such descriptions and analysis, and, if you have an analytically inclined class, you might want to pick up one of these books (Janet Burroway's *Writing Fiction* is a college text that is readable and interesting). It is fun to find the elements of the story line and put them on the board for the class. Essentially the classical story line or plot is a complication or knotting up (*nouement* in French), a crisis and conflict, and a long or short untangling (the *dénouement*). You can experiment with a couple of stories everyone knows, such as "Goldilocks and the Three Bears" or "Cinderella," and make them fit the little chart, but I don't think this approach does much to help anyone's writing. Most students, in fact, grasp intuitively that a story has some problem and a climax.

This isn't to say that students can *write* one well, but their problems in story writing don't come from their not knowing what a story is. On the contrary, most students know only too well what a story is, and they will, if the teacher makes the mistake of saying "Let's write a story," do just that: write an imitation of whatever books are popular with children this year, or the standard plots of television melodramas, or a traditional fairy tale. Writing TV plots or retelling fairy tales can be respectable assignments, but if that is what the children write, I want to have assigned it myself so it will be clear what we're doing. I don't want it to exclude other types of writing.

Some students, from about the fourth grade up, can write near-professional family problem fiction—the sort of thing done so well by Judy Blume. Some will write reams and reams of stories about girls with impossible younger siblings or a problem with braces. These student imitations are usually full of conversation, focus on real life conflict and humor, and have some lesson to teach. Here is a miniature example of the genre.

A DARK STREAK OF GREEN

It was at recess time after lunch at P.S. 223. A girl named Lisa was playing double dutch with her friends. But another girl named Yvette was playing too. Lisa could jump very good. Lisa was so good in double dutch that she was interviewed on the news program "Live at Five" and also because she became the star in the class. The teacher admired Lisa too. A dark streak of green came before Yvette of envy towards Lisa.

So one day Yvette said to Lisa, "How did you get so good, Lisa?"

Lisa said, "I'm just good!! And anyway, what do you want to know for, I'm the best and that's that."

Yvette said in her mind, "Well, that's what you think," and got on the elevator.

Lisa said, "I didn't want to say this, but I'm jealous of you because you can ride on the elevator by yourself."

Yvette sat there with her mouth open, and then said, "Uuh, uuh, I'm jealous of you too because you can jump wonderfully. Well, I'll help you gain your courage to ride the elevator if you help me jump good."

"Well okay," Lisa said.

That day the dark streak of green went away as the light green streak came in with happiness and friendliness.

—Karen·Duhart, 5th, P.S. 124, Queens

Karen's story would not be mistaken for writing by an adult, but it does have the conflict and solution necessary for a "realistic" kids' story. My favorite part of the story is the careful distinction between the two shades of green, and the moment when that dark streak gets between Yvette and her friend.

Story form, then, is easily accessible to most student writers. If there is any problem with their "story" writing, it is that many of them have trouble finishing what they start. The energy runs out; they get bored and end with one of those famous truncations: "And then he shot the bad guys and got the money and was famous. The End." Period. What I call the "Get-off-my-back" school of story writing. The more serious challenge is how to make sure the students are really writing about essential material and not just filling in the outline of what they think is a story.

Conflict

I think that a better way of approaching story writing is to begin where the energy is — at the heart of why the student wants to write this particular story. Thinking of conflict first is one good way to do this (see chapter 5). Every real story (as opposed to a vignette or a prose poem) needs some sort of conflict. Conflict is a nice word in its derivation, too: it comes from the Latin and means "strike together." This gives me the image of stones striking together to make a spark, or even cymbals being clashed. The word is also used to mean everything from a genteel disagreement ("We had a conflict over the placement of the forks") to a full-scale world war ("The threat of global conflict..."). I like to do a brainstorming on the blackboard with all the kinds of conflict the students can think up, under headings such as conflicts at home, conflicts at school, conflicts with friends. What causes conflicts? Money? Food? Love? Conflicts within oneself are fruitful for writing. I like to make a huge list, with plenty of ideas for anyone who doesn't have one already, and then I often read one of the following two tiny but complete stories with strong central conflicts.

From NERVOUS PEOPLE

We're sitting at the table and eating pancakes.

Suddenly my father takes my plate and begins eating my pancakes. I howl.

My father is wearing glasses. He has a serious look. A beard. Nevertheless, he is laughing. He says, "You see how greedy he is. He won't give his father one pancake."

I say, "You're welcome to one pancake, go ahead and eat it. I thought you were going to eat them all."

The soup is brought in.

I say, "Papa, do you want my soup?"

Papa says, "No, I'll wait till they bring the dessert. Now, if you give me your dessert, then you're really a kind boy."

Thinking dessert is cranberry pudding with milk, I say, "You're welcome to it. You may eat my dessert."

Then they bring in a Bavarian cream, to which I am not indifferent.

Pushing my plate of Bavarian cream over to my father, I say, "Go ahead and eat it if you're so greedy."

My father frowns and leaves the table.

My mother says, "Go to your father and ask his forgiveness."

I say, "I won't go. I didn't do anything wrong."

I leave the table without touching dessert.

At night when I'm lying in bed, my father comes in. He is carrying my plate of Bavarian cream.

My father says, "Well, why didn't you eat your pudding?"

I say, "Papa, let's eat it together. Why should we quarrel over this?"

My father kisses me and feeds me the cream with a spoon.
— Mikhail Zoshchenko

"A Little Fable"

"Alas," said the mouse, "the world is growing smaller every day. At the beginning it was so big that I was afraid. I kept running and running, and I was glad when at last I saw walls far away to the right and left, but these long walls have narrowed so quickly that I am in the last chamber already, and there in the corner stands the trap that I must run into." "You only need to change your direction," said the cat, and ate it up.
— Franz Kafka, *The Complete Stories*

Story Building

Another method of teaching story writing, one that does not depend on the students' previous knowledge of plot from popular literature and television, uses the chapters of this book as an outline for building a story. I use this method when I want a fiction writing project that extends over a period of time. I begin with Place, insisting that no one should do more than a beginning the first day. I make a game of my insistence on this point, but it is essential to the method that the students get involved in the action only gradually. I want the students to take a long time visualizing the setting and working out the sense details of a place. This sort of writing prepares the reader better for what is to come later, but, more important, it encourages the writer to imagine thoroughly the setting for the story. The intense description can act as a sort of meditation, too, and sometimes a new idea crops up that would never have occurred to the writer had he or she plunged into the plot and action at once.

At the second session we introduce people into the setting where the story is taking place. Again the emphasis is on description and on thinking through the characters of the people being described. Karen Duhart's piece above would probably have profited from more time spent on describing the school yard and then letting us know what the girls looked like, how they

165

dressed and moved.

When the place and the people have been described, it is time to get to some action. A discussion of conflict and climax would probably help pull the story together (at this point I often use *Nervous People* on page 164), but the emphasis is on using a leisurely, descriptive beginning to give the student time to feel through the material of the story. For most children, by the second or third writing session, the categories of elements of fiction begin merging as they properly should; the child is off on a tear, plunging ahead, or else has lost interest and is ready to try something else.

Here is a sample of writing that was done by Story Building in a third grade class. You'll notice that from the beginning the writer mixes in his action with sense details and description.

•

I was in the deep green forest. I heard gunshots as the leaves shattered below my feet. I gripped the fur of my horse. I lifted my rifle. The birds were singing. A hawk circled around. I could hear the rattling of a rattlesnake. I aimed my rifle as my feet shook in my boots. I heard foot steps. My legs were ready to dash, but my head wouldn't let them. Just at that very second a big bear rose in front of me. Then my legs just couldn't take it. I shot one bullet and jumped upon my horse and fled, but the bear was close behind. Finally I was racing up the mountainside where my cabin was. I quickly put my horse in the stable and raced into the house and slammed the door behind me. I could smell fresh biscuits and soup my mother was cooking in the kitchen. My father just came in by the door and asked what's that banging on the door. I tried to tell him, but no sound came out. Finally sound came out. I told him about the bear. When my father heard that, he ran for his rifle. He came back with a rifle in his hand. Quickly he shot the bear! My father smiled, Boy that was a biggy. I smiled too. My father was a tall man with brown hair and a moustache. He wore buckskin pants and a fringed leather shirt. My father was a kind man. Just then, Ma called us for dinner, so I had dinner, and then I went to bed.

– Joel Kafka, 3rd, P.S. 321, Brooklyn

I think Joel probably could have come up with the action of this story without any intervention from a teacher, but I suspect that the detailed description of sounds and smells would not have come to him on his own.

•

Most of the assignments and samples from adult and children's writing in this book suggest other strong and natural forms for organizing material as well as from story. Consider for example the idea in chapter 2 of describing a place by seeing it from a distance and then walking gradually nearer and nearer and finally into it. This movement is a highly structured

166

way of choosing which piece of information goes where. Describing how a person looks, and at the same time revealing the narrator's feeling about that person, is another sophisticated way of pulling together observations. Even something as simple as describing a place or person by using all the senses offers a form that could, in fact, be too rigid if overused. It is essential to realize that organization is not a cookie cutter, but an interaction between the creator and material. It is not a grid on which a story is laid out but a part of the very process of thinking and perceiving and writing. One of the writer's greatest challenges is to find a way of embodying and developing the form that grows from the original conception. All the best techniques for getting students started are also the ones that help them discover the important subjects and find the subject's natural shape.

Some of the best ways of finding that natural shape begin with what I like to think of as naturally occurring forms, such as dreams, memories, and life stories.

Dreams

One of my favorite forms to use with students of all ages — and this includes college students and adults — is dream writing. A discussion about dreams opens up the mouths of children who never talked before; almost everyone has been gripped by the power of a dream. Dreams are a good source for writing: they have emotional power and a vivid content and they often come with their own built-in structure. A dream is complete when you wake up in the morning; it is as much of a whole as "Cinderella" or "The Three Bears," and it has some of that same quality of inevitability — as if it could have happened only that one way.

As a teacher you have to be prepared for the violence and weirdness of dreams. Sometimes dreams bring disquieting material to the surface, but most children are reassured to discover that many people have nightmares, that they are a common fact of human life. I should also add that I don't use dream writing with a new class because dreams *are* intimate, best written and read in a supportive situation where the people have some familiarity with one another.

Below are two of my favorite stimulus pieces for dream writing. Because everyone knows what a dream (or nightmare) is, the examples in this case are much less necessary than a good discussion.

A DREAM THAT MY DOG WAS CHOPPED TO BITS

It all started in a meeting, and I brought my little dog. So I let my dog go thinking that she won't go anywhere. But she went where some kids were and the kids scared her into a house that I've never seen before. I ran very fast, and when I got to the house, I was exhausted. But I ran into the house, and I saw the kids, and one of them gave me a tail. It was my dog's tail; so I started walking slowly till I got to this room where there were a lot of kids. And a lady came out with a platter, and on the platter was my little dog cut to bits. The lady told me, Too late, Luis, she is dead. I was so angry that I went to hit her, but just as I was going to hit her, she disappeared. I walked slowly out of the house, and I went to my house. Very sadly I open the door, and there was my little dog licking my face, and when I woke up, she was licking my face.

—Luis Tapia, 5th, P.S. 75, Manhattan

HANDS

I

When I fall asleep
my hands leave me.

They pick up pens
and draw creatures
with five feathers
on each wing.

The creatures multiply.
They say: "We are large
like your father's
hands."

They say: "We have
your mother's
knuckles."

I speak to them:
"If you are hands,
why don't you
touch?"

And the wings beat
the air, clapping.
They fly

high above elbows
and wrists.
They open windows
and leave

rooms.
They perch in treetops
and under bushes
biting

their nails. "Hands,"
I call them.
But it is fall

and all creatures

with wings
prepare to fly
South.

II

When I sleep
the shadows of my hands come to me.

They are softer than feathers
and warm as creatures
who have been close
to the sun.

They say: "We are the vessel,"
and tell of journeys
through water.

They say: "We are the cup."

And I stir in my sleep.
Hands pull triggers

and cut
trees. But

The shadows of my hands
tuck their heads
under wings waiting
for morning,

when I will wake
braiding

three strands of hair
into one.

—Siv Cedering Fox

Some children responded:

•

I once dreamed that there was an election for leader of a children's world. All the kids were voting for me or Rebecca. I won. We had a big celebration. Everybody went down into the subway station and rode on small dinosaurs.

All my friends were there. There were tin swings with graffiti on them. A wooden structure stood in the middle of the station. If you climbed a ladder you could stand on top of it.

We sang for joy. We sang hymns and sang to God, rejoicing for me to be their leader.

After the celebration, I went outside. Evil faces looked at me. Swearing that they would get back at me.

169

I ran and ran. I ran to my mother and father, and they ran with me to the subway station.

When we got there, we saw the dinosaurs. The tin swings were gone. A train was coming. It was roaring at us. Screeching brakes. Silence.

My mother, father and I continued to walk. We couldn't stop. I tried to scream, but nothing came out. The tracks were getting closer and closer. I could see the garbage on the tracks. There was a boy and a man climbing on top of the tracks. I saw the faces. The idea of dying frightened me.

All of a sudden my feet stopped moving. We were safe. My mother, my father, and I started running. We ran till we were out of the station.

My mother and father went home. I stayed outside on Carroll Street. I was in the Children's world now. All of my friends came out and I played a reed-pipe. I thought I saw Pan come out of his cave.

We sat outside till late in the evening. I watched the stars and felt happy. Joy ran through my body, warming me with love for the world.
　　　　　—Simone Dinnerstein, 5th, P.S. 321, Brooklyn

MY GOOD NIGHTMARE

I had a very good nightmare. It was about my niece and me walking in a park. Then black and gray creatures came out of the ground. There were about three of them surrounding us. My niece was six and I was sixteen. She yelled for her mother who is my sister. Then the creatures said, "There ain't no use my chil', ain't nobody gonna hear ya anyway." One of them grabbed my niece. Then I broke wild and said, "Listen here you, you...." Then a nymph walked up and said, "Don't ever fight a demon of the devil, my child." So the nymph pointed her finger at my niece and said, "My Holy God, Lord in Jesus name, release this child from the devil's chain." Then my niece appeared and the nymph told us to run home. Then I told my niece, "You know the nymph wasn't a nymph. She must have been an angel!" Then my niece said, "What's a nymph?" Then I woke up.
　　　　　—Govai Jones, 5th, P.S. 183, Queens

I like the way these dream writers plunge into the experience in their writing. They don't fool around with Once-upon-a-time's. The style seems assured and more sophisticated than much of student writing. This is the strength of dream writing— it has a quality that encourages concise and vivid writing.

There are many assignments using dreams:

•**Idea 324:** Collect your dreams for a week or ten days. Write in the present tense as if the dream were happening to you at this very moment.

•**Idea 325:** As an experiment, choose one dream, and write it in the third person, as a story, and compare that version with the first person version. Do you like one better? What changed?

•**Idea 326:** Write a dream or nightmare that you *might* have had. Is it different in some way from your regular dreams?

•**Idea 327:** Make up the dream or nightmare of a famous person.

•**Idea 328:** Make up the dream of an animal or a plant.

•**Idea 329:** Make up the dream of an inanimate object like a desk, a revolver, a Christmas angel.

•**Idea 330:** Imagine that some part of you flies off in the night or takes a trip like the hands in the poem "Hands." Describe what happens.

•**Idea 331:** Write a dream from your distant past.

•**Idea 332:** Write the beginning of some real dream you have had, and exchange papers with a friend. Finish the friend's dream while she or he finishes yours.

•**Idea 333:** Turn one of your dreams into a play and act it out.

•**Idea 334:** Make one into a comic book; a poem; a picture.

Memories

Just as dreams often have a wholeness, a natural shape, so do memories. They, too, often result in finished pieces of writing with a beginning, middle, and end. Often these memories, especially early memories, are associated with sense impressions or important events. I have a powerful word memory from when I was around two-and-a-half years old and was told my dog had been poisoned with "ground glass." The words stuck in my mind; I didn't understand that there can be two meanings to a word. So I squatted down in the back yard and looked at the earth, the "ground," for the poison glass that killed my dog.

One example of an early memory I like to use is the following selection by the great American painter Georgia O'Keeffe, who writes from a perspective of being more than ninety years old.

From GEORGIA O'KEEFFE

My first memory is of the brightness of light — light all around. I was sitting among pillows on a quilt on the ground — very large white pillows. The quilt was a cotton patchwork of two different kinds of material — white with very small red stars spotted over it quite close together, and black with a red and white flower on it. I was probably eight or nine months old. The quilt is partially a later memory, but I know it is the quilt I sat on that day.

This was all new to me — the brightness of light and pillows and a quilt and ground out beyond. My mother sat on a bench beside a long table, her back turned to me. A friend called Aunt Winnie stood at the end of the table in profile. I don't remember what my mother looked like — probably because she was familiar to me. Aunt Winnie had goldish hair done high on top of her head — a big twist of blond hair and lots of curly bangs. My mother was dark, with straight hair and I had never seen a blond person. Aunt Winnie's dress was thin white material, a little blue flower with a sprig of green patterned over it. The bodice was close fitting with long tight sleeves, the skirt straight and plain in front and very full and puffed and ruffled at the back — a long dress touching the ground all around, and even trailing a little extra long in the back.

Years later I told my mother that I could remember something that I saw before I could walk. She laughed and said it was impossible. So I described that scene — even to the details of the material of Aunt Winnie's dress. She was much surprised and finally — a bit unwillingly — acknowledged that I must be right, particularly because she, too, remembered Winnie's dress.

         — Georgia O'Keeffe

It is not surprising that light and color should organize a painter's earliest memory. This one appears accurate, too — first the overall impression of light, then the near objects: pillow, quilt. At a little distance, and passed over quickly, the familiar figure of the mother, then the striking blonde stranger. Finally details of the stranger's clothing. The movement of the passage follows the track of the baby's eye.

•**Idea 335:** Write that kind of memory, one that follows the mind as it apprehends each thing, but do it with something other than an event — perhaps with a memory of an early, beloved possession or a memory that begins with a strong sense impression.

    •

    Once there was this little fire engine. Actually, I had two engines, one plastic and one metal, but I liked the plastic fire engine more. Mainly because I can keep it inside the apartment. The metal one was too old and big to keep inside the house. I liked this fire engine. It had many different knobs and levers. At that time it made me feel important. I had fun going around the house and making a sound similar to a huge locomotive. It was just big enough so I could sit on it. It relaxed me everytime I was near that damn thing. The engine and I had a lot of good times. The best was crashing into walls and people.

         — David Chait, 10th, Stuyvesant High, Manhattan

    •

    I remember the first time I had been in the company of a now-close friend. There was a certain smell about him, a kind of boyish smell. I didn't mind it at all, it seemed sort of personal to me. Now that spring has arrived, we were walking together without our jackets and I smelled that smell again. For some reason, whether I was glad it was spring, or I was in

a good mood, I felt very happy and secure. The smell just reminded me of rolling in hay, or someone who just finished participating in an exerting sport. I probably like it because I like what it reminds me of. Smell is like that. Smell something bad and you'll scrunch up your nose and say, "Boy that reminds me of . . ." Memories are conjured up, association occurs, etc. etc. I really don't know what I'm saying. I simply felt happy to smell that smell of my friend as opposed to the other things I could have smelled.
—Anonymous, Stuyvesant High School, Manhattan

The latter piece is a good example of the sort of touching real life material that can be turned into fiction. The writer begins with something striking, vivid, or important, and builds on that. One of the most famous of these memory-elicited works is Marcel Proust's enormous and magnificent novel *Remembrance of Things Past,* which is in part about the action of memory—how incidents are forgotten, how people are remembered differently in different contexts. The cornerstone of Proust's whole vast edifice is a memory recalled to his narrator by the taste of a bit of cake that has been soaked in a spoonful of tea.

The more usual and less ambitious type of memory writing is the incident: some event with a beginning, a middle, an end. This gives the writer a plot which can then be fleshed out or changed and fictionalized. The strength of starting with memory material, like starting with dream material, is that the overall plan is given by the material itself.

•**Idea 336:** Write an embarrassing or unpleasant incident from your memory. Change the ending of it in any way you want. Perhaps put it in the third person—give the character a name different from yours and make her or him say or do what you failed to.

•**Idea 337:** Write a memory a day for five days, using as a starting point a different sense each day.

•**Idea 338:** Make an individual or class memory collection. You might include everyone's Earliest Memory, Three Memories Before I Started School, My First Day of School (see model on page 115), My Best/Worst Birthday, Trip, Vacation, Party, etc.

•**Idea 339:** Draw a box. Into it sketch from memory a favorite snapshot of you when you were younger. Write what you were thinking at that moment.

•**Idea 340:** Do the same thing with a real baby snapshot of you.

•**Idea 341:** Have everyone bring in snapshots and mix them up, pass them around so that, if possible, no one knows whose they have. Write a story based on the situation in the snapshot you end up with.

•**Idea 342:** Do the same thing with snapshots of your family when they were younger.

•**Idea 343:** Collect the childhood memories of all the members of your family, but especially from grandparents and great-grandparents. What was the most exciting thing that happened to your grandfather when he was a child? What is your grandmother's earliest memory?

•**Idea 344:** Write some of these pretending you are the person having the memory.

•**Idea 345:** Find out and write down the story of how your parents met.

•**Idea 346:** Find out and write down the story of your birth.

•**Idea 347:** Collect other people's memories of you when you were a baby.

Life Stories

Another form with a natural wholeness that is particularly good for more extended writing is the biographical or autobiographical piece. Many of the suggestions for writing assignments in the Memories section above feed into such a project.

One's own life often seems untidy — certainly hard to have a perspective on — but the life of someone else can be seen as one of the great natural structures for a piece of writing. Biographies all use the form, of course, and so do many novels, ranging from *David Copperfield* to *The World According to Garp:* birth, childhood, initiation into adulthood, struggles for success, change, and then death or some other form of stasis. One of the reasons I like biography as a form is the opportunity it offers to consider and record change, development, growth, degeneration. Turns of fortune and reversals of fate are always gripping material — the natural source of plot.

Junior high and high school students seem especially drawn to writing life stories. Puberty is one of the most drastic physical changes we go through, and students of that age are also facing decisions and choices and further changes that will direct the whole course of their lives. They begin to see that they are in the middle of a continuum, and they see other people's lives as good and bad examples, having meaning for them in their choices.

I first used the idea of life stories when I was working with seventh graders in the South Bronx. They had written descriptions of people that shocked me with the intensity of their cruel humor. I had neglected to make any ground rules about not writing about classmates, so I got some of the most vivid writing I had ever had from them — pimples you could see, bad breath you could smell. What I wanted was to keep some of the vigor of the language but to get more compassion from them, so I brought in part of a year-end report from a storefront school on the Lower East Side of Manhattan where I used to teach a creative writing workshop. This piece by an adult, whose name I have since lost, was not written for publication; it is a report written for work.

PAPO: BY HIS TEACHER

Papo came to the school last year. Sixteen years old, he couldn't read, write or do basic math. His health was very poor — he had asthma, chronic bronchitis and colds, and during the first part of the year, he was hospitalized several times for other health problems. Papo was convinced that he was "stupid" and couldn't learn; his frequent and prolonged absences reinforced his sense of failure and despair. Outside of school, he was involved in a lot of very negative acting out, which constantly pulled him further away from a sense of growing and achieving. Still, he finished the year at the school and, despite a great deal of hostility and paranoia, seemed to feel that he belonged here.

The first semester of this year seemed like a re-run of the last: great frustration and resistance combined with repeated absences kept him from progressing in his work — although there were small changes, signs that he felt more secure. Papo smiled more often; he was less likely to provoke fights, and he studied furiously for the tests I gave. (Last year he stayed home whenever a test was scheduled.) He was in trouble because of his absences and lateness, and was on "probation" when, before Christmas, he got hepatitis and was out for six weeks. When he came back, he was a different person — fairly regular in his attendance, very serene, and extremely serious about his work. It was a joy just to look at him. His face, which once had been tight and drawn with suspicion and anger, was sweet and peaceful. Physically, he was growing rapidly, and his once-frail body was becoming strong and mature. His progress in class was extremely slow and difficult, but — for the first time — he allowed himself to be aware of and take pride in his small victories. He even participated enthusiastically in a few group activities, such as Yoga (for which he showed a remarkable natural ability), First-Aid, and Filmmaking. Papo's self-confidence had been so shattered that he could not work unless I was sitting next to him, silently reassuring him that yes, he could do it and was doing it. The beauty of the school is that, when he needed my presence, he and I were given the "luxury" of being able to work together one-on-one. Within a few months, he was spending long periods of time working on his own.

Papo was reading on a second grade level and making steady progress when suddenly, in late April, he stopped coming to school. He had taken a full-time job working in a factory. Papo had become such a calm and steady presence in the school that we missed him a great deal, but working full-time seemed the best thing for him. He was 18 now, moving into new worlds. Whenever we saw him, he seemed very happy. Then, several months after starting the job, he lost two fingers of his right hand in an accident at the factory.

Thinking about Papo raises many unanswerable questions for me. The rage and impatience of his first year here seem so clear and understandable. What forces led to the great change in him in the middle of the year? Papo had been into some heavy stuff that could have led him to jail or worse. Why does one kid find his way through this, when so many do not? And then, after such a long and difficult struggle, why is he stopped so tragically?

Papo cannot go back to work. He has applied for disability, and says that now he will come back to the school to work on his reading. We will welcome him back, although going back to school at this time will mean, for him, being thrown back to a level he had already left behind and will raise serious conflicts for him. Hopefully we will be able to help him work them through.

This spring, after my reading class had a sensitive, spontaneous talk about the dangers of rooftops (Papo had seen a friend plunge to his death as they played there several years ago), he dictated the following thoughts: "Up on the roof, there's many things to do. You could have a lot of fun. But it's very dangerous cause you could fall off the roof. Up on the roof I like to fly birds. I like to feed them. I like to fly them. But most of all, I would like to be one of them."

•**Idea 348:** After reading this, write about someone you know who changed.

HOW RODNEY CHANGED FROM SCAREDY CAT TO ALMOST BRAVE

When Rodney first came to our school, I thought he was retarded (no offense) but later on I found out he was all right so I started to be his friend.

Later on I noticed that he let a lot of people push and beat on him. So I started to tell him he shouldn't let people hit on him like that, but he didn't pay any attention to what I said, so I let him do what he wanted. And later on he started to improve, whenever a boy hit him he would hit them back. Then about a week or so ago he started hitting some girls back, except Lavander, Yvette, Kecia and me. But sometimes he wanted to knocked the devil out of Kecia, but he's scared. Hopefully when he grows older he'll learn to hit almost everyone when they hit him.
— Gina Coward, 7th, I.S. 184, Bronx

MY BROTHER

My brother, when he was 6, he used to be considerate to my mother. He used to help her go shopping; he was low in his grades (although he was good in school he hardly ever passed a test.) When he was 9 or 10 he put his leg out of place when he fell off the bump-beds. (He got left back in the fifth grade cause of his leg.) After that he lost his kindness and wasn't considerate anymore. He never helped my mother since then. Although he isn't kind anymore, he improved in his grades, rapidly too. In fact he was once a 3.7 reader, now he's a 7.8 reader.
— Richard Morales, 7th, I.S. 184, Bronx

•**Idea 349:** A variation on this assignment is to write about the change itself. The idea is to tell how the person was, what happened, and how he or she is now (another neat and natural structure).

The students who wrote the following pieces were in a remedial reading skills class and they asked a lot of questions after I read "Papo": Was he a real boy? Did I know him? What happened to him? We had two class periods to work on the pieces, and the students thus had far more time than usual to extend, reconsider, and correct the pieces. Willie Lee Young writes a straightforward narrative with a simple conclusion: his friend is what he is because his brother taught him. Vanessa's piece takes place more in her own mind as she goes back and forth about this man Skip, why he is the way he is, what he says, what she thinks about it. Deborah's is the basic plot for a whole story, or even a novel. All three pieces show acute observation of what happens to people in our world.

•

I know a man. His name is Skip. He is a "wine-old." He said the reason being that way is that his wife left him. And she took all the furniture and beds. He had nothing but himself. And I guess he was lonesome. But I don't understand that because he can always get married again. But I guess she was the only one he loved very much. He was so happy. When she left, it was sorrow for him.
— Vanessa Wise, 7th, J.H. 258, Brooklyn

•

My friend named Ronnie was once a good little lad. He is only 12 or 13. He never stole anything or beat up on anyone. But now that he found new friends, he steals cars and robs people. None of my friends like him anymore.
It all started when he first moved on the block. He would steal candy and things like that. His bigger brother was in jail. Then he got out, then Ronnie and his brother would go out and steal mini-motorcycles. But now that he knows new friends, he steals cars and things like that. So his brother taught him these things.
— Willie Lee Young, 7th, J.H. 258, Brooklyn

•

It all started when she first went there. She didn't know any of the boys and girls who went there. In about a week or two she knew about the kids. And they became her friends. In about a month they started her to smoke, and smoke pot, and stuff like that, and her grades were getting poor, and she started not doing her work, and cutting classes like she was out on the street, and then she dropped out of school. But now since she dropped out, she doesn't smoke or smoke pot. She met this cute boy, and now they have been going together for about a year. And then she got pregnant by him. When it was time for the baby to be delivered, the doctor said that the baby is dead, and my cousin was crying, and now she goes to another school, and she is doing very well in her new school. And she met some very nice friends in school.
— Deborah Williams, 7th, J.H. 258, Brooklyn

•

177

There are, then, assignments that will encourage wholeness and completion just as there are assignments that will encourage experimentation and fragmentation. The teacher needs to develop a sensitivity to what form might be most appropriate to a given piece of writing. This sensitivity comes, of course, from working with children and texts, and it is as delicate and difficult a work as writing itself. Teaching is an art too, one whose actual successes are often so subtle that they are lost from view in the growth and development of the students. I doubt, in fact, that we ever know the most far-reaching effects we have had on our students.

The aim in teaching should always be first to encourage the initial plunge into thinking, imagining, and remembering, and then to offer ways to deepen, extend, tighten, and complete the work. To a large extent, though, writing is always a self-taught discipline. This can be a comfort to us as teachers: we create an atmosphere and make suggestions about the work directly or through our proferred models and exercises, but in the end, it is the student, reviewing and imagining, playing and struggling, who writes. We are joyous witnesses, not the most important part of the process, but vital to it.

•

I want to end this book by telling how another book grew and found its own natural form. Some years ago I published a story in a small literary magazine. It was, as it always is, a thrill to see my words in print, but I didn't really expect anyone to pick up the tiny magazine and read it unless I personally handed them a copy. A few weeks after the magazine appeared, I received a phone call from an editor at *Esquire* magazine. He had read and liked my story and wanted to see more. We made an appointment, and I immediately mailed him everything I had written in the last five years. In my fantasy, this was the Big Break. This was It. I was going to be published in something besides little magazines; I was going to appear in a slick magazine that strangers could buy in airport newsstands all across the country, and probably in foreign countries too. I was, in this fantasy, on my way to prizes, wealth, book contracts, my picture on the cover of *Time* magazine, the Nobel Prize.

It turned out that although the editor liked my writing, he didn't think I had anything suitable for his magazine. But he definitely wanted me to write something new and send it to him. Looking back now, I think that what he mainly wanted to do was encourage me. I, however, took what he said as a challenge. I acted as if I'd been given an assignment that I didn't like. Nothing of mine was suitable? Fine, I'd write something just perfect for him and his precious magazine. I must have had a pretty poor opinion of the magazine, though, because I decided to write something very contemporary (so I thought) in that it would be sexually explicit and ugly. Using a cynical voice that was not natural or comfortable to me, I wrote a story that I thought was the ultimate in nasty sophistication of a sort that I myself don't enjoy at all. I called the story "Fat Marsala," and it was about a girl from a small town who goes to the big city and has some grotesque experiences eating artichoke hearts in olive oil and having sex in a bathtub. I didn't like the girl much, and I think the story secretly embarrassed me. But I was sure it was just what they would love at *Esquire*. The editor, however, had the good taste not to like it, and neither did my friends. My feelings were terribly hurt: I had been a good girl, tried to please people, and they had not been satisfied.

Some months passed, and I reread the story when I had a little distance on the thing. As I read it, I admitted to myself that there was only one part of the story that I liked, and it occurred to me that I could hardly expect other people to like something I didn't like myself. I learned two things from this reading of the story, one general and one specific. The general one was that I could not write well unless I was authentically connected to what I was writing. I realized that even with college term papers, the best ones were those I was most involved in, the ones that I actually got excited about. I vowed never again to write anything that I did not feel, at some level, truly gripped by. This general lesson underlies my approach to teaching writing.

The specific thing I learned from rereading "Fat Marsala" had to do with that one passage that I liked. It was a brief flashback to Marsala's childhood when she was baptized by immersion. In the context of the story this was supposed to be shocking and blasphemous, but instead, when I reread it, I went musing back on my own baptism, and the kind of experience it had been. Then I started wondering: What if, I thought, what if, on top of being afraid of drowning, the girl had also to contend with the fact that it was her own father, a Baptist minister, who was the one baptizing her? My own father was a school teacher, and I remembered the feeling of being in his classes in high school. What if, I thought. What if?

So I started again, to make a new short story, based on a fictionalized memory: the story of a little girl who has a struggle with her father, a preacher, over her baptism. I wrote the story, and then started playing What If some more about the stubborn little girl. What would she be like when she got older? I wrote a draft of another story, and by the time I was finished, I knew I wanted to write a novel because I was getting interested in the other characters, the minister, the girl's mother, and sister. Starting from a tiny flashback in a failed story, I came up with the manuscript of my first published novel, *A Space Apart*. The book never soared onto the bestseller charts, but it received encouraging reviews and had a respectable sale. It is certainly a book of which I am proud.

The point I want to make is that *A Space Apart* grew and took shape in its own jerky, idiosyncratic way. I discovered its organization and many of its subjects in the process of writing it.

I think this process of writing holds true in some general way for essays and other nonfiction too. The book you are now reading began with my work with children — with my memories of days in classrooms, and with a mass of material written by adults and children. Out of looking over the material and mulling over the experiences came a certain order, or at least a progression in my mind — an outline of five or six words: Introduction, Place, Person, Inside and Out, Dialogue, Action. Conclusion. Then came a plunge in, rough sketches, adding new parts, and then taking away and re-arranging. If the book has any coherence, it comes from an internal logic that developed little by little, during the very act of writing.

Appendix A: Notes on Revision

As a writer, I feel that revision is so closely entwined with the other elements of writing that I can hardly imagine separating it out. For me revision doesn't mean editing for grammatical errors, or even polishing the surface of a piece of writing (although those things certainly need to be done). My idea of real revision involves a rechewing and redigesting of material over and over again until it comes as close as possible to its own best form. The result rarely satisfies me completely, although I am often pleased. This impossibility of perfection is perhaps a lesson for adults rather than for children. Children will learn it in good time, if not about prose, then about life. I really believe that the ability to go back and plunge into the work — to start over repeatedly — is the most difficult and advanced lesson in writing.* In my teaching I tend to be more concerned that students find a fruitful way to begin their writing and then find the forms natural to what they want to express.

Because of their fear of making mistakes, children don't revise easily. They associate change in their written work with having failed to get it right the first time. For this reason, what is needed is a way of creating the same kind of experimental, playful feeling about revising (adding to, taking away, choosing different words) that a child might have when facing a ball of modelling clay. I want to find ways to show my students that *words and sentences are malleable.* This is one of the most important things a teacher

---

*One interesting approach to teaching writing works directly with the idea of constant revision. This is the "writing process method" developed by Donald Graves and others. I recommend Graves' book *Writing: Teachers and Children at Work* to any classroom teacher looking for a complete program that focuses primarily on revision and writing out of actual experience.

181

can share with students: that a piece of writing can be manipulated and molded like clay.

One of the first kinds of revision I find myself suggesting to students is the addition of more details — the part the writer saw or heard mentally and assumed that the reader would also see and hear without being told. One important lesson to learn in writing is how much must be made explicit. For young adult writers, interestingly enough, often the opposite thing happens: the writer tends to tell too much and insults the reader's intelligence. Learning to balance how much to tell and how much to leave to the reader's imagination is a lifetime endeavor, but, for younger children, it usually begins with telling more.

I approach this essential concept of revision with a game in which the students manipulate someone else's words. It then becomes clear that students are also free to change their own writing.

•**Idea 350:** I call this game the Cat and the Box, although any two short, concrete, common nouns could be used in place of "cat" and "box." Divide the class into Group A and Group B and have the A's write on their paper the word "cat." The other groups gets "box." The game is to take the boring little word and, during a five-minute period, make it interesting by adding anything you want: a story context, lots of adjectives, or whatever. Typically you will get descriptive passages ("A huge red box with gold stars and silver moons on the side and a sign that says Do Not Open"), or slightly longer, miniature stories ("The black cat with the weird eyes hissed as it jumped on the back of the huge German shepherd"). I usually finish the session with a contest in which I or students read some of the writings and the class votes for the most vivid "Cat" and "Box."

•**Idea 351:** A more elaborate version of the same idea is something called "Four Boring Stories." Each student chooses one of the following brief plots and turns it into something interesting and exciting by adding absolutely any details he or she wants.

FOUR BORING STORIES

1. I met my friend. We had fun.
2. I took a walk. I saw a dog.
3. I rode in the elevator with a man.
4. There was a box in my living room. I wasn't supposed to open it.

This one also could be a contest, but is probably better as a simple writing assignment because of the different amounts of time it will take individual students to finish their stories.

One important lesson about revision that I want younger students to learn, then, is that their writing can usually be made more interesting and alive by *adding details*. A second lesson about manipulating material is that a piece of writing can be put in a *better order*.

Generally when students get a new idea late in a piece of writing, they tack it on at the end: "... And when Rover finally came home safely, the whole family celebrated. Rover was a kindly big gray dog with silky hair. The End." This student clearly doesn't realize that writing can be rearranged." Or else doesn't want to face copying the whole piece again. This is a child who needs a pair of scissors and a roll of tape. I have always loved the sheer power of being able to run the scissors through my work, to tape on flaps of new words and to draw arrows indicating insertions. One of the best methods I know for teaching revision is simply to have available a pile of scissors, tape, and large sheets of extra paper. The teacher then demonstrates by taking something (preferably something she has written herself) and cutting it in two. She then tapes the two halves, in reverse order, on a big paper and perhaps writes a few more words in the extra space. Such a simple demonstration plus the available materials can be all the motivation a class needs for beginning to change and move paragraphs and to try different beginnings and endings. I have had whole classes so enamored of the cutting and taping that they rearranged *everything* — good writing along with bad.

•**Idea 352:** A lesson for practicing rearrangement is to pass out duplicated copies of the following scrambled story along with scissors and tape. The assignment is simply to cut it apart and rearrange it in the way that seems to make the most sense.

> My heart pounding, I took another step.
> I said, "I'll never go down there again!"
> I put my feet down very carefully and clutched the rail.
> I screamed and ran up the stairs as fast as I could.
> I didn't want to go down there.
> The sound sent a chill up my spine.
> The thing squealed!
> The light in the basement was broken.
> It slithered past me, touching my leg.
> My foot landed on something soft and squishy.
> I heard a noise like something scurrying.

This story has a pretty clear "best" ending, so I often begin a discussion after the students have made their arrangements by talking about the ending. I don't think the best beginning is that obvious, though. I wrote the story beginning with "I didn't want to go down there," but one class almost convinced me it was better to start with "The light... was broken." The object here is not, of course, right answers, but practice in manipulating and consideration of what makes a good beginning, middle, and end.

•**Idea 353:** Here are two more scrambled stories to use. The first one was written by a third grader, and the second one by a sixth grader.

THE STORY TELLING CONTEST

Ellen and I won.
As Ellen told a story, her voice sounded funny.
The judges looked at you funny.
Next came my turn.
Everyone had their fingers crossed.
Ellen and I got to go to the district contest.
The day of the story telling contest, I was nervous.
It was March 17, 1982.

●

A man was riding on a sleek, black motorbike with a swastika on it.
He wore black boots with mud caked on the bottom.
I was walking my dog late one Saturday night when I saw him for the first time.
He wore a black shiny jacket and a hard hat with a long point on top.
His low deep voice echoed in my head, as he laughed continuously.
Whenever I see him I think of all the Jews that died in Nazi Germany.
He was constantly riding up and down on the sidewalk.

●**Idea 354:** Sometimes after the rearrangement exercise of "The Story Telling Contest" above I ask the class to make any changes they want, including adding things, turning the girls into boys, or whatever. This kind of open-ended changing is closest to the act of rewriting one's own work.

●**Idea 355:** One of my all-time best assignments is to give students another student's piece and ask them to do anything they want to it, to make it, in effect, their own. A piece I often use for this is a description of a street woman written by a seventh grader. I have always liked this description—particularly its rhythms of repetition—although I feel strongly that the last sentence is out of place.

> She was very old and had bummy clothes and she had long hanging lips. She drinks a lot of wine and begs and also she doesn't have any shoes. She has no house, no kids, not even a husband. Her clothes do not match, and also her clothes have a lot of holes. She has on a man's pants with holes in them and also she is very dirty, and she has an overcoat with holes in it and she begs and begs and begs. And plus she has brown eyes, a big long nose, a man's voice, a scarred-up face, no hair and green teeth.

Things that go together need to be grouped here—the details about her appearance and clothes—and probably the part about having no husband or kids should be a culmination of her woes, although perhaps there is something about the clothes that is even more poignant. At any rate, I have always had surprisingly good results with giving this to a class to rework. I usually precede the writing with at least some discussion and practice in adding details and rearranging parts, so I have had my say as to what I think is important in rewriting, but I ask the students to do whatever they want to make the piece better.

At the end of one residency I was letting students choose which of their various pieces they wanted to put in a publication, and I was amazed by the number who chose as their best piece not one of their original writings but rather their rewriting of the lady with the bummy clothes. I have never quite understood why they would choose that piece rather than something all their own, but I suspect they hardly remembered the original anymore, that they had made this thing so true to their own experience and imagination that it no longer was someone else's at all. This is, of course, the experience we want to have with revisions of our own work too: that the reworking becomes so *right* as it grows that the original disappears completely.

Here are some samples of how students revised:

•

She is old with bummy clothes. With long hanging lips going down to her shoulders, she is also an alcoholic and also begs too much. Has no shoes, no house, and not even some children or a person to take care of her. Her clothes have holes, she also wears man's pants and is also very dirty. Her overcoat has holes and she still does beg and beg and beg. She has brown droopy eyes and has a green pupil with a big long nose like some sort of beak. Has terrible green teeth. She begs and still begs.
  —Leah Weinberger, 5th, P.S. 87, Manhattan

•

She was very beautiful, and she had long pretty hair. She doesn't drink, and doesn't beg at all. She has so many shoes, she doesn't know what to do. She has a very nice house, 2 kids, and a husband who lives with her. Her clothes look nice on her, and don't have any holes in them at all. She wears lady's clothes, and she is very clean. She wears an overcoat, and has a beautiful sweater that goes with it. And she has beautiful brown eyes. A lady's voice, a lovely face, all her teeth are straight, and brushes her teeth everyday. And loves everybody on the block, buys them all ice cream, cakes, sodas, pies, and treats them all to McDonald's after she comes home from work. And she also has a job.
  —Althia Faber, 5th, P.S. 87, Manhattan

•

This woman is just like a mouse with no hole because when she gets money, all she does is buy drugs and take them. She wears the same old holey clothes everyday. She doesn't have a house or kids. Nobody likes her because all she does is beg. This lady is also very ugly. She has brown eyes, an ugly scarred-up face, a big, long, doofy nose, a man's voice — baldheaded, big dragon long lips, and green teeth from drinking so much. All she does is talk and beg, beg and talk, talk and beg.
  —Ashaki Rucker, 4th, P.S. 87, Manhattan

•

Every morning, 6:00 her torn-up figure appears on the street near the old West Alley. She wears old ripped up clothes with a lot of holes. She also wears men's clothes and an overcoat much too large. Her face fits her appearance in a terrible, frightening way. It is scarred up with no hair. She also has brown eyes, green teeth, and a long bony nose. She has no family and lives on the street with no money or belongings. She screams at children and throws bottles at adults. She is as unhappy as she is terrible.
— Molly Chatain, 4th, P.S. 87, Manhattan

Appendix B:
Writing Ideas by Grade Level

This appendix groups together some of this book's writing ideas that are particularly successful with certain grade levels. Some exercises are obviously inappropriate for beginning readers and writers because they require too much reading and writing. Other exercises may seem too gamelike for older adolescents and adults. I want to emphasize, however, that even though I recommend a particular Idea — say, writing about monsters — as being particularly successful with fourth through seventh graders, this doesn't mean that you couldn't use the material with your class of third graders or even your high school students. *Most of the exercises and Ideas in this book have been used with people of all ages from young children to older adults.* I believe, in the end, that a six-year-old writer is more *like* an adult writer than *unlike.* This belief underlies most of the Ideas in this book; they are based on what writers of the past and present have done and are doing.

But, at the same time, you know your students, and you know their interests. As you read this book you will be struck by exercises that fit their interests and yours. I hope that your instincts for what would work with your class will be your primary guide. The categories in this appendix are meant only as suggestions, as one way to begin reading this book, or as a quick reference for a teacher in a hurry.

I hope that, after using the Ideas, you will make your own categories for this Appendix: Ideas That Worked Best in Groups; Ideas Perfect for Seasonal Writing; Ideas That Sounded Better Than They Worked in Practice; Ideas That Started Us on Long Projects; etc.

•

(Note: all numbers, unless specified otherwise, are Idea numbers, which run consecutively through the book. Particularly appropriate Ideas are marked with an asterisk.)

Ideas Especially Suited to Younger Students (Up to Third Grade)

Ideas 3, 4, 6, 7, 16, 30 31, 49, 55-57, 63, 65-67, 71, 74, 82-84, 89, 125, 131, 195 198, *207, 213, 219, *220, 241, *246, 250, 288, 350.

Drawing a Self-portrait (pages 38-39)
Portraits of Real Animals (page 41)
Inside/Outside Writings (page 41)
Talking Things (pages 108-112)

Writing Ideas Especially Suited to Intermediate Students (Fourth through Seventh Grades)

Ideas 17, 20, 24-26, 33, 37, 50, 59, 75-81, *89-94, 98-105, 110, 122, 131, 137-142, 163, 169, 181, 198, 199, 206, 213, 221-224, *229-231, 241-245, 246-251, 252, 254, 270-272, 275-282, 286, 288-293, 294-311, 317, 324-334, 336-347, 350, 351.

Monsters (pages 43-45)
Fiction Diaries and Disasters (pages 137-142)

Writing Ideas Especially Suited to Secondary Students and Older

Ideas 5, 33-36, 38-44, 48, 59, 85, 88, 95, 106, 111-121, 123, 124, 145-150, 154-157, *182, 183, 202-204, 221, 232-236, 241, 254, *257-263, 282, 284, 285, 289, 299, 302, 303, 318, 319, 324, 325, 335.

Freewriting (chapter 1)

Ideas Especially Suited to Intermediate and Secondary Students Who Are Reading below Grade Level

Ideas 3, 4, 6, 13, 15, 60, 64, 71, 125, 129, *132-136, 144, 151, 187, 196, 210, 214-216, *218, 220, 241, *252, 286, 348, 349.

Self-portraits (pages 37-39)
Introductions (pages 145-150)
Life Stories (pages 174-178)

For Everyone

Dreams (pages 167-171)
Memories (pages 171-174)
Describing a Place (pages 9-30)

Describing a Person (pages 31-60)
Pretending to Write the Thoughts of Another Person (pages 150-154)
Capturing in Words Your Own Thoughts (pages 2-3, 130-137, 145-148, 150-154)

Index of Authors

(Adult authors' names are in italics.)